traveling

Three Months on the NBA Road

⭐ ⭐ ⭐

John E. Nordahl

Macmillan · USA

MACMILLAN
A Simon & Schuster Macmillan Company
1633 Broadway
New York, NY 10019-6785

ISBN 0-02-860438-5

A catalogue record is available from the Library of Congress.

Manufactured in the United States of America
10 9 8 7 6 5 4 3 2 1

CONTENTS

ACKNOWLEDGMENTS

Writing this book was the most difficult thing I've ever chosen to do, and there was no way I would have completed either my travels or my manuscript without the assistance of a variety of people.

With regard to my basketball travels, all of the NBA teams provided invaluable contributions, including access to game tickets and team information. Specifically, I'm indebted to Arthur Triche and Kim Coleman of the Atlanta Hawks; Jeff Twiss of the Boston Celtics; Harold Kaufman of the Charlotte Hornets; Dennis Macklin, Kevin Riley, and Joe O'Neil of the Chicago Bulls; Bob Price and Dorothy Lockwood of the Cleveland Cavaliers; Kevin Sullivan of the Dallas Mavericks; Tommy Sheppard and Jay Clark of the Denver Nuggets; Matt Dobek and Sue Emerick of the Detroit Pistons; Julie Marvel of the Golden State Warriors; Rose Pietrzak, Tim Frank, and Jeff Gaines of the Houston Rockets; Dale Ratermann of the Indiana Pacers; Cary Collins and Mike Williams of the Los Angeles Clippers; John Black of the Los Angeles Lakers; Mark Pray of the Miami Heat; Bill King of the Milwaukee Bucks; Kent Wipf and Bill Robertson of the Minnesota Timberwolves; John Mertz of the New Jersey Nets; Chris Brienza of the New York Knicks; Alex Martins of the Orlando Magic; Joe Favorito and Zack Hill of the Philadelphia 76ers; Tom Ambrose of the Phoenix Suns; John Christiansen of the Portland Trail Blazers; Phil Hess of the Sacramento Kings; Tom James of the San Antonio Spurs; Cheri White of the Seattle SuperSonics; Kim Turner of the Utah Jazz; and Maureen Lewis and Matt Williams of the Washington Bullets. In addition, Jan Hubbard and Ellen Brandon of the NBA's media relations department provided me with media credentials for the 1995 All-Star Weekend, and assistant Evan Silverman worked diligently to ensure that I enjoyed that event in Phoenix.

A number of NBA fans contributed as well, both by offering their insight and observations about different teams, and by helping me overcome the occasional obstacles that arose during my trips. It would be impossible to list them all here, but special acknowledgment goes to Patricia Bender (a Mavericks fan), William Detoy (Clippers), John Einstoss (Warriors), David Fahey (Blazers), Keith Galipo (Bucks), Julie Hughes (Spurs), David Hunter (Cavaliers), Jim Nagle (Bullets), and Ted Reijonen (Sonics).

Friends in Orlando and around the country provided help in a wide variety of ways, including acting as hosts when I visited their cities; providing lodging, transportation, and company at games; and offering support and input while I wrote the manuscript. My thanks go to Heidi Burnett and her sister Stephanie; Rachel Darnell; Jarel Davidow; Sally Dunbar; Sherrie Hahn; Jeff Hand; Ken Hauptman; Donovan Johnson; John McConnell; my aunt, Betty Nordahl; Christine Pfeiffer and Dan Stocke; Geoff Rogers; Richard, Joan, and Chris Rogers; Dawn String; David Weaver; and Jennay Wooley. Todd Trubey deserves special thanks for his contributions; I was truly blessed to have his mix of basketball experience and editorial talent at my disposal.

I couldn't ask for a better literary agent than Bobbe Siegel. Even though she's not much of a basketball fan, Bobbe appreciated the idea of traveling the NBA, and it is only because of her efforts that I've been able to fulfill my goal of not only experiencing such adventures but also sharing them with fans across the country in this book.

After Bobbe completed the deal, Traci Cothran of Macmillan Books quickly demonstrated that I had found the right publisher. Traci proved not only to be a skilled editor but an able counselor as well, providing me with encouragement and support while not losing sight of our tight schedule. By the end of the project, I considered her not just an editor, but a friend as well.

And finally, I'd like to give special thanks to my parents. In spite of my uncertain professional future, they fully supported my efforts to travel the NBA and write a book about my experiences, even as the project stretched from a planned six months to more than two years. Their patience has been extraordinary, especially for two people who wouldn't know the difference between Muggsy Bogues and Manute Bol. To them, and to all the people who made my dream a reality, I offer my sincere gratitude.

National Basketball Association teams and arenas, 1994–95 season:

TEAM	*ARENA*	*CITY*

EASTERN CONFERENCE
Atlantic Division

Boston Celtics	Boston Garden	Boston, Massachusetts
Miami Heat	Miami Arena	Miami, Florida
New Jersey Nets	Meadowlands Arena	E. Rutherford, New Jersey
New York Knicks	Madison Square Garden	New York City, New York
Orlando Magic	Orlando Arena	Orlando, Florida
Philadelphia 76ers	The CoreStates Spectrum	Philadelphia, Pennsylvania
Washington Bullets	USAir Arena	Landover, Maryland

Central Division

Atlanta Hawks	The Omni	Atlanta, Georgia
Charlotte Hornets	Charlotte Coliseum	Charlotte, North Carolina
Chicago Bulls	United Center	Chicago, Illinois
Cleveland Cavaliers	Gund Arena	Cleveland, Ohio
Detroit Pistons	The Palace of Auburn Hills	Auburn Hills, Michigan
Indiana Pacers	Market Square Arena	Indianapolis, Indiana
Milwaukee Bucks	Bradley Center	Milwaukee, Wisconsin

WESTERN CONFERENCE
Midwest Division

Dallas Mavericks	Reunion Arena	Dallas, Texas
Denver Nuggets	McNichols Sports Arena	Denver, Colorado
Houston Rockets	The Summit	Houston, Texas
Minnesota Timberwolves	Target Center	Minneapolis, Minnesota
San Antonio Spurs	The Alamodome	San Antonio, Texas
Utah Jazz	The Delta Center	Salt Lake City, Utah

Pacific Division

Golden State Warriors	Oakland Coliseum Arena	Oakland, California
L.A. Clippers	L.A. Memorial Sports Arena	Los Angeles, California
L.A. Lakers	The Great Western Forum	Inglewood, California
Phoenix Suns	America West Arena	Phoenix, Arizona
Portland Trail Blazers	Memorial Coliseum	Portland, Oregon
Sacramento Kings	ARCO Arena	Sacramento, California
Seattle SuperSonics	Tacoma Dome	Tacoma, Washington

DEDICATION

To those who made me strong enough to travel:
my family and friends.

To those who inspired me to travel:
the members of the National Basketball Association,
especially the Orlando Magic.

To those who ensured that my travels were worthwhile:
the NBA fans across the United States.

And to the only girl I ever think of with regret.

"I'm looking for a wonderful, wonderful woman
to marry me and have children.
But until that happens, I love this game."
—Richard Lewis
in an NBA commercial

INTRODUCTION

It all started with a hat.

In the late 1970s my father went to San Francisco on a business trip, where he bought a Giants cap for me as a souvenir. I was a casual if not very knowledgeable sports fan in the ninth grade, and the Giants hat was only the second baseball cap I'd owned. I remember feeling that the hat was very special, simply because it had come from the team's city, and not from the sporting goods shop in my hometown of Lexington, Massachusetts.

I began collecting many other baseball caps over the next few years, but the Giants cap was always my favorite. I had a terrific idea: What if my father could start getting me caps from every city he visited? Eventually, I would have a complete set of authentic, bought-in-the-city hats, a collection which was about the neatest thing I could imagine having.

Unfortunately, my father didn't travel that often, and I quit collecting baseball caps during high school. Around that time, the Boston Celtics won the first of three league championships in a span of five seasons. The year was 1981, the man leading the way was a second-year forward named Larry Bird, and suddenly I began to learn a great deal more about basketball. My days as a serious baseball fan were numbered, but I never forgot how much I loved the Giants cap that my father got me in San Francisco.

It's one thing to somehow get your hands on a souvenir from every city in a professional league. It's quite another to go on the road and get those mementos yourself.

My name is John Nordahl, and I'm a basketball fan. To be specific, I'm a fan of the National Basketball Association, where the best basketball in the world is played. Most specifically, I'm a fan of Orlando Magic basketball, ever since I moved to Orlando a few months before the Magic began to play in the NBA.

I'm a single male with a college degree in broadcasting and film from Boston University. Born in 1965, I was told a few years ago that I was among the last of the baby boomers, but since then I've learned that I'm actually a member of Generation X. My biggest qualification as a basketball expert is my experience with the Magic: Since moving to Florida in 1989, I've seen more than two hundred Magic games at Orlando Arena. That probably doesn't qualify me as an expert on the NBA, but I won't argue the point, because I don't claim to be one.

But I am an observant person, with a sense of adventure and a natural curiosity about things, and in 1991 I got the idea to go on a trip around the country and see a basketball game in every city in the NBA. I had questions that, even as a devoted fan, I'd never really had answered. Most concerned the arenas where the game is played: Do all the arenas look the same? Are most games presented the same way as Magic games? How many teams have mascots? Do the fans really leave early at Lakers games in Los Angeles? Does the Portland Coliseum, the smallest in the NBA, really seem especially tiny? What about the Charlotte Coliseum, the largest? Who has the best fans? And what is it like to spend a night cheering at a home game for every single team in the league?

During the first three months of 1993, I took to the road and found my answers, and in the process fulfilled my dream of seeing at least one game at every NBA arena. I knew that what I saw and experienced would be of interest to basketball fans across the country, and as a result I made plans to write this book upon my return. As I soon learned, however, the writing and selling of a manuscript can take quite a long time, and when the good people at Macmillan agreed to publish my book, it was with the condition that I do the whole trip again. That's how I came to travel around the NBA twice: the first time during the latter half of the 1992–93 season, and the second during the middle of the 1994–95 campaign.

THE IDEA: FALL 1991–SUMMER 1992

The first time I heard about someone taking a cross-country trip solely to visit ballparks was in the mid-1980s, when a man named Bob Wood appeared on *Late Night With David Letterman*. Wood, a schoolteacher from Seattle, had spent two months one summer driving all over the country to see games in each of the twenty-six professional baseball stadiums. He had written a book about his experiences, mostly focused on comparing the different food and facilities in each city, and actually brought to the Letterman show some samples of ballpark franks from cities he'd visited. Sure, collecting hot dogs couldn't compete with collecting hats, but I was still pretty impressed. In 1991 a couple did a similar trip in a camper, although they expanded their itinerary to include minor league ballparks in their travels. ESPN featured videotape of the pair as part of their coverage of the major league baseball season.

Near the end of that summer, I was sitting in the trailer that serves as the home of the Studio Guide department at Universal Studios Florida, talking with a friend named David Weaver. David (don't call him Dave) and I had trained together to become studio guides at Universal in July of 1990. That afternoon in 1991, we were talking about the couple's trip, and David, knowing that I was a fan of the Orlando Magic, asked me what I thought such a trip around the NBA might be like.

I guess it wouldn't be immodest to say that I was more than an average Magic fan. I'm not one of those wild fans who paints his face or carries a sign on game nights, but at that time the Magic were about to begin their third season, and I hadn't missed a home game in their first two years. (I had moved to Orlando from Boston in August 1989, about three months before the Magic began play.) I wasn't obsessed with my streak, but my schedule had been flexible enough to give me the chance to see all the games.

To answer David's question, I drew a crude map of the United States and marked the approximate locations of all the NBA cities. Looking at the map, we realized that if you drove around the country in a big circle, you could visit all the cities along the way. In fact, it was almost as if the teams were arranged in clumps: three in Texas, three in the Southwest, six on the West Coast, five in the Midwest, six in the Northeast, two down the Atlantic seaboard, and two in Florida.

I had been to games in Boston while I was growing up and while at Boston University, perhaps a dozen overall. Besides Orlando Arena and Boston Garden, the only other place where I'd seen a game was Miami Arena, which I'd done while visiting Geoff, my best friend from Lexington who had moved to Florida while we were in college. Looking at the map, I told David that, if I were to do the trip, I'd want to go in a clockwise fashion, starting with Houston and ending in Miami. David and I began to talk about other elements of such a trip, including different methods of travel. He suggested that a person could fly, but I thought that would be very difficult.

"What you'd want to do is drive," I explained to him. "There's a lot of reasons that flying doesn't make sense. It's much more expensive, because you'd not only have to buy a bunch of plane tickets, but you'd also have to pay for taxis or rental cars or whatever. Also, you wouldn't be able to take much stuff if you had to load it onto twenty-seven flights to twenty-seven cities."

We agreed that creating an itinerary wouldn't be a problem: Just chart a rough outline and then plug in home dates once the NBA schedule was announced.

We talked about it at length, and the idea grew more and more intriguing. I'll never forget what he said to me when the time came for our conversation to end..

"Don't just let this idea drop, John," he told me. "Look into it."

And so I did.

The Rand McNally Road Atlas lists the distances between cities, accurate distances that tell you how many miles it is when you drive, not when you fly. I bought a copy and made up this chart:

Trip Leg	Miles	Approx. Travel Hours (at 50 mph)
Orlando to Houston	978	19.5
Houston to San Antonio	193	4.0
San Antonio to Dallas	271	5.5
Dallas to Denver	797	16.0
Denver to Salt Lake City (Utah)	497	10.0
Salt Lake City to Phoenix	646	13.0
Phoenix to Las Vegas	287	6.0
Las Vegas to Los Angeles (2 teams)	288	6.0
Los Angeles to Oakland (Golden State)	377	7.5
Oakland to Sacramento	85	1.5
Sacramento to Portland	600	12.0
Portland to Seattle	173	3.5
Seattle to Minneapolis	1,691	34.0
Minneapolis to Milwaukee	335	7.0
Milwaukee to Chicago	95	2.0

Chicago to Indianapolis	182	3.5
Indianapolis to Detroit	273	5.5
Detroit to Cleveland	163	3.5
Cleveland to Boston	643	13.0
Boston to New York City	215	4.5
New York to E. Rutherford, New Jersey	30	1.0
East Rutherford to Philadelphia	90	2.0
Philadelphia to Washington, D.C.	140	3.0
Washington to Charlotte	384	8.0
Charlotte to Atlanta	249	5.0
Atlanta to Miami	662	13.5
Miami to Orlando	224	4.5

So the trip totals, according to Rand McNally, came out to 10,568 miles, which averaged out to roughly 215 hours of driving.

Piece of cake.

As crazy as it was, the idea wouldn't die, and by New Year's Day 1992 I had decided to go through with it. No compromises, no fantasy trip planning, no what-ifs, but instead a real adventure that perhaps nobody had ever done before. But how to do it? Without any self-help books to tell me how to get tickets to NBA games in cities all across the country, I had no idea how to proceed.

In February, the NBA held its annual All-Star Game in Orlando. As a Magic season-ticket holder, I was able to buy tickets to the weekend events, and come Saturday I found myself sitting among people from the NBA, one of whom was named Steve. He explained to me that he was from New York City, and that his wife Bruni worked in the NBA's publicity department.

It was too good an opportunity to pass up, so for the first time I explained my idea of a trip around the NBA to someone other than my friends. Steve was enthusiastic, and although he had no more idea of how to organize it than I did, he gave me his wife's phone number at the NBA offices and suggested that I call her to talk about possible ways to make my idea a reality.

On a Monday morning in March 1992, I made the first of dozens of phone calls regarding the trip. Bruni was at the NBA offices in New York City, and I was relieved to find that Steve had told her about my idea. She informed me that, unless I was doing the trip in association with NBA product licensing or had some other connection to the league, I would have to contact each team individually and request that they help me by arranging for a ticket to whatever game I was going to see in their city.

Finding names and addresses was no problem. Every team creates a media guide each season, a glossy book that provides newspaper, television, and radio professionals covering the club with a single source of important information. With a copy of the Magic media guide, I had a resource that listed every team's address and the names of front office personnel. Since the media guide was designed to help members of the press, it listed a person to contact on each team, usually the media or public relations director, and I decided to address my initial letters to them.

As the 1991–92 season continued, I drafted letters to the NBA team offices. In each, I explained my plan and asked for the name of the person I should contact when I knew what game I would be seeing in their city. I sent these letters in one big bundle on Monday, April 6th, then sat back and waited for the replies to begin rolling in.

The first came exactly a week later, a note from the Dallas Mavericks that was enthusiastic and personal, and I was filled with unbridled optimism. Three others soon followed within a few days, and all promised to help me arrange for a ticket to whatever game I wanted to see in their city.

Then, suddenly, the replies stopped. I'd gotten one on Monday, one on Wednesday, and two on Thursday, and that was it. After all those letters, I had succeeded in getting a commitment from only four teams. And so, as much as I dreaded it, as much as it felt like a job hunt, and as difficult and time-consuming as it was, I began to call them all, one by one, to ask if they'd gotten my letters.

Over the next few days, I talked to about a dozen of the people I'd written, and nearly all told me the same thing: They would be happy to either sell or give me a ticket to a game, but they really couldn't do anything until the schedule was released.

So I quit calling teams in early May, content to wait and plan what I could before I got the NBA schedule and contacted the rest of the teams. I went to my local American Automobile Association and got a complete set of their TourBooks for the continental United States, which gave me information about AAA-approved lodging along my intended route. In early July I began making a mock trip itinerary, charting a route using maps and the TourBooks to try to get a rough idea of how long I'd be traveling and how much money it would cost me. I was guessing between two and three months on the road, at a cost between four and six thousand dollars for lodging and gas.

It was hard to believe: I was 26 years old, working as a tour guide at a jazzed-up $600-million theme park, about to drop everything for a few months and jump in my car to drive around the country and see a lot of basketball games. All I had to do was make a schedule, contact the teams, shut down my apartment, and hit the NBA road.

THE FIRST TRIP AND BEYOND: JULY 1992–NOVEMBER 1994

On a Friday morning in mid-July of 1992, the NBA announced its schedule for the 1992-93 season, and the whole thing began to take shape.

With a rough outline of the trip in mind, I wrote down home dates for each team during the period I might visit their city. I'd decided to leave a couple of weeks after New Year's Day so that I wouldn't have to travel during the holidays, and once I found a suitable starting date I simply consulted my earlier notes and created a schedule that allowed me to visit each team without having to double back or face an excessive amount of driving during any leg of the trip.

In planning my travels, I checked only the dates of home games for each team, not looking to see who the opponent would be until I'd finished the schedule. The way I figured it, such a system would shield me from any accusations that I was trying to scam tickets to high-profile games, and would also be a good random sample of what the NBA had to offer. I was initially disappointed that I wouldn't see the Magic play outside Orlando, but I realized that if I did I wouldn't be able to root for the home team, something I planned to do in each city.

Once I knew the dates and games I would see, I wrote back to each team that summer, mentioning my first letter and asking if they could "reserve" me a ticket to one of their home games. I figured that my careful wording would let them decide whether to sell or give me a ticket. I also mentioned that I planned to write a book about the trip, in case that could influence their answer.

It took me nearly three months, but by the end of September I'd finished my calls. Every team except two had agreed to either sell or give me a ticket to a game in their city, and I was fortunate to have friends in both the holdout cities to help with those tickets.

I spent the first half of the 1992–93 season preparing for the trip and studying up on the league. One thing I wanted to do was contact fans in each NBA city, which I did through a couple of national computer services. By posting messages on the electronic bulletin boards, I was able to compile a list of fans who were willing to help me learn about their teams and arenas, and even though I would end up contacting only a portion of them the list gave me a complete resource for fan information. I wrote big checks to cover the rent and utilities, including an especially hefty advance to Sprint to cover the numerous phone calls I would be making from the road. My girlfriend Jennay agreed to help me by watching my mail for any important correspondence, and by convincing her mother to take care of my cat while I was gone. I began my leave of absence from Universal a few weeks before I was scheduled to take to the road, and as New Year's Day 1993 rolled around I entered the final phase of my preparations.

In the last days before I left, I took my car to be inspected and tuned at two separate garages, gathered my gear, and shopped for supplies. After a hectic final day of errands and planning, I went to Orlando Arena on the night of January 12, 1993, to see the Magic play the Chicago Bulls. It was the Magic's 141st regular-season home game, not including the dozen or so exhibition games at Orlando Arena, and I had seen them all, preseason included. When I'd planned the trip, I'd pictured that night as a time to quietly reflect on my three and a half years without missing a game, but the proximity of my departure for a three-month journey was too much of a distraction, and my mind wandered during almost all of the last game of my streak. It was not just an ordinary game, either, but the first-ever meeting between Michael Jordan and Shaquille O'Neal, the player many predicted to be the next great NBA superstar. Yet Shaq was a rookie and the Jordan-led Bulls were the defending champions, and when Jordan blocked O'Neal's first shot the tone was set. The Bulls led from beginning to end, running away to a 122–106 victory, so perhaps my distraction was a blessing.

January 13th was a Wednesday, and I spent most of the morning and early afternoon packing my bags and loading my car. Once I'd finished with my preparations, I was pleased to discover that, despite the amount of stuff I was bringing along for the trip, none of my windows were blocked, giving me a clear field of vision for driving. Satisfied that I'd packed everything I needed, I took one last look around my apartment before closing the blinds and locking up. It was just after 2 PM when I pointed my car north on the highway, taking the Florida Turnpike toward I–10. Before long my favorite AM station began to fade out, and the reality set in that Orlando truly was behind me, with the road ahead as my home for a long time.

For three days I drove to Houston, and on January 16th I saw the first game of my tour at The Summit. From there I traveled to the league's other two Texas cities, then through the mountain time zone to Denver, Utah, and Phoenix. After a brief stop in Las Vegas, I began the month of February by spending two weeks working my way up the West Coast, seeing the four California teams, Portland, and Seattle. As the NBA held its All-Star Game in Salt Lake City during the third week of February, I was crossing the Plains from Washington to Minnesota, a 1,700-mile drive that lasted nearly a week.

After closing out the month in Minneapolis, I visited the midwestern teams in Milwaukee, Chicago, Indiana, Detroit, and Cleveland during the first two weeks of March. After a close call with a memorable storm on March 13th, I began the East Coast leg with stops in Boston and the New York area, and then drove to Philadelphia, Washington, Charlotte, and Atlanta, where I completed my dream of visiting every league arena. All that was left was to travel to Miami Arena to complete my second goal: to see every team play a home game in a single season.

This is a quick summary, of course: I could have written an entire book about my experiences during the tour, and after I returned to Orlando on April 13th I began to do just that. I'd hoped to finish the text in a few months, using that time to find a literary agent and publisher in order to get the book on the shelves as soon as possible. But I was unfamiliar with how slowly things work in the publishing world, and nearly a year passed before I was able to find an agent who shared my enthusiasm for the project.

When I finally signed with an agent, I learned that publishing houses usually take almost a year to bring a book to the shelves, a discouraging revelation that left me concerned about the timeliness of my material. The only new arena for the 1993–94 season was in San Antonio, and in the spring of 1994 I flew to Texas to see a couple of games at the Alamodome, so that I wouldn't have any gaps in my knowledge of NBA facilities.

The summer of 1994 rolled around, and on a July afternoon my agent called and told me that Macmillan Books was interested in my manuscript. They liked the idea of a book that would detail my observations of the league after traveling to each arena, but they were concerned about timeliness as well, and I began to consider possible ways to improve the book.

It was a frustrating situation, and I remember thinking about it one afternoon while driving home from my friend's apartment where I did my writing. I was turning off the highway when the answer came to me quickly, like a flash of lightning; in the first few moments I considered it, I wondered if I was crazy.

Why not do the whole thing again?

It made perfect sense. If I were to travel around the country to every NBA arena a second time, with a publisher ready to bring out the book a few months later, any specific information in the text would be as up-to-date as possible. The first trip had been less expensive than I'd anticipated, and I still had all the materials I'd used on the road, like extra duffel bags and a laptop computer. In the months since my return, I'd been working full-time on the book, and a second trip would only be an extension of that time in an effort to complete what I started.

Regardless of all the logical reasons, I realized that I'd wanted to go again all along. Not because I didn't feel familiar with the different arenas, or because I felt unsatisfied with the conclusion of my first NBA trip. Instead, I wanted to travel again because so much of the trip was over quickly, and it seemed that many of my visits were only glimpses into what other teams had to offer. I always believed that anyone who visited Orlando Arena for only one night couldn't possibly get much of an insight into how things happen at a Magic game, and I yearned to spend more time seeing games in other NBA cities.

In addition, I had paid my dues the first time, and was now familiar with the locations of the teams' arenas. I was no longer a novice to the experience of moving from city to city on a relatively small budget. And I knew how to plan a schedule that would take advantage of my experience with traveling around the NBA. The bottom line was, I was convinced that a second NBA trip would be easier, better, more detailed, and, in many ways, more exciting.

It would also make me much more qualified to write this book.

A couple of weeks later, the NBA released the schedule for the upcoming season, and I began my work once more. What I came up with was a masterpiece: a schedule that allowed me to see 38 games outside Orlando, gave me many opportunities to see teams more than once, let me visit my family at Christmas, and put me in Phoenix for All-Star Weekend. Following the same basic route but traveling the other direction, I would first visit the teams in the Eastern Conference and then make my way to the West, finishing in Texas rather than starting there.

The results of my work on the schedule were overwhelmingly positive, and I found myself filled with even more hope that I'd have the chance to put it to use.

Macmillan reviewed the material I'd sent them for almost six weeks, then called me in mid-September and asked for a few more details on my proposed second trip. I gave them my pitch, and two days later we had a deal. My contract included the typical advance, plus extra money to pay for the expenses of my second tour, an amount based on what I'd spent on the first trip. It was going to happen all over again, and so I pulled out my old notes and began to make the calls to start the process of requesting tickets. A quick two months later, and I was off once again, knowing what to expect and how to do it right.

I was determined to make this trip the ultimate exploration of NBA action throughout the league, and to use this book to relate my experiences during the 1994–95 season and also provide a few highlights of my 1993 trip as well.

Now let's go traveling.

—John E. Nordahl
May 4, 1995

DECEMBER 1994

12 Sun	Mon	Tue	Wed	Thu	Fri	1994 Sat
		NOVEMBER 29 Sacramento at Miami 7:30p.m.	NOVEMBER 30	1	2	3
4	5	6	Cleveland 7 at Orlando 7:30p.m.	Drive 8 426 Miles	New York 9 at Atlanta 7:30p.m.	Drive 10 240 Miles
11	12	Milwaukee 13 at Charlotte 7:30p.m.	Drive 14 382 Miles	Utah 15 at Washington 7:30p.m.	(Drive 143 Miles) 16 Cleveland at Philadelphia 7:30p.m.	Detroit 17 at Philadelphia 7:30p.m.
(Drive 100 Miles) 18 Miami at New Jersey 7:30p.m.	19	(Drive 40 Miles) 20 New Jersey at New York 8:00p.m.	Detroit 21 at New Jersey 7:30p.m.	Cleveland 22 at New York 7:30p.m.	(Drive 222 Miles) 23 Philadelphia at Boston 7:30p.m.	24
25 Christmas Day	Drive 26 657 Miles	27	Washington 28 at Cleveland 7:30p.m.	Drive 29 172 Miles	Boston 30 at Detroit 8:00p.m.	Drive 31 284 Miles

JANUARY 1995

1 Sun	Mon	Tue	Wed	Thu	Fri	1995 Sat
1	2	3	Washington 4 at Indiana 7:30p.m.	Drive 5 185 Miles	Seattle 6 at Chicago 7:00p.m.	7
8	9	Orlando 10 at Chicago 7:30p.m.	(Drive 90 Miles) 11 Sacramento at Milwaukee 7:30p.m.	Drive 12 337 Miles	Detroit 13 at Minnesota 7:00p.m.	Drive 14 1724 Miles
15	16	17	18	Phoenix 19 at Portland 7:00p.m.	20	21
Sacramento 22 at Portland 7:00p.m.	Drive 23 174 Miles	Denver 24 at Seattle 7:00p.m.	25	Utah 26 at Seattle 7:00p.m.	Drive 27 758 Miles	28
29	30	San Antonio 31 at Sacramento 7:30p.m.				

FEBRUARY 1995

2						1995
Sun	Mon	Tue	Wed	Thu	Fri	Sat
			1	Chicago at 2 `Sacramento` 7:30p.m.	(Drive 82 Miles) 3 L.A. Clippers at `Golden State` 7:30p.m.	4
Chicago at 5 `Golden State` 5:00p.m.	Drive 371 Miles 6	Utah at 7 `L.A. Clippers` 7:30p.m.	San Antonio at 8 `L.A. Lakers` 7:30p.m.	Houston at 9 `L.A. Clippers` 7:30p.m.	Drive 376 Miles 10	All-Star Saturday (Phoenix) 11
All-Star Game 12 4:00p.m.	13	14	Phoenix at 15 `Phoenix` 7:00p.m.	16	Golden State at 17 `Phoenix` 6:00p.m.	Drive 645 Miles 18
19	20	21	L.A. Clippers at 22 `Utah` 7:00p.m.	Drive 534 Miles 23	24	25
Utah at 26 `Denver` 1:30p.m.	Drive 784 Miles 27	Houston at 28 `Dallas` 7:30p.m.				

MARCH 1995

3						1995
Sun	Mon	Tue	Wed	Thu	Fri	Sat
			1	Cleveland at 2 `Dallas` 7:30p.m.	(Drive 270 Miles) 3 Orlando at `San Antonio` 7:30p.m.	4
Houston at 5 `San Antonio` 12:00p.m.	Drive 199 Miles 6	Phoenix at 7 `Houston` 7:00p.m.	Drive 978 Miles 8	9	Portland at 10 `Orlando` 7:30p.m.	11
12	13	14	15	16	17	18
19	20	21	22	23	24	25
26	27	28	29	30	31	

The South
November 29–December 13, 1994

NBA standings as of Tuesday, November 29, 1994:

EASTERN CONFERENCE
Atlantic Division

	W	L	Pct	GB	Home	Away
Orlando Magic	9	2	.818	—	5-0	4-2
New York Knicks	6	4	.600	2.5	4-1	2-3
Boston Celtics	6	6	.500	3.5	2-4	4-2
New Jersey Nets	6	8	.429	4.5	4-1	2-7
Washington Bullets	4	6	.400	4.5	2-3	2-3
Philadelphia 76ers	4	8	.333	5.5	3-4	1-4
Miami Heat	3	7	.300	5.5	2-2	1-5

Central Division

	W	L	Pct	GB	Home	Away
Cleveland Cavaliers	7	5	.583	—	4-2	3-3
Detroit Pistons	7	5	.583	—	5-2	2-3
Indiana Pacers	7	5	.583	—	4-1	3-4
Chicago Bulls	6	6	.500	1	2-2	4-4
Charlotte Hornets	5	6	.455	1.5	3-3	2-3
Milwaukee Bucks	5	6	.455	1.5	2-3	3-3
Atlanta Hawks	4	8	.333	3	2-4	2-4

WESTERN CONFERENCE
Midwest Division

	W	L	Pct	GB	Home	Away
Houston Rockets	9	3	.750	—	3-2	6-1
Utah Jazz	8	5	.615	1.5	7-1	1-4
Dallas Mavericks	6	4	.600	2	3-2	3-2
Denver Nuggets	6	5	.545	2.5	4-4	2-1
San Antonio Spurs	6	6	.500	3	5-3	1-3
Minnesota Timberwolves	1	12	.077	8.5	0-7	1-5

Pacific Division

	W	L	Pct	GB	Home	Away
Phoenix Suns	9	3	.750	—	7-0	2-3
Seattle SuperSonics	8	5	.615	1.5	5-1	3-4
Golden State Warriors	7	5	.583	2	4-1	3-4
L.A. Lakers	7	5	.583	2	2-2	5-3
Portland Trail Blazers	6	5	.545	2.5	3-2	3-3
Sacramento Kings	5	5	.500	3	4-3	1-2
L.A. Clippers	0	12	.000	9	0-6	0-6

Miami Blues

MIAMI HEAT

Founded: 1988
1993–94 Record: 42–40
Team Colors: Red, Yellow, Black, White

Tuesday, November 29

The players and team officials deny it, but NBA fans in Florida recognize the natural rivalry between Miami and Orlando, and as a Magic fan I've had my heart broken by the Heat many times. It was no surprise, then, that the Magic's biggest rivals would fail to have any home dates that fit comfortably with the rest of my schedule for the trip.

Miami lies about 230 miles south of Orlando, in the opposite direction from all the other NBA cities, and as I juggled dates and distances I realized that I would have to make a special trip to South Florida sometime either before or after my big circle around the rest of the country. After checking for conflicts with the Magic's home schedule, I decided to head down and spend a day traveling the Florida Turnpike and quickly visiting Miami Arena before I left on the big trip. It was the last Tuesday of November, nine days before the start of my three-month tour. I told myself that the short excursion to Florida's other NBA city would serve as a good warmup for the thousands of miles of travel I faced in the months ahead.

Previous Heat Games at Miami Arena:

1989–90 season: Detroit (Heat 88-84)/New York (Heat 128-121)/Milwaukee (Bucks 113-108)/Orlando (Heat 122-105)

1990–91: Minnesota (Timberwolves 108-107)/Orlando (Heat 104-102)

1991–92: Orlando (Heat 113-102)/Orlando (Heat 105-101)

1992–93: Golden State (Warriors 125-119)/Philadelphia (Heat 119-114)/Milwaukee (Heat 106-95)

Before I dreamed of traveling around the country, my basketball trips consisted of brief visits to South Florida. The motivation wasn't purely basketball, because my best friend lived in Miami. Both Geoff and I had grown up in Lexington, our houses only a quarter-mile apart, and we were rooming together in college when his parents moved from Massachusetts to Florida. We're such close friends that I can forgive him for becoming a Heat fan, and during my previous visits we managed to catch a half-dozen games at Miami Arena. On a couple of occasions, I drove to Miami and bought a single ticket from a scalper to see the Heat play the Magic. My extensive travels across the country might have been more dramatic, but those day trips to see the Florida teams battle at Miami Arena will always have a special place in my heart, even if the Magic never managed to win any of the games I saw.

I love the distinctive nicknames of the Florida NBA teams, because they seem to reflect the characteristics of each city. The Heat play in a big, exciting tropical metropolis, a collection of skyscrapers and beaches nestled against the ocean. Meanwhile, the Magic make their home in one of the world's favorite travel destinations, only a few miles from Disney World (with its Magic Kingdom), Universal Studios, and the countless other attractions that make Orlando magical to visit. Perhaps I'm sentimental, but to me the cities seem to be represented not only by their teams' names, but also by their arenas and fans.

Take Miami. Every Florida city has plenty of Northern transplants, but Miami seems to have most of the New Yorkers. The brazen attitude associated with the Big Apple is so common in Miami that it wouldn't surprise me to find out that the two are sister cities. In addition, Miami's proximity to Cuba has given the city a huge Hispanic population that makes it home to two distinct cultures and languages.

I've always thought of Miami as New York's southern branch—a Big Apple with palm trees. Just like New York, Miami is unique, exotic, and exciting. It's also big, loud, and dangerous. And just like its city, Miami Arena is all those things as well.

Located a short distance from the downtown skyscrapers, Miami Arena opened in 1988, the year that the Heat joined the NBA as one of the four expansion teams of the late 1980s. Although only a half-dozen years old, the Arena has generated plenty of bad publicity, but it remains one of the league's more interesting buildings. For one thing, no other arena is the same distinctive color, a hue known as "coral" that resembles a sandy pink. It contributes to the building's smooth, tropical appearance, although coral gives way to brown in the rough stone that makes up the arena's base.

From a distance, Miami Arena appears oval shaped, but a closer look reveals that much of the building is square. The main entrances—steep brick staircases leading to a large group of doors—are located at the east and west ends of the arena, while the north side contains a row of ticket windows. Miami Arena has a distinctive combination of light and dark colors and smooth and ragged textures, making it a stylish and pleasant arena, nicely framed by the nearby buildings of downtown.

But an arena is just like a house: It doesn't matter how pretty it is if it's in a bad part of town. Miami Arena is just east of Overtown, one of the city's more dangerous neighborhoods, and the location has contributed to several unpleasant incidents over the years. For example, to the best of my knowledge Miami Arena is the only facility in the league outside Los Angeles to have had a game postponed due to rioting.

Although Miami Arena is easily accessible by public transportation, its proximity to Overtown means that on game nights vendors, panhandlers, scalpers, and police descend on the building to mingle with the crowds, which adds to the New York feel of the experience of seeing a Heat game. Miami's public transportation system is convenient and safe, eliminating the need to drive to the arena (and expose your car to any potential risk), but the walk to the arena from the local stations west and south of the building is one of the more unsettling strolls outside an NBA building.

Despite its close proximity to Overtown, Miami Arena has hosted a team that enjoyed success with attendance in its first six seasons, and the frequent scarcity of tickets has brought complaints about the building's capacity. Constructed at a time when the NBA favored more intimate arenas, Miami's home court holds just over 15,000 people, making it the smallest modern building in the league. The Heat need only look north to Charlotte, where the other expansion team of 1988 has been consistently filling a 24,000-seat arena, to realize that they could have sold a great many more tickets over the years if they had built a larger building. To make matters worse, the team's luxury boxes, the plush suites usually rented by wealthy corporations, are located above all the regular seats—a position high among the rafters that may be preferable for a penthouse apartment but not for people trying to watch a basketball game.

With these problems a constant irritation for Miami fans, long-standing rumors hint that a new arena will be built near Joe Robbie Stadium in the north part of the city. Blockbuster Video mogul H. Wayne Huizenga owns Miami's three other major sports teams, and if he shares these concerns about Miami Arena (home to his hockey team, the Florida Panthers) he may finance such a facility, giving the Heat a bigger, safer place to play.

And if that happens, the distinctive coral building that is Miami Arena will no longer be a part of the NBA. A new arena, with plenty of extra seats and conspicuous luxury boxes closer to the action, will open in the spacious land far north of downtown Miami, surrounded by miles of parking spaces and little else. For better or worse, the building that opened in 1988 will quickly become obsolete, and the heart of Miami will no longer be the place where fans go to see the urban game of basketball.

Tuesday, November 29, 1994—7:30 PM

MIAMI HEAT (3-7) VS. SACRAMENTO KINGS (5-5)

Best friend or not, Geoff won't be at the game tonight: He's no longer a bachelor living in Miami, but as of six months ago a married man settled on Florida's west coast. Still, I won't be lonely: His brother Chris, also a Heat fan, has agreed to come along as I attend my twelfth game at Miami Arena. We decide to take advantage of the new Metromover system, an automated elevated train that opened in the downtown area only a few months ago.

✪ MIAMI ARENA
Opened: 1988
Capacity: 15,200
Miami, Florida

Chris and I board the train for the quick trip to the arena, and near us is a young man wearing a baseball cap decorated with the Heat logo. The stylish design shows a flaming basketball dropping through a hoop, and the sight of the logo reminds me of how close Chris came to designing it.

Like many teams, the Heat used fan voting to determine how the franchise would be shaped. After a contest to chose a name, the newly-christened Heat asked fans to submit designs for a team logo. A graphic designer by trade, Chris entered the contest and had his logo picked to be one of twelve finalists chosen from more than a thousand entries. For weeks the candidates were displayed on television and in newspaper ads, with the winning designer taking home a pair of season tickets as the grand prize. Even though his entry didn't win the final vote, Chris came very close to being part of NBA history. Talk about your immortality: What fan wouldn't want to name their city's team or design its logo?

In a familiar routine for me while traveling the NBA, I make my way to the "will-call" window to pick up our tickets, enjoying the moment where I discover what seats the team has given me. Although the Heat made me pay for my tickets during the first trip, their media director has graciously offered to "comp" us for tonight's game, and a quick check of a seating chart reveals that we're dead on the end of the arena, a few rows back in the permanent seats of the lower bowl.

Like most arenas, Miami's building is shaped in an oval, built to follow the boards of a hockey rink. For basketball games, temporary bleachers are added to the floor, and as a result we find the view from our seats partially obstructed—we can't see the players from the waist down on the near end. It's not my favorite location to watch a game, but I shouldn't complain, as the Heat have treated me pretty well in the past, especially considering that I'm from rival Orlando.

Some things are unique from the very start. During warmups, Heat scouting coordinator Tony Fiorentino offers "Tony's Tips," where he analyzes that night's opponent in a video message broadcast on four giant screens that hang in the corners above the upper level. (During halftime, we will be treated to "Tony's Tips" about the Nets, the Heat's opponent in their next home game.) The video screens fascinate me: Added after the Heat's first season, they consist of square pieces formed into a grid. The quality of the image is adequate, but the striking thing is their shape: rather than being close to square, like the shape of a television, Miami's monitors are more rectangular, cutting off part of the video image and creating strange framing of the game pictures and replays. I'm looking forward to wide-screen television as much as the next guy, but Miami's version leaves something to be desired. In addition, there are no video monitors on the concourse level, which is a rarity in modern arenas and makes it much more difficult to keep up with the action while visiting the concession stands or restrooms.

Miami Arena is also one of the few NBA buildings to regularly include a live band. In past games, I've seen them launch into song during every break in the action, at times even accompanied by a live singer, but tonight only the drummer is on duty. Using an electric drum system, he provides the rhythmic beats to lead the chants of "de-fense, de-fense" at several times during the game. Much like the video screens, I can't say that I'm a fan of the idea of live music at an NBA game, but the concept is another unusual part of the Miami Heat experience.

The differences continue as the game begins. Miami Arena is one of only two NBA buildings where a singer performs a song other than the national anthem before each game—in this case, it's "America the Beautiful."

After that, things get much more traditional: the Kings' starters are announced first (accompanied by the song "King of the Road"—a cute choice), then the lights drop, music plays, and the Heat's starting five get their turn. As the lights come up and the game begins, I am shocked to see that huge sections of the blue-and-green seats are unoccupied.

I've been to games in half-empty arenas before, of course, but never in Miami. The reasons for the poor attendance are pretty easy to pinpoint, as Miami's season has started slowly after the team traded several key players in an effort to win more games. Most fans don't have a problem with the trades, but as Miami's new personnel learn to play together, the club is struggling at the bottom of the Atlantic Division. Add in an opponent like the Sacramento Kings (never a huge draw on the road) for a Tuesday night game, and a below-average crowd is understandable.

Even with an abundance of empty seats, the crowd is buzzing. It's clear that the people at the game are the Heat faithful, and most seem to be knowledgeable, hard-core fans.

The Heat have dominated the Kings in Miami, losing only their first home game against Sacramento and winning six straight since then, most by a wide margin. In the first quarter it looks like this night's game will have a similar result, as the Heat execute well and jump out to a 33-22 lead. Yet as the reserves for both teams get some playing time in the second quarter, the Kings begin to battle back, and at halftime trail only by two.

Chris and I take advantage of the break to pick up a couple of Miami Heroes, my favorite arena food in all the NBA. Although I'm not enough of a gourmet to have an interest in sampling all of the concession items offered across the league, I'd still put my money on Miami Arena's signature sandwich as the favorite to be the best. It's a combination of ham, roast pork, Swiss cheese and dill pickle slices, oven baked on a roll of Cuban bread. I've enjoyed the sandwich at just about every game I've seen at Miami Arena, and it's always fresh and delicious, if not especially healthy.

We take our sandwiches to the upper level, where we've decided to spend the second half in some seats where we can clearly see the whole court. Miami's small capacity means that just about every seat offers a decent view of the action, free of obstructions and relatively close to the floor. Once settled in the upper bowl, we're able to appreciate the game much better, following the flow from end to end as the second half gets underway.

Like most arenas, Miami Arena has a four-sided scoreboard hanging over midcourt that displays the score, time remaining, and timeouts left. In addition, the Heat's center scoreboard contains the player boards—displays that list the uniform numbers, points scored, and personal fouls of each player on the court. The largest part of each side is the message boards, the graphic screens found in virtually every arena that show logos, messages, and advertisements. With the exception of the awkwardly shaped video screens, most of the other elements that make up Miami Arena are pretty standard, including smaller scoreboards that line the base of the upper bowl. The only distinctive board is one that shows the total number of 3-pointers made by each team, and as we watch the second half it becomes painfully clear that the Heat could use a few more of them.

Sacramento takes the lead in the third, making shots and grabbing every rebound that falls close to them, and Miami's lack of shared playing time begins to show as the Heat miss one bad shot after another. Still, the home team keeps it close, and with less than a minute left are only down by six. After a timeout, Miami forward Brad Lohaus hits a three with 21 seconds left, then Harold Miner steals the ball from the Kings and feeds it to Glen Rice, known for his deadly range. He is the perfect choice to take the shot that can tie the game, and as Rice lets fly from just behind the newly shortened three-point line, Chris rises in the seat next to me, ready to raise his arms in triumph. The Miami crowd, desperately hoping for a bright moment in what appears to be a dismal season, begins to rise with him, shouts of "Three!" on their lips, but the ball bounces off the back iron and the Kings grab the rebound. As if on cue, the arena begins to empty in a mad rush of spectators. After such high hopes during the building process of their expansion team, Heat fans obviously can't stand to see any more of what will be another loss, even though less than twenty seconds remain.

The Heat end up scoring only 14 points in the fourth quarter, and the final result is a 5-point Kings victory, making it clear that the new Heat squad will need some time to gel. The announced attendance is 14,301, although that figure seems somewhat inflated, and I will later read in an Orlando newspaper that the crowd is the second smallest in Heat history. After being a part of sellout crowds containing obnoxious fair-weather Heat fans, one bright side to this night is my feeling that most of the people in the stands are true basketball fanatics. It's too bad they have to leave disappointed. Final score: Kings 94, Heat 89.

Average 1994–95 ticket cost: $24.62 (23rd highest in the NBA)

Beer: $3.50 (16 oz.)

Soda: $1.75 (14 oz.—Coca-Cola products)

Hot Dog: $2.35

Parking: $10.00

Mascot: Burnie (cartoon-like guy with flaming hair)

Cheerleaders: Miami Heat Dancers

Remote-controlled blimp: none

Other professional teams that play full-time in Miami Arena: Florida Panthers (National Hockey League), Miami Hooters (Arena Football League)

What I'd change about Miami Arena: Get some big-screen monitors the right shape.

What I love about Miami Arena: What else? The coral paint job and the Miami Hero.

Statistics from Team Marketing Report, Inc.

Do You Believe?

Founded: 1989
1993–94 Record: 50-32
Team Colors: Electric Blue, Quick Silver, Magic Black

Wednesday, December 7
About a week after I returned from Miami, I once again found myself on the eve of a massive trip, and just like the first time, I had too many things to think about and not much time to plan.

Jennay, who had looked after my apartment and mail during the first trip, had since moved up north, so I'd convinced my friend Dawn to move in while I was gone. In return for living rent-free for three months, she would be responsible for feeding my cats, checking my mailbox for any important items, taking phone messages, and handling the packages of NBA stuff that I would send home during the trip.

I spent the last full day packing and moving things around to give Dawn space for her stuff, as well as making calls and running errands. Although I'd done it once before, the process of shutting down everything for three months was still a hectic and taxing one, and I was looking forward to finishing the tasks at hand and taking to the road, where my life would be neatly self-contained in my car, and any distractions would be kept to a minimum.

Of the many similarities between my two trips around the NBA, the first was that I would once again see a Magic game on the night before I left. Dawn would join me for the game, but the guest of honor had to be my friend John.

John is a few years older than me, settled in Orlando with his wife and their baby boy, and during the previous year he and I had become close friends. We'd been guides at Universal together until he had auditioned for and won a position as a performer—singing and dancing in the Blues Brothers stage show as Elwood Blues.

One summer afternoon John and I were talking on the phone when he mentioned that he had found a strange lump on his throat. Soon after that casual admission, John began weeks of tests, and by the end of the summer the doctors had diagnosed that he had Hodgkin's disease and had to undergo six months of chemotherapy.

Although Hodgkin's is a kind of cancer, it can often be treated successfully, and John kept up his spirits during the difficult process. For four months he had continued his treatments faithfully, never seriously complaining about his misfortune and working when he could.

It was the first game that we'd seen together all season, but John had been following the team closely, enjoying Orlando's sudden development into an NBA powerhouse. Although his first love would always be football and the Denver Broncos, it still made me happy that he was able to watch the Magic during his difficult time, whether at the arena or on television. John had faced many uncomfortable nights with his treatment, and was hospitalized for a time, but wherever he was he would always look forward to the games.

There are times when the business side of sports seems dominant, and people cynically dismiss the games and their players, but this was a case where it was easy for me to forget that aspect of professional sports. I knew the Magic were important to John, just as they were important to me. If I were ever in his situation I know that the opportunity to focus on the team, to root for them and not think about my predicament, would be welcome.

So there was no one with whom I would rather see the final game before my trip began.

> **Previous Magic Games at Orlando Arena:**
>
> 192 regular season games, two playoff games, too many preseason games.

The Magic arrived in Orlando at the same time I did. It was the fall of 1989, and one of the first things I did after settling in Central Florida was plunk down the money for a single season ticket to the newest game in town. The brand-new Orlando Arena had opened only a few months earlier, and in October the Magic played Detroit in the first NBA game in the building. With the frenzied support of a full house, Orlando went on to beat the defending world champions, an accomplishment somewhat diminished because it was a preseason game. Regardless of the circumstances, I was hooked, and each time I went to a game I learned more about the sport.

Some of my friends fail to understand how I could become a Magic fan after growing up in the land of the Celtics, but I'd never immersed myself in the game while in Boston. After I moved to Orlando, I was going to games an average of twice a week from November to April, watching and learning as the Magic went through the expected growing pains of any expansion team. Once I'd established myself in Orlando and made some friends, I bought two more season-tickets, giving me one in the lower bowl (for when I went alone) and a pair in the upper bowl. I spent three years rooting for the boys in pinstripes while they were doormats, enjoying the action while hoping that smart decisions and good fortune would someday make my team into a winner. For those first three years, however, there were many nights when the main attraction was not the game but the show around it inside Orlando Arena.

Downtown Orlando is not a huge metropolis, but the few skyscrapers do provide a background to the nearby arena. Located just west of I-4, the major highway that snakes through the city, Orlando Arena is part of the Centroplex, a compound which includes a theater, convention center, and major hotel. While several parking lots and garages surround the area, the grounds around the arena are lush and landscaped well enough to blend in nicely with the central Orlando neighborhoods.

The building is a striking combination of straight lines and curves. Made of huge white concrete blocks, the O'rena (as Magic fans call it) is basically rectangular, swelling into solid concrete nodes that jut out at each corner. The short east and west sides curve outward, blending with the nodes to minimize the appearance of straight lines. The courtyard surrounding the arena, made up of light and dark bricks arranged in a wavy pattern, continues the pattern.

The roof and sides provide the lines. The top of the arena is a plain rectangle, while the long north and south sides are flat, dominated by stairs that run the full length of both sides, the most distinctive exterior stairs in the NBA. Fans use them to climb to the concourse level, where several entrances are open on each side.

The location is certainly a plus, as the arena is not only incorporated into the downtown area but also has plenty of parking and relatively easy access for the thousands of cars that bring in the Orlando faithful on the nights the Magic play.

Wednesday, December 7, 1994—7:30 PM

ORLANDO MAGIC (12-3) VS. CLEVELAND CAVALIERS (9-7)

It is a grand and glorious night, a night to remember. Not because of the trip, although my impending departure is never far from my thoughts. Not even because, to my astonishment, the Magic have the best record in the NBA. No, tonight is special because of John.

In a tremendous quirk of timing, John has just received his test results a few hours before the game, and the doctors have told him that the cancer is gone. He'll have to continue with his chemotherapy for another two months, and there are more detailed tests to be done later, but every single indication is that he is cancer-free. On a day when I'm so busy with last-minute preparations, the news cuts through the clutter of my thoughts and keeps things in perspective.

The game tonight marks only the third time in the six-year history of the Magic that they will play the same team on back-to-back nights. Last night Orlando faced the Cavs in Cleveland's brand-new Gund Arena and won easily, jumping out to a huge lead before cruising to a 114-97 victory. With such a convincing victory on the road, I figure that the game will be an easy win, with the Magic blowing out the Cavs at the O'rena. As it turns out, I will be only half right.

From the very start, Orlando's front office decided that seeing a Magic game would be an entertainment event, not just an NBA game, and as a result the show begins early and continues until after the final buzzer.

Before the game, the sound system blasts music while the Magic Dancers perform on the baselines. The player introductions are done in the typical fashion (visitors first with the lights up, then lights down for the home team), but the Magic use indoor fireworks, spotlights, a

✪ ORLANDO ARENA
Opened: 1989
Capacity: 16,010
Orlando, Florida

disco ball, and video clips to spice up the moment. During the introduction and throughout the game, p.a. announcer Paul Porter slurs the names of Magic players, exclaiming "Shaaaaaquillllllllle O'Nealllllllllllllllllllll!" when Shaq scores, for example. Fans watching a game on TV may hear Porter's voice in the background and think he sounds obnoxious, but at the arena his vocal styling really adds to the experience.

Despite all the hoopla happening in the building, the interior of the arena follows the standard pattern, laid out in the same oval design found in Miami. Both the Florida arenas have their luxury boxes located above the upper bowl, and while the teams may wish they'd built them closer to the floor, the design allows the fans to sit anywhere in the stands and have a good view. There are bad seats in every NBA building, of course, but in Miami and Orlando they're kept to a minimum.

The Magic go through their flashy opening routine to start the game, complete with loud music and indoor fireworks, but from the start the basketball is sluggish. Although Orlando has always been a running team, pushing the ball into a fast-break offense whenever possible, the Cavs have dedicated themselves to a slowdown game, and for three quarters it works. The game is a comedy of errors, as both teams miss passes and shoot horribly, swinging at each other like two punch-drunk fighters unable to connect with a knockout. Horace Grant is sitting out a game for the first time all season due to tendinitis in his knee, and Anfernee Hardaway is limited due to early foul trouble. In short, the game is a mess, and at the end of three the Magic lead is a pitiful 61-60. Just like the last time, my final Magic game before the trip is tough to watch, but I guess I shouldn't complain—at least they're still ahead.

The Magic will need all the entertainment they can muster off the court on this night, and the Sports Magic Team comes to the rescue. The Team is a group of young men and women who dress in decorated blue-and-black jumpsuits and roam around the seats and on the court during timeouts, amusing the crowd by letting fans toss a mini-basketball at a helmet-mounted hoop perched on a volunteer's head. A variation has them using an entire goal mounted on their backs (smaller than a regulation goal, of course) as a target, which they can adjust in height to increase the chance of a shot going in. They also launch balled-up T-shirts to the crowd with a makeshift slingshot consisting of rubber tubing stretched between two Sports Team members and pulled back by a third. The slingshot flings the shirts to the upper bowl with ease, and occasionally even reaches all the way to the luxury boxes.

The Magic are too good to be held in check for long, and use a 7-1 run at the start of the fourth quarter to open up a 68-62 lead. With only a 6-point edge, the game is still in doubt, but in the middle of the quarter we finally get to see some of the action the NBA is known for. Shaq scores inside, Hardaway hits a three, Brian Shaw nails a jumper, and Anthony Avent, starting in place of Horace Grant, hits a fast-break bucket that puts them ahead for good at 80-65.

It is indicative of this game that the best moment occurs after the final buzzer. Shaw has the ball outside the three-point arc, dribbling as the last ten seconds run out. Shaq stands to his left, posted up for a three, but Shaw only smiles as O'Neal signals for the ball. With a second left, Shaw bounces a pass to the big man, far too late to attempt a shot, but as time runs out Shaq goes into a jump shot motion anyway. His form is decent, and even though the buzzer sounds before the shot leaves his hands, I watch the hulking center closely. The joke is whether Shaq will ever hit a 3-pointer, and this time he does, demonstrating a solid shooter's touch and hitting nothing but net. Naturally, it doesn't count, just as a flailing three he hit in the preseason won't be found on his career stats either, and Shaq will have to wait for another day for his moment of satisfaction, much like those of us who sat through this ugly matchup.

The final score is 90-75, setting a record for fewest points by a Magic opponent, and also establishing the mark, in my opinion at least, for the most sluggish game at Orlando Arena in the past two years.

Orlando Arena has a beautiful parquet floor, just like the famous hardwood of Boston Garden, which is nicely detailed in the team's colors. Both the lower and upper bowl sections have two rows of lights above them, which are not only functional but also provide the arena with a distinctive background detail.

Even with my fondness for Orlando Arena, the simple truth is that things used to be better. Not the team, of course—the Magic are playing the best basketball in their brief history. No, I mean the atmosphere used to be better.

One thing I miss is the Fat Guy running around the arena. Orlando has one of the great NBA fans, a loyal season-ticket holder named Dennis Salvagio. Salvagio, a local attorney, looks as if he's a twin separated at birth from George Wendt, the actor who played Norm on the TV show Cheers. During the second overtime of a game against the Bullets in the Magic's first season, cameras caught Salvagio enthusiastically dancing to the music during a timeout, and the crowd roared with approval at the sight of his rotund frame on the big-screen monitors. Newspaper articles and other publicity soon followed, and Salvagio is now known as "The Fat Guy." He's at almost every game, and takes part in several promotions with the team.

The best part was his trademark method of pumping up the crowd. If the score was remotely close, Salvagio would wait until a proper moment in the fourth quarter to do his stuff. When a timeout was called at a crucial juncture, he would leap from his seat, make his way down to the aisle around the court, and proceed to run a lap around the arena, stopping along the way to exhort the crowd to get on their feet and cheer. Salvagio usually circled the arena twice, and I couldn't help but think that some night the trip might do him in. I guess his doctor felt the same way, because Dennis was ordered to quit his strenuous cheerleading by his family physician. He's still at the games, but you have to look for him in the lower bowl to spot him these days.

The worst change, though, was the Magic's decision to replace the seats in the O'rena. When the team was first recruiting season-ticket holders, one selling point was our brand-new arena, which included extra-wide seats among its luxuries. Once the team signed O'Neal, Hardaway, and other high-priced players, however, it was less important that the arena's seats have more room for fans' backsides than it was to have a greater number of backsides in the seats. During the summer of 1994, the wider seats were taken out of the upper bowl and replaced by ones of minimum size, a process that added about 800 spots to the building's capacity. A similar procedure was planned for the lower bowl in the summer of 1995, which means that an arena that once held 15,077 will have a capacity of more than 17,000 for the 1995–96 season.

The change hasn't been a major hassle to me as a season-ticket holder (although I'm thankful that my butt isn't very wide), but I wish I could believe that the measures would help keep ticket prices down, rather than simply line the Orlando players' and owner's pockets with even more money. As long as the modification to the lower bowl doesn't hurt the location of my single seat, I guess I'll only occasionally think about how much better some things used to be. Final score: Magic 90, Cavaliers 75.

Average 1994–95 ticket cost: $34.91 (sixth highest in the NBA)

Beer: $2.75 (12 oz.)

Soda: $1.75 (16 oz.—Pepsi products)

Hot Dog: $2.00

Parking: $5.00

Mascot: Stuff the Magic Mascot (big green dragon)

Cheerleaders: Orlando Magic Dancers

Remote-controlled blimp: yes

Other teams that play full-time in Orlando Arena: Orlando Predators (Arena Football League), Orlando Solar Bears (International Hockey League), Orlando Rollergators (Roller Hockey International)

What I'd change about Orlando Arena: Not much—perhaps I'd put in blue seats to match the team colors.

What I love about Orlando Arena: Just about everything—after all these years, it's practically my second home.

Statistics from Team Marketing Report, Inc.

On the Road Again

Founded: 1949
1993–94 Record: 57-25
Team Colors: Red, White, Gold, Black

Thursday, December 8–Friday, December 9

With my first game of the trip a short 30 hours away, I had hoped to be on the road sometime around noon on December 8th, but as I continued the slow and methodical preparations for my journey the hours stretched into late afternoon before I was ready to depart.

I'd established a system on the first trip which had worked well enough that I decided to use it again. First, I filled my trunk with the things I wouldn't need every day: compact discs to provide music on the road; a bag of books, writing materials and other supplies; a box filled with AAA TourBooks and NBA media guides; a snow shovel, ice scraper, and tire chains for the winter weather I'd be facing; and a couple of jackets for different temperatures.

Next, I loaded the things I wanted to take in my hotel room each night into the back seat: two small suitcases, one packed with shirts and the other with pants; a pouch containing a folder for each city in the NBA with the names and phone numbers of the people I'd want to reach on the road; and a plastic trash bag containing my favorite blanket, two pillows, and an alarm clock. Finally, I filled the front passenger seat with a knapsack that held my Macintosh PowerBook 160 laptop computer, the indispensable and highly recommended *Rand McNally Road Atlas*, a binder with computer-generated routes for each leg of the trip, and my address book; and a bag of supplies including my notebooks, camera, and maps. In addition, I had three duffel bags, each with one week's worth of boxer shorts, socks, and undershirts, and I threw one bag in the back seat and packed the other two in the trunk. This system gave me three weeks' worth of clean clothes, and limited the amount I had to unpack in each city.

At last I made my final decisions about what to take and what to leave, then packed everything as efficiently as possible. Atlanta is seven hours north of Orlando, but with the sun beginning to set I knew that I was too exhausted to make it very far that night. I left Orlando at 5:30 PM, driving on the Florida Turnpike to I-75. After a couple of hours on the highway that would take me to Atlanta, I gave my aching body a rest and pulled over at a roadside motel in Lake City, Florida. My first stretch of driving had been only 150 miles, and I was tired and behind schedule, but I was glad to be on my way, finally finished with the hassles of planning and packing.

Refreshed by my first good night's sleep after a week of late-night preparations, I continued on my way Friday morning, still about 300 miles south of Atlanta. An overcast day couldn't dampen my spirits, and even though I wouldn't arrive in the Georgia capital until the start of rush hour, I was looking forward to my return to The Omni. If nothing else, I had a date for the game.

> **Previous Hawks Games at The Omni:**
>
> 1992–93 season: New York (Hawks 109-104 in OT)

Atlanta has an impressively large downtown area, and among the tall buildings near the center of the city is The Omni, home of the Atlanta Hawks. Many downtown arenas dominate the area around them, but The Omni is an exception. Found at the end of a street, the Hawks' arena is surrounded by other buildings, roads, and a subway station, all of which combine to dwarf The Omni in a mass of gray and white. Across the street to the east is CNN Center, not only the headquarters of Hawks owner Ted Turner's vast broadcast empire but also a full shopping center. A short distance west is the Georgia Dome, the new indoor stadium that is the home of the NFL's Atlanta Falcons and was the site of a recent Super Bowl. A platform to the south contains a bus drop-off circle and a stairway to a MARTA stop, part of the city's subway system. And in the middle of all this is The Omni, a subtle mixture of black-and-brown metal that looks more like a warehouse than an NBA arena.

Built in the early 1970s, The Omni is perfectly square, constructed with black steel walls that have ridged patterns running across each side. The walls are windowless, but the four corners contain large sections of glass indented about five feet from the outer wall, which extend a short distance down the side of the arena and keep the building from looking too gloomy. The roof of The Omni holds a group of twenty-five large triangular knobs, each rising like a miniature version of an Egyptian pyramid done in dark brown and connected by metal beams to one another. These knobs may be smaller than their counterparts in the Mideast, but they are large enough to make the roof of The Omni look like an upside-down egg carton. The roof structure is called an "Ortho-Quad-Truss," which allows the building to be free of support columns for a span of 360 feet in each direction. With its huge black walls, mysterious roof pyramids, and steely appearance, The Omni reminds me of the monolith in the film 2001: *A Space Odyssey*: cold, strong, intimidating.

There are four rows of railroad tracks between The Omni and the Georgia Dome, and I can't help but think that their presence is appropriate, because the atmosphere around The Omni feels like the building sits on the wrong side of the tracks. The crowds I've witnessed before each game seem to be exceptionally boisterous, to use a kind term. During one of my visits to Atlanta, I saw a group of teenagers hanging out near one of the street corners around the arena, and as I watched they quickly scattered at the sound of an approaching police siren. As both of the Hawks games I saw in Atlanta were against the Knicks, it's possible that the unsettling atmosphere around The Omni was due in part to a crowd of unruly Knicks fans. Even so, being outside The Omni made me somewhat nervous, which is not necessarily a bad thing: At least I felt like I was in a big city.

○ **THE OMNI**
Opened: 1972
Capacity: 16,368
Atlanta, Georgia

Friday, December 9, 1994—7:30 PM

ATLANTA HAWKS (7-10) VS. NEW YORK KNICKS (10-5)

My suspicion that the area around The Omni isn't very safe is reinforced early. Rachel and I park in a lot a few blocks from The Omni, and the unseasonably warm night has prompted me to leave my jacket in her car. The attendant overhears my plan and warns me to put my jacket under a seat, to reduce the chance that somebody might try to pull a smash-and-grab for it.

Rachel manages the art gallery of the Warner Brothers Studio Store in Atlanta, a position she held in Miami before being transferred. A few weeks ago, she'd called me to let me know about a new item she had for sale, and after I told her about my trip she offered to be my guide in Atlanta.

We head to the will-call window, where the Hawks have left a pair of tickets for us—terrific seats located about halfway up the lower bowl along the baseline above the Knicks' bench. I'm only slightly surprised at the quality of the tickets, however, as the Hawks were also very kind to me on the first trip, giving me a single in the corner of the lower bowl. It's tough to get them on the phone, but the Hawks are a very nice organization.

The game is between the Hawks and Knicks, the same teams that played during my other visit to The Omni, making Atlanta the only city where I would see a repeat of a matchup from my first trip. Even though the Hawks have been a relatively good team in recent seasons, attendance in Atlanta has never been very strong, and the main thing that bothers me about tonight's game is that a major portion of the crowd will be rooting for the visiting team. Even so, with the Knicks in town I have high hopes that the second game will be almost as good as the first, which the Hawks won in overtime.

The Omni is as dark as ever, but the light from inside spills out brightly from the corner windows. We enter into the concourse level, where things are pretty standard: concession booths line the inner walls, while extra food and souvenir stands are set up in the corners.

But the biggest thrill is the plaque found near the southwest corner of the building. "In Loving Memory Of ELVIS AARON PRESLEY," it reads, "For All The Joy And Happiness He Brought To The People In Atlanta's Omni" and lists the eleven dates that The King played The Omni between June 21, 1973 and December 30, 1976. The plaque concludes: "Thanks Elvis For The Memories—Happiness Is . . . Elvis Fan Club And The Over 260,000 Who Experienced These Phenomena." For those looking for interesting peculiarities in NBA arenas, Atlanta's Elvis plaque shouldn't be missed.

The Omni is distinctive in other ways than the Elvis tribute. For one thing, the Hawks' home arena is the most square building in the league, not only on the outside but in the seating design as well. Although the arena is basically laid out in the lower bowl/upper bowl design found in most arenas, the design has no curves at all. The lower sections have sharply cut corners, with stark white fronts which slant at a sharp angle down toward the ends of the arena. The front of the upper level is also cut with sharp angles, as the court runs diagonally to the outer walls of the arena.

Another unique design characteristic is found in the upper bowl. While several NBA buildings have an upper bowl design with varying heights to the sections, every other arena has more seats in the middle of the level than the ends. In Atlanta, however, the upper bowl runs high in the middle, shrinks in number of rows in the corners, then increases back to full size on the ends. Although it keeps with the square design of the building, the layout nevertheless creates some less-than-desirable seats in the last few rows in those end sections of the upper bowl.

In general, though, The Omni is not a bad place to see a game. The upper bowl only slightly overhangs the lower bowl, but the luxury boxes are unobtrusively located at the top of the lower sections, and as a result the upper seats offer a good view of the action. In addition, the upper bowl contains a separate front row of seats, which are more expensive than other seats in the upstairs sections but have a nice private feel.

One interesting and rare characteristic of The Omni is that the seats are all different colors: red, yellow, orange, and purple, each seat a single color but with no overall discernible pattern. A friend suggested to me that the color scheme was designed to camouflage a lack of people in the seats. Whatever the reason, the multicolored design is not one of my favorite things at The Omni.

As an older arena, The Omni lacks a fundamental feature that makes a game much more enjoyable: a set of big-screen monitors to broadcast the action and show replays. In a sport like basketball, where several key plays in each game demand immediate playback (especially if they involve a call by the officials), it's unfortunate that The Omni has no such monitors. (Even the misshapen screens in Miami are preferable to none.) The Hawks do broadcast the radio play-by-play on the concourse level, however, which is nice for fans visiting the concession stands. In addition, there are monitors on the concourse that show the current action, as there are in almost every arena in the league.

Instead of big-screen monitors, the Hawks have a center scoreboard with space for player information and a small message board, and two larger message boards in opposite corners of the arena. The boards come into play even before tipoff, as Rachel and I watch a woman perform the national anthem. Amazingly, she forgets the words to the song, despite the fact that they are being projected onto the huge screens in both corners. I try to keep from laughing out loud, but it's hard for me to imagine that anyone could ask for bigger cue cards.

During the routine player introductions (visiting team first, then lights out for the Hawks starters), it's obvious from the cheers that the arena is full of Knicks fans. But this time there is some support for the home team, and I manage to convince Rachel to join me in rooting for the Hawks. (She is initially leaning toward the Knicks, mostly because she thinks they're going to win.) I explain the two reasons why she should root for the Hawks: one, they're the home team, and as such deserve respect from the crowd; and two, as a Magic fan I had to encourage her (and anyone else) to root against the Knicks whenever possible. It's a full-blown rivalry now, and we need every game we can get.

The Hawks get off to a fast start, and by the end of the first quarter are leading by nine. Midway through the quarter a pair of Knicks fans move into the seats next to us, college-age guys who are carrying small white signs proclaiming their loyalties to New York. They are Chris and Chris, Northerners enrolled in school in Alabama, and the first thing they do is try to rally the Knicks fans in our section. Despite their actions, they seem like pretty decent guys, and I have to give them a break: They've driven four hours to see the game. Still, I tell Rachel they're going to be so disappointed when the Knicks lose.

Even though I'm somewhat kidding, it seems like I may be right. The Hawks manage to maintain their lead into the third quarter, withstanding a couple of Knicks runs, but the Hawks' offense runs cold in the fourth quarter, and the Knicks overcome an 11-point deficit to take the lead with less than four minutes left. As the tempo of the game shifts from one team to the other, the crowd seems almost perfectly divided, with large groups of fans cheering for each play, no matter what the result. The Hawks tighten their defense, manage a couple of key steals and timely stops, and swing the ball to Mookie Blaylock, who hits a 3-pointer with 39.2 seconds left. The Knicks fail to score on their next possession, and after a couple of free throws the game is over. Despite only scoring 33 points in the second half, the Hawks have held on for an improbable win.

They may not have many full-time fans, but after seeing them beat the Knicks twice, the Hawks can count me as an honorary member of their supporters. Final score: Hawks 89, Knicks 85.

Average 1994–95 ticket cost: $25.05 (22nd highest in the NBA)

Beer: $3.00 (16 oz.)

Soda: $1.75 (16 oz.—Coca-Cola products)

Hot Dog: $2.00

Parking: $7.00

Mascot: Harry the Hawk

Cheerleaders: Atlanta Hawks Avia Dance Team

Remote-controlled blimp: yes (giant Harry the Hawk)

Other teams that play full-time in The Omni: Atlanta Knights (International Hockey League)

What I'd change about The Omni: A bunch of things, starting with the multicolored seats.

What I love about The Omni: The Elvis plaque.

Statistics from Team Marketing Report, Inc.

The Hive

Founded: 1988
1993–94 Record: 41-41
Team Colors: Teal, Purple, White

Saturday, December 10–Tuesday, December 13

The night of the Hawks game had been relatively warm, at least for Atlanta in December, but by Saturday the temperature plummeted back to what was typical, and it was clear that I was no longer in Florida. Accompanying this drop in the mercury was a hard, nasty rain, and I spent most of my day in the comfort of my hotel room.

In a bizarre coincidence, the Hawks traveled to Orlando to play the Magic the night after they beat the Knicks, and so I was able to watch on television the first home game I would miss during my travels. The circumstances had been quite different during the first trip, as the team had gone on an extended road trip after I left Orlando in January '93. It was only after I'd traveled for ten days and seen games in Houston, San Antonio, and Dallas that I missed a Magic home game. It was on a Friday night as I rushed from Dallas to Denver, one of the few times I had to drive far into the evening to keep to my schedule, and I was on a lonely road outside Amarillo when the tipoff took place at the O'rena almost 1,300 miles away.

The end of my perfect attendance streak was painful, of course, but one reason I took to the road was to conclude my run in a positive way, rather than have some misfortune put a stop to it. I must admit, however, that I wasn't entirely disappointed when the Magic lost to the Heat that night. In my way of thinking, it served them right for having the audacity to play a game without me there.

But the 1994–95 Magic had yet to lose a home game, and to nobody's surprise they crushed the Hawks. One advantage to the timing of my second trip was that most of the home games I would miss would be blowouts—everyone was looking for the real show at Orlando Arena to start in the playoffs.

On Sunday I went holiday shopping for the only time during my trip, using Rachel as a guide to lead me to a convenient shopping mall located near my hotel. I was staying just off the highway in the northern part of the city, a suburban area with lush hills and twisting roads. Rachel's navigation was invaluable to me, as is any help I can get when in an unfamiliar city.

When first planning my travels, I never realized how difficult it can be to function on the road. It's easy to find food and lodging, for example, but locating something specific can be a nightmare. As much as I take for granted the local shopping malls, post offices, supermarkets, drugstores, and movie theaters, in an unfamiliar city they never seem to be around when I'm looking for them. In Atlanta, for example, while running some errands, I spent almost three hours with a letter in my pocket before I found a mailbox. Before the first trip, I never would have imagined how lost I could get during a five-minute drive to a mall in a strange city.

As it was two weeks before Christmas, the mall was a madhouse of activity, and I decided to escape while I could and shop for gifts later. I did find the time to buy a big, hooded sweatshirt to wear on the trip (my idea of holiday shopping—buying something for myself), and Rachel agreed to wash it at her apartment that evening.

On Monday I drove back into the city to the Warner Brothers Studio Store where she worked and picked up the shirt from her. We'd had fun hanging out, and even though I'd met her briefly before, I still thought of her as the first new friend I made on the trip.

That afternoon I drove to Charlotte, a trip of 250 miles that lasted until after sundown because of my late start. I crossed into South Carolina just before 5:30 PM, then entered North Carolina almost two hours later. The highway ran into Charlotte on the north side of the city, and it was there that I found a motel near the airport for my two-day visit.

Previous Hornets Games at the Charlotte Coliseum:

1992–93 season: Houston (Rockets 111-103)/Portland (Trail Blazers 121-114)/Miami (Heat 116-89)/Cleveland (Hornets 114-113)

1993-94: L.A. Lakers (Hornets 141-124)

One thing I love in sports is when a facility is nicknamed after a team, and in the NBA there's only one example of this practice. The Nuggets don't play in the Mine, the Kings don't play in the Castle, and the Rockets don't play in the Launch Pad, but travel to Charlotte and you can see the Hornets play in the Hive. I realized when I first saw the Charlotte Coliseum that the nickname fits perfectly.

In the western outskirts of Charlotte, settled among the woods south of the airport, the Billy Graham Parkway takes NBA fans to Tyvola Road, a six-lane street that snakes through the gentle hills of the North Carolina countryside. This side street runs to the base of the gradual hill on top of which sits the Hive, a hill with thousands of paved parking spots in the numerous lots to the west and south of the arena. Patrons are quickly shuffled into a space through the access roads, and once parked can gaze with wonder at the building at the top of the hill, an arena with a capacity of nearly 24,000 people, making it the NBA's largest.

Just as worker bees pack into their nest, NBA fans stream to the Hive to watch one of the league's most exciting teams, selling out all but five games since the Hornets began play in 1988. Even with such an impressive capacity, the arena doesn't appear to be anything more than a well-designed building in which to see a game. Not especially big, the Hive is round, made of rough brick that varies from dark to light brown from base to top. Lines of white trim separate the different-colored sections, and the building is topped by a white roof. There is only one entrance for most ticketholders, a huge vestibule that extends out from the west side of the building. This entrance is an attractive combination of white columns and large windows, rising above a half-dozen steps and facing the main road for incoming traffic. Set in the walls of the Hive are diamond-shaped windows, which are found between the very slight corners that keep the building from being smoothly round.

I have no idea if the architects of the Charlotte Coliseum had it in mind when they designed the arena, but the rough, tan walls and round shape certainly make it look like a hive to me.

Not only did I see four games in Charlotte during the first trip, I also found myself in the Queen City eight months later on the eve of Thanksgiving 1993. A family wedding was to take place that weekend in Virginia, and my mother had asked me to fly to North Carolina and drive my grandmother to the event.

That night against the Lakers turned out to be the only Hornets game when I had trouble finding a ticket. During the first trip, I'd bought tickets in front of the arena for all four games, never having to look very long to find something in the lower bowl at face value. With a capacity approaching 24,000, usually there are plenty of season ticket holders selling extras in front of the Hive, but on that night it took me twenty minutes even to find somebody with a pair.

The reason I'd bought scalped tickets for all the games I saw in Charlotte was that the person I spoke to in their front office always referred me to their ticket manager. It's not that the Hornets' front office was rude or anything, it's just that they never even considered giving me a ticket or letting me buy something better than what I could get at Ticketmaster. Instead, I chose to partake of the quality items that I could find at what felt like a ticket market in front of the arena.

Tuesday, December 13, 1994—7:30 PM

CHARLOTTE HORNETS (9-9) VS. MILWAUKEE BUCKS (6-12)

It has rained all day in Charlotte, and the night air is far too cold for my taste. Even the local Hornets fans are grumbling about the temperature, and as I park in the lot on the west side of the gradual hill below the arena I pray to the god of scalping that I can find a good seat quickly. Once again there are a bunch of tickets out front, but most are in the upper bowl, and tonight I am discriminating in what I buy.

✪ CHARLOTTE
COLISEUM
Opened: 1988
Capacity: 23,698
Charlotte, North Carolina

Eventually I find a $31 seat between the baskets, about a third of the way up in the lower bowl. I can tell that the guy who sells it to me is a pro, but he is exceedingly polite and honest about the ticket's location, so I give him face value even though I probably could bargain him down.

How do they put 24,000 people in the Hive? Is there an extra level, seats in every corner of the arena, fans packed in from the rafters to the floor?

Not really. I was surprised when I first walked into the Charlotte Coliseum and saw the same oval upper bowl/lower bowl design found in most NBA arenas. The difference, of course, is that the two levels are huge, and fans sitting at the top of the lower bowl have a view more like that found in the upper bowl of some arenas. And despite what I've read in some publications, the simple truth is that the slope of the seats is slight enough that in most locations the head of the person in front of you will slightly obstruct your view of the court. The angle is satisfactory, of course, but any fan familiar with other arenas will recognize the difference.

Still, there are huge advantages to such a large arena. For one thing, there are plenty of good seats at reasonable prices, making a Hornets game one of the better values in the NBA. For another, a sold-out Charlotte Coliseum is as loud as one might expect of such a huge crowd, and even though the Hive opened only six years ago it has few luxury boxes to get in the way of the action. (The designers had the good sense to put the suites at the top of the lower bowl, where they offer a good view without intruding on the standard seats.) And finally, the sightlines are decent throughout the building, even if you might have to peek over the person in front of you.

Making my way through the concourse, I am awash in teal and purple. Not only is the lower level roomy and well-designed, there is an upper concourse as well, providing a second group of concession stands and restrooms for the folks in the upper bowl. Depending on the time of the game, it's sometimes worth your while to dash upstairs to get your popcorn, as the lower concourse is usually more crowded during any break in the action.

I make my way down to the seat, and am delighted to find that I'm in the front row of my section, with a wide aisle in front of me offering plenty of legroom and opening up my view quite a bit. Next to me are a couple and their son. They are dressed casually, but around us are a ton of men and women in business clothes.

The man and his son leave to get some refreshments, and after the high-tech introductions you'd expect in a modern arena, the woman and I are alone in our row. An usher appears and asks to see our tickets. I'm somewhat surprised, considering that the ushers in the Charlotte Coliseum never seem to care about checking tickets, but since I'm in a sweatshirt among the suits and ties I don't let it bother me. I show my stub, and the woman next to me explains to the usher that her husband has her ticket. The usher appears unconcerned and leaves (I'm sure she was only worried about me—the woman was dressed well enough to blend in), but the woman is furious. Her husband returns, and she tells him the story, expressing her desire to take the stub from her husband and make a point of showing it to the usher, whom she described with a word that "rhymes with rich," to borrow a phrase. The man calms her down, and within a few minutes we are talking basketball and I am telling him all about my trip.

The man's name is Jim, and in the middle of the first quarter he points out the reason why the usher was so diligent. Making a grand entrance, complete with a camera crew in tow, is George Shinn, owner of the Hornets and big wheel in Charlotte. He sits down one row behind us, only about six seats away, and Jim nudges me with his elbow.

"You should go over there and introduce yourself," he says. "Then ask him why the Hornets have never given you a free ticket to a game, like every other team in the league."

I laugh and consider his idea, but in the end I pass. I still think of myself as a typical fan, and every free ticket I get is a bonus, not something I'm owed.

Shinn has a religious background, and perhaps that's why the Hornets take part in a ritual that I find amazing. At the start of every game I've ever seen in the Charlotte Coliseum, right before the national anthem, a local clergyman has led the crowd in an invocation. It's a short prayer, usually asking for blessings on the players or fans (or both, although on this night the invocation only addresses the players). Religion is something I never thought I'd need to mention in a book about basketball, but the Hornets manage to combine the two subjects, however briefly, at each home game. I guess some people think of it as only an extension of the national anthem, a mass ritual that anyone can ignore if they chose to, but still I wonder if many Charlotte fans are as uncomfortable with the practice as I am.

Tonight's opponent is Milwaukee, a young team rebuilding around top draft pick Glenn Robinson, but neither the Hornets nor the Bucks are tearing up the league. The Charlotte newspapers have expressed concern that the Hornets have slowed down their typical running game to shift toward a half-court offense, and in the first half the Hornets respond by pushing the ball on the break and building a 15-point lead. Home after a five-game road trip, the Hornets seem to be cruising, and I complain to Jim that the game will be a blowout. I tell him that I'm rooting for the Hornets, of course, but first and foremost I want to see a close game.

As if responding to my complaint, the Bucks cut the lead to six at half-time. Then the bottom falls out on the home team in the third quarter, as the Hornets go an amazing six minutes without scoring, and the Bucks build a 73-69 lead.

"Hope you're happy," Jim says amiably, not yet too worried. "Now you've got your close game."

Much like Orlando, games in Charlotte are big and splashy: Music blares, cheerleaders dance, a mascot plays with the crowd. The arena offers an eight-sided hanging scoreboard, the sides alternating between video screens and message boards. Lining the bottom of the lower bowl is a healthy number of scoreboards and message boards, and the team has even gone so far as to include a three-sided shot clock above each backboard so everyone in the building can quickly check its status.

My favorite of all the glitzy elements involves Alonzo Mourning. Every time Charlotte's starting center reenters the game after his first stint on the bench, the message boards show a picture of a dark castle with the title "Tower of Power" emblazoned above it. While the graphic is on-screen, the speakers blare the Darth Vader theme from *Star Wars*, giving an added rush to the ritual of his return to action.

Mourning is on the bench for much of the game, as he struggles with foul trouble from early on, but Larry Johnson steps up after a quiet first half and hits some crucial baskets in the fourth quarter. It's a game the Hornets should win, and for Jim's sake (not to mention the thousands of other Charlotte fans) I'm happy when they pull it out in the final minutes. The result is a six-point Hornets victory in a game that is the 243rd straight home sellout at the Charlotte Coliseum, the fifth longest streak in the NBA.

I met Jim by chance, but his story is one of the most amazing I heard during all my NBA travels. He's a sales manager at a car dealership in Princeton, West Virginia, almost 175 miles from Charlotte. Even so, he's had season tickets for the Hornets since their first year, and for about three-quarters of their games he's packed his wife and nine-year-old son into the car and driven for three hours to get to the Hive. If it's a weekend game, the family might stay overnight in Charlotte, but most of the time Jim turns around and drives back to Princeton right after the game ends, with his wife by his side and his son sleeping in the back seat. For

Jim, a game night starts at three or four in the afternoon and ends at one in the morning.

And perhaps most astounding is that he's an average fan. He's not one of those creepy people who seem way too wrapped up in the game, but a knowledgeable and pleasant guy with a good sense of humor. I can't imagine the odds of meeting him at random in a crowd of almost 24,000 people, but it certainly was a pleasant surprise.

By the way, if you're wondering if I'd drive six hours round-trip to see the Magic play, I can tell you that I certainly would—maybe three or four times a year, anyway. Final score: Hornets 107, Bucks 101.

Average 1994–95 ticket cost: $22.43 (26th highest in the NBA)

Beer: $2.25 (16 oz.)

Soda: $1.00 (16 oz.—Coca-Cola products)

Hot Dog: $1.50

Parking: $4.00

Mascot: Hugo (a hornet, obviously)

Cheerleaders: The Honey Bees

Remote-controlled blimp: yes (Air Hugo, a giant version of the Hornets' mascot)

Other teams that play full-time in the Charlotte Coliseum: Charlotte Rage (Arena Football League)

What I'd change about the Charlotte Coliseum: Take out a few seats and increase the slope from the floor.

What I love about the Charlotte Coliseum: The prices, the loyal fans, the team's colors, and the fact that it looks like a hive.

Statistics from Team Marketing Report, Inc.

NBA standings as of Wednesday, December 14, 1994:

EASTERN CONFERENCE
Atlantic Division

	W	L	Pct	GB	Home	Away
Orlando Magic	15	4	.789	—	9-0	6-4
New York Knicks	11	7	.611	3.5	7-2	4-5
Boston Celtics	9	11	.450	6.5	5-6	4-5
Philadelphia 76ers	8	11	.421	7	5-6	3-5
New Jersey Nets	9	13	.409	7.5	6-5	3-8
Washington Bullets	6	11	.353	8	3-4	3-7
Miami Heat	5	13	.278	9.5	3-5	2-8

Central Division

	W	L	Pct	GB	Home	Away
Indiana Pacers	12	6	.667	—	6-1	6-5
Cleveland Cavaliers	12	8	.600	1	7-4	5-4
Charlotte Hornets	10	9	.526	2.5	5-3	5-6
Chicago Bulls	10	9	.526	2.5	5-4	5-5
Atlanta Hawks	9	11	.450	4	5-5	4-6
Detroit Pistons	8	11	.421	4.5	6-3	2-8
Milwaukee Bucks	6	13	.316	6.5	3-5	3-8

WESTERN CONFERENCE
Midwest Division

	W	L	Pct	GB	Home	Away
Houston Rockets	13	6	.684	—	6-3	7-3
Utah Jazz	12	8	.600	1.5	8-4	4-4
Denver Nuggets	10	7	.588	2	6-4	4-3
Dallas Mavericks	9	8	.529	3	5-6	4-2
San Antonio Spurs	9	9	.500	3.5	6-5	3-4
Minnesota Timberwolves	3	16	.158	10	0-9	3-7

Pacific Division

	W	L	Pct	GB	Home	Away
Phoenix Suns	14	5	.737	—	8-0	6-5
Seattle SuperSonics	12	6	.667	1.5	8-1	4-5
L.A. Lakers	12	7	.632	2	4-3	8-4
Sacramento Kings	11	8	.579	3	7-3	4-5
Portland Trail Blazers	9	8	.529	4	6-4	3-4
Golden State Warriors	8	12	.400	6.5	5-4	3-8
L.A. Clippers	2	17	.105	12	1-10	1-7

Shooting Blanks

Founded: 1961
1993–94 Record: 24-58
Team Colors: Red, White, Blue

Wednesday, December 14–Thursday, December 15

To drive from Charlotte to Washington in one day is a pretty long haul, and since I had the night off I decided not to push it. On Wednesday I covered 320 miles, entering Virginia just before 4 PM and stopping for the night at a budget motel in Ashland, a few miles north of Richmond. Thursday was brisk but clear, and I enjoyed the midday sun as I continued north toward Maryland, crossing the state line at 2:30 PM and reaching Landover a half-hour later, a quick day's travel of 105 miles.

One of my strategies on the first trip was to limit the number of times when I had to drive and see a game on the same day. I was concerned about spacing out my stops, not only to avoid cramping the schedule but also to give me a fighting chance to deal with any minor emergencies I might encounter. For my second tour of the NBA, however, I decided to push things a little more, planning to see as many games as I could since I'd visited all the teams before.

Even so, my experience on both trips was that games were much more enjoyable on the days I didn't drive. Traveling to a city, even if many hours before the game, doesn't offer me the chance to relax, settle in, and concentrate on the team and arena. It's not that watching an NBA game takes a great deal of energy, it's just that if I go into the area without taking a little time to focus, the game often seems a blur. Whenever possible, I like to read the newspaper, glance at the two teams' rosters, and maybe get a little background on the players I'm going to see.

Still, one thing that excited me about traveling a second time was the chance to pick up the pace a little bit and see how much NBA action I could watch. With my previous experience at traveling, I figured that a few more days with both driving and games would be acceptable. Tinkering with the dates and locations, I was able to pack in thirty-eight games outside Orlando, only three short of the amount each NBA team plays at home during a season. It would require many days of extensive driving, and the most intense leg would be on the East Coast during my stops in Washington, Philadelphia, New Jersey, New York, and Boston. At those five arenas, I would see a whopping eight games in nine nights, starting with my return to USAir Arena.

> **Previous Bullets Games at USAir Arena:**
>
> **1992–93 season:** New Jersey (Bullets 97-92)
> **1993–94**: Boston (Celtics 100-88)

Once I had visited every NBA arena, it was no surprise that people wanted to know what I thought were the best and worst among the league's venues. I didn't have a single hands-down favorite, but when it comes to the worst arena in the NBA, one building stands out: USAir Arena, formerly the Capital Centre, home of the Washington Bullets.

Although the Bullets represent the District of Columbia, their arena is just across the district's eastern border in Landover, Maryland, near a part of the highway loop that surrounds Washington. Only a few minutes from downtown, the area surrounding USAir Arena is downright suburban, a thickly wooded landscape spoiled only by roads laden with the typical indications of a nearby city—an assortment of fast-food restaurants, motels, and department stores. Driving east from the city, Bullets fans pass under a highway and turn onto a side street, weaving past a hotel, retirement complex, and some corporate buildings on a small road that leads to USAir Arena. It's a strange place to have an arena, in the middle of what seems like a sleepy suburb.

The arena is visible from the highway that passes nearby, but unless you're familiar with it you might not recognize it as an NBA facility. Built in 1973, USAir Arena looks as if the only thing that has changed since the day it opened is its name. Surrounded by parking lots that have cheesy red, white, and blue signs marking the different rows, the arena is a tan, white, and gray building that is both a marvel of unique design and a celebration of ugliness. Rising high on its east and west sides, USAir Arena curves down to a sunken middle, giving the arena an appearance more traditional for an outdoor stadium than an enclosed building. Stretching across the top of the building is a series of thick black wires whose function I couldn't fathom, because the huge concrete pillars that support the elevated east and west sides make me think that the structure has proper support without the wires' help. Whatever the reason for the design, I can't imagine anyone would want to have their city represented by an arena that appears to be masquerading as a football stadium.

Built into the corners of the arena are the entrances, with the ticket windows located on the southwest corner, closest to the main entrance road. The wall containing the ticket windows is painted a deep blue, with white stars and red trim. The four lots around the arena, obviously named in a frenzy of patriotic spirit, are designated Stars and Stripes, Capitol, Eagle, and Liberty Bell Parking. I guess with a hockey team called the Capitals sharing the building, the folks at USAir couldn't avoid such touches, but around such a battered building they are rather sad.

During my first visit to Landover, right in the middle of basketball season, I saw something in a USAir parking lot that made me think that even the Bullets don't care much about their arena's appearance. It was a burned-out Camaro, a charred shell of a vehicle with smashed windows and a decimated interior that had been stripped and set on fire, with its hood popped in an ugly testament to urban decay. The car clearly had been sitting in the lot for a long time, and even though it was a fair distance from the entrances, as I looked at it I could only shake my head in disbelief. Didn't somebody want to have the car removed?

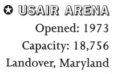

○ **USAIR ARENA**
Opened: 1973
Capacity: 18,756
Landover, Maryland

Thursday, December 15, 1994—7:30 PM

WASHINGTON BULLETS (6-11) VS. UTAH JAZZ (13-8)

For the second game in a row, I'll be sitting with a guy named Jim. The Jim in Washington is a molecular biologist who happens to be a Bullets fan, and when I contacted people in the basketball newsgroups on the Internet he was one of those who responded. I invited him to join me for tonight's game, and he meets me at the hotel where I will be staying for the night, just down the street from the arena.

The prospect of seeing the Bullets play has become much more positive since the team acquired Rookie of the Year Chris Webber from the Warriors, but in his first weeks with the club the second-year star forward has yet to lead the team to glory. Still, he's having an immediate impact in one department: The Bullets are selling a lot more tickets.

As we walk to the arena, Jim tells me that attendance was increasing even before Webber arrived. Amazingly, the Bullets in recent seasons have been breaking records for tickets sold, despite consistently poor play and a subpar arena. Jim tells me that the increase was mostly due to the tireless effort of Bullets President Susan O'Malley, the league's only female team president. In each of her first three seasons in that capacity, the Bullets have broken the team record for average attendance, and last year they had over 15,000 fans per game. Although I shudder to think of what Bullets games must have been like before she took over, Jim tells me that one of their main strategies has been to promote the opposing teams. The sad truth is, the Bullets just don't have the fan base that the other Washington teams do, but fortunately for them, NBA basketball is the perfect game to hype the visitors.

The hotel is less than a mile from the arena's turnstiles, and after walking through the cold night air I'm relieved when we reach the entrance to the heated building. The Bullets have left us a pair of comp tickets, and I feel a little guilty about my negative opinion of their arena. The truth is, one of things I like most about the Bullets is their front office—they've always treated me well.

The pair is in the lower bowl, almost on the dead end about halfway up behind a basket, and we walk through the arena's concourse level to make our way to the seats. The walls are constructed of concrete blocks painted with red, white, and blue trim, while similar designs hang over each of the corner entrances. Every pillar and beam has a small flag design as well.

The concourse has a typical number of concession stands, but the Bullets are woefully lacking if you're looking to shop for a souvenir. Only a couple of small booths are set up on the concourse, each offering a mere handful of merchandise. Although the demand for Bullets souvenirs might be limited, I still think the team's image would improve if they stocked their stands in a way that suggested somebody might want to buy something with their logo on it.

Just like the Hornets two nights ago, the Bullets are playing their first home game after a road trip, but they still should be much more rested than Utah, tonight's opponent. The Jazz played last night in Minnesota, and in a brutal twist of scheduling immediately had to fly halfway across the country for a second road game less than 24 hours later. But every other indication is that this will be a tough matchup, as the Jazz are healthy and playing well, and the Bullets are missing Rex Chapman and Don MacLean, two of their top scorers.

Even though our seats are behind the basket, we're up high enough to have a decent view of the court. The arena is the first I've seen on this trip that isn't tiered, with both lower and upper levels. Instead, USAir Arena has a stadium design, with the higher sections located behind the lower ones. Because the roof slopes down in the middle, fans sitting in the top seats can't see across the arena to the other side, and during the game the lights are turned off upstairs, giving the upper seats a cramped and dim atmosphere. At least the last few rows of the end sections are spared such a claustrophobic view, as the number of rows shrinks in the corners and on the ends.

Hanging over center court is a typical four-sided scoreboard, complete with big-screen video monitors that offer a decent picture of the action. Around the rest of the arena are other message boards and scoreboards, including some that are rather distinctive. In opposite corners are two message boards that only show advertisements throughout the game, while two unmarked center scoreboards hang over entrance portals and display total rebounds for each team. But the most curious are two score-boards located in the opposite corners from the advertising boards, which continuously show a two-digit number that changes frequently and hovers around 80. Jim explains that they are sound meters, register-ing the noise made by the crowd. In theory they're a good idea, but they rarely seemed to fluctuate much, and I doubt that they're accurate. Unfortunately, despite the sellout crowd, the game will offer little chance for much cheering anyway.

The Bullets announce the starters in typical fashion, accompanying their lineup with an original rap song that must have been recorded pretty recently, as it mentions Webber in the lyrics. The most memorable thing about the start of a game in Washington, for me at least, happens during the national anthem. When the performer reaches the final lines and sings "Oh, say does that..." the crowd shouts "Oh!" at the proper moment. Jim tells me that the ritual is borrowed from nearby Baltimore, where Orioles fans perform it at the start of their baseball games. It's a neat touch, although it would be nice if the Bullets had a similar tradition of their own, not one borrowed from another team.

The game is close through one quarter, but the action is sloppy as the Jazz build a 20-16 lead. Although the Bullets show signs of life in the second quarter, some typically solid play from Utah's John Stockton and Karl Malone leads to an eight-point Jazz lead at halftime.

We're on the end of the arena near the visitor's bench, and as a result we get a good view of the NBA's most famous fan, Robin Ficker. Just like the Fat Guy in Orlando, Ficker is an attorney, but their style of rooting for their teams is markedly different. The Fat Guy uses his fame to unify the crowd in cheering for the Magic, but Ficker has opted to single-handedly attack the opposing team. From his seat a few rows behind the visitor's bench, Ficker wages a one-man war, carrying signs and noise-makers in an attempt to disrupt their concentration. His actions have led to some radical maneuvers by the subjects of his wrath, including moving team huddles onto the floor and holding up a large banner between him and the court. In addition, the NBA added a rule a few seasons ago prohib-iting fans from disrupting communication between the coaches and their teams. The league denied that it had any connection to Washington's rabid fan, but the new edict still became known in some circles as the "Ficker Rule."

Tonight Ficker is flashing a sign that serves both to support the Bullets and degrade the Jazz. On one side it reads "Lil' Gheorghe is our Romain Hero," and he holds up a head of lettuce as he displays it to the court. (It's a reference to Gheorghe Muresan, the Bullets' second-year center who is Romanian.) On the other side is printed "Wimp List: Mailman/Benoit/ Spencer/Hornacek," a message that shows a surprising lack of wit. Although he's relatively low-key on this night, in the past I've seen him pull out a trumpet and start blowing the "Charge!" theme. He hasn't given up all his props, though, and still has a small plastic megaphone that he uses to amplify his voice. After witnessing his act in person, I have the feeling he could get along without it. All I can do is wonder: What kind of person would make such an effort to prove that he's the biggest jerk in a crowd of 18,756 people?

It is the worst kind of game to watch, a night when the visiting team jumps ahead and maintains a lead right around ten points. No matter what the Bullets do, they just can't seem to put together a stretch of strong offensive play, and whenever they show signs of life they are brushed back by Utah's powerful tandem of Stockton and Malone. To make matters worse, Utah guard Jeff Hornacek is in a zone, draining one jumper after another.

On a night like this, the entertainment during breaks in the game becomes important, and the Bullets offer plenty of it. Besides the cheerleaders and mascot, the team has a series of live segments with a host who heads into the crowd to interact with the fans during breaks in the action. He's got the kind of manner usually found in a low-key game show host, and as part of his duties he conducts a couple of short interviews and contests. At one point, he asks a fan a trivia question, and later goes up to host a segment where the crowd votes on the "fan of the game" by applauding after a series of photos.

The host's actions are broadcast on the video screens, and he's followed by a spotlight. In addition to the remote segments, the Bullets have a full complement of fan contests, but they take place in an unusual environment. Most of the events are pretty typical, but the crowd quickly turns on anyone who fails to win. What's most shocking to me is that the p.a. announcer encourages the negative reaction. If I ever take part in an NBA contest, I pray that it's not in Washington—I don't need the pressure of the Bullets fans, who are among the most merciless in the league.

Jim and I hope that the Jazz might be winded from their game last night, but they are never really threatened in the fourth quarter. The Bullets are young and have little experience together, and without two of their top scorers they can't put up much of a fight. As Jim and I walk past the gridlock of cars leaving the arena (like in Charlotte, the isolation of USAir Arena's parking lot slows down traffic after a game), I can't help but think that the best time to watch the Bullets play the Jazz will be in a season or two. Final score: Jazz 95, Bullets 85.

Average 1994–95 ticket cost: $25.18 (20th highest in the NBA)

Beer: $3.25 (14 oz.)

Soda: $1.90 (16 oz.—Coca-Cola products)

Hot Dog: $1.95

Parking: $6.00

Mascot: Hoops (sunglasses-wearing guy with basketball head and hoop body)

Cheerleaders: The Bullettes

Remote-controlled blimp: yes

Other teams that play full-time in USAir Arena: Washington Capitals (National Hockey League), Washington Warthogs (Continental Indoor Soccer League)

What I'd change about USAir Arena: Gee, just about everything?

What I love about USAir Arena: That it will be the Bullets' home court for only a few more seasons. Several weeks after my visit to see the Bullets during my second trip, team owner Abe Pollin announced firm plans to build a new, updated arena for the Bullets and Capitals closer to downtown Washington. All I can say is, the sooner the better.

Statistics from Team Marketing Report, Inc.

Rocky Weekend

Founded: 1949
1993–94 Record: 25-57
Team Colors: Red, White, Blue

Friday, December 16–Saturday, December 17

Another day, another arena, another game.

The ritual was the same that morning as every day that I checked out of a hotel. First, I unplugged my alarm clock and placed it between my two pillows, wrapped them up in my blanket, and stuffed the package into a garbage bag for easy transportation. Next, I disconnected my computer from the phone line and packed it into a knapsack, along with my *Rand McNally Road Atlas* and a notebook containing detailed routes between cities. After filling up my small bag of toiletries, I then stuffed it into the duffel bag I'd brought in, which contained that week's worth of T-shirts, socks, and boxer shorts. Newspapers, game programs, and folders with notes for each team went into the fake-leather pouch, and then the other items I used during my stay had to be returned to my small all-purpose bag with the Magic logo on it. Finally, I packed my pants and shirts in the small suitcases.

I had two choices when leaving a hotel: either use one of the carts in the lobby or make two or three trips by foot from the room to my car. By the second tour, I was pretty familiar with the routine, and could usually streamline the process into two trips. The trick was to have enough stuff to feel comfortable, but not so much as to make packing and unpacking difficult.

The process of moving so frequently can quickly become tiresome, but my hasty tour of the East Coast demanded it, so for the third day in a row I packed up my Volkswagen late that morning and continued north.

The good news was that Philadelphia is a quick and easy drive from Landover, a short 130 miles straight up I-95. Although the day started sunny outside Washington, by the time I was underway it had clouded up once again. Passing through Baltimore, I looked from the elevated highway toward the downtown area and got a brief glimpse of Camden Yards, the Orioles' new facility that had become the model for recent baseball stadiums. I considered pulling off the road to get a closer look at the ballpark, but some errands had put me on the road later than I would have liked. Not to mention the fact that I, like most fans, wasn't really enthusiastic about devoting any time or energy to baseball. Nothing like a long, ugly, greedy strike to discourage loyalty to a sport.

At about a quarter of four I entered Delaware, and a half hour later I was in Pennsylvania settling into a hotel in Essington about three hours before the Sixers game was to start. Even though Philadelphia's team was struggling to rebuild after losing Charles Barkley, I was still looking forward to cheering them on at the Spectrum. Not only were the Sixers one of the nicest organizations in the league to me, they were also one of only six teams I had never seen win on their home court. One of my goals was not only to have seen a game in every NBA arena, but also to have seen every NBA team win at least one home game.

Although such a feat sounds improbable, I thought there was a good chance of it happening. In the 32 games I saw outside Orlando on the first trip, the home teams had a record of 21-11. Of those eleven losses, three were by the Hornets and one by the Timberwolves, both teams that I saw win other home games during my visits to their cities. Of the other seven losses, one was by the Celtics, but I'd seen them win several games at the Garden while I lived in Boston. So I was only six teams shy of fulfilling my second goal: the Sixers, Pistons, Bulls, Trail Blazers, Warriors, and Mavericks.

It looked quite possible on paper. The Sixers weren't a great team, but I would see them play twice. The Pistons could probably beat the Celtics at home, the team they would face when I visited Auburn Hills. The Bulls, Trail Blazers, Warriors, and Mavericks were all playing decent basketball when I began my second trip, and in all four cities I would see two games. I couldn't help but feel confident that it could happen, expanding my accomplishments as an NBA fan even more. Maybe some other fan has been to every arena to see a game, but I couldn't imagine that anybody else had seen a home win in all 27 cities.

> **Previous 76ers Games at the Spectrum:**
>
> **1992–93 season:** Dallas (Mavericks 89-87)

If you ever travel the NBA, you'll probably find yourself cheating in a few cities. I started my adventures thinking that I would go sightseeing whenever possible, but by the end of my travels I was doing everything I could to conserve energy and make things as simple as possible.

With such a philosophy in mind, Philadelphia was a piece of cake. The Spectrum is located south of downtown, a short distance from I-95, which runs across the outskirts of the city before looping north toward New Jersey. Roughly ten miles west of the arena is the airport, and if you don't mind hiding out during your visit, you can avoid most of the hassles associated with a major city while staying a quick ten-minute drive from the game. Just look for a hotel in Essington, where you can find the perfect room to match your budget among the half-dozen hotels.

The area around the Spectrum is relatively barren, a landscape of parking lots and empty blocks with only a few trees to break the monotony. Downtown is to the north, and on that side of the Spectrum is Veterans Stadium, the home of the Philadelphia Eagles and Phillies. The two sports facilities, which between them house four major league franchises, look strikingly similar in design, certainly much more so than the arena–stadium pairings found in Denver or Oakland, for example.

The Spectrum is an oval building, constructed of brown brick accented with white trim, with a ring of windows near the top that make the upper bowl visible from the outside. Although the design is unspectacular, it's not unattractive either, and there are a couple of neat touches on the outside of the Spectrum. On the north side is a statue of Rocky Balboa, the fictitious boxer made famous by Sylvester Stallone in the movies. On the south side is another statue of a larger-than-life figure, the late diva Kate Smith. As if those two weren't enough, a courtyard on the south side that leads to the ticket windows is dominated by a complex re-creation of a hockey scene. A skater, arms raised in victory, is depicted moments after scoring a goal, and the intricate work includes the figure of an opposing goaltender and the net that the puck has just entered. All three displays are pretty impressive, considering that only a handful of arenas have any statues as decoration.

South of the Spectrum is an empty lot that was used for parking during my first visit, but is now the site of a brand-new facility under construction. Called the CoreStates Center, it will be a 21,000-seat arena to be occupied by the Sixers and Flyers, currently the two main tenants of the Spectrum. Scheduled to open in 1996, the CoreStates Center will be the latest in a string of new NBA arenas with plenty of luxury boxes and an increased capacity.

What's unfortunate is that, of all the arenas scheduled for replacement, the Spectrum is the only one where I didn't see much of a need for change. Even though the arena opened in 1967, in my opinion it's a traditional eastern NBA building that isn't a bad place to see a game.

Friday, December 16, 1994—7:30 PM

PHILADELPHIA 76ERS (8-12) VS. CLEVELAND CAVALIERS (13-8)

I park near the site of the CoreStates Center, which has just begun to take shape. CoreStates is a local bank, and as part of the agreement to put their name on the new arena they have also added their moniker to the current building. Although I was completely unaware of the change, the Spectrum is now officially known as the CoreStates Spectrum. I only hope that they didn't pay too much extra for the change, as the only place where anyone uses the new name is at the arena. All the newspaper and TV coverage that I come across, even in Philadelphia, still refers to the building as "the Spectrum," without any mention of CoreStates.

The concourse of the Spectrum continues the brick motif, and near one entrance is a big painting that depicts the future of the area, showing Veterans Stadium, the Spectrum, and the CoreStates Center once the whole complex is completed.

✪ THE CORESTATES
SPECTRUM
Opened: 1967
Capacity: 18,168
Philadelphia, Pennsylvania

As I make my way to my seat, it's almost time for tip-off, and a quick look around makes me think that the new arena probably wouldn't be built if it weren't for the Flyers. The simple truth is, Philadelphia is a hockey town, and the Sixers struggle to bring fans into the arena on the nights they play. Philadelphia averaged only 12,425 people per night in '93–94, the second-worst attendance in the league. On this night, there are just under 10,000 fans in the seats, making the Spectrum almost half-empty (or half-full, if you're an optimist).

The arena is designed in the typical oval layout, with the upper bowl hanging over the last few rows of the lower bowl. In addition, a third level runs around the top of the arena, five rows of discount seats priced at $10. They're actually not a bad option, one of the few opportunities in the league to buy a seat between the baskets for little more than the cost of a movie ticket.

The center scoreboard is six-sided, each showing a video picture of the game. The player boards are built into the base of the upper bowl on the ends of the arena, and are arranged along a horizontal line instead of the traditional vertical design.

The Sixers don't need to move to have some luxury boxes, as the Spectrum has suites built into the top of each lower bowl section. The seat they've given me is a few rows in front of one of the corner suites, close to the same location they gave me on my first visit to their arena. It's a decent seat, as once again the Philadelphia front office has been extremely kind to me.

The opening announcements follow the typical pattern, although the highlight is a computer-generated graphic showing a basketball flying through the city streets to the Spectrum. The most interesting element of the pregame tonight, however, is the presentation of the game ball from the Sixers' last home game to Willie Burton. While I was watching the Hornets play in Charlotte on Tuesday night, Burton and the Sixers were squaring off against the Heat, the team that had waived him earlier in the season. In a historic example of payback, Burton lit up the Heat for 53 points, leading the Sixers to a blowout win. On top of all that, Burton's total was the highest ever recorded at the Spectrum, surpassing the old mark of 52 set by Michael Jordan. As I wait for the game to start, I can only hope that Burton will stay in the zone tonight against Cleveland.

The Cavaliers are wearing their new uniforms, the ugliest jerseys introduced in the NBA in a long time, and once again they start things off with the same style of basketball that lulled the Magic to sleep in the game in Orlando the night before I left. With the Sixers struggling to improve and the Cavs slowing their game, I figured that the atmosphere in the Spectrum would be less than electric, and it turns out that my guess is correct. It's the second of three games I'll see in Philadelphia during my travels, and even though all three are on weekend nights, the Spectrum never seems like an NBA arena.

The crowd is an unusual mixture of people. There are some Sixers fans, of course, but they are outnumbered by two other types of people at the Spectrum. A large percentage of the crowd is groups, many of them from local schools and youth organizations. In addition, a huge number of

people seem to be at the arena just to watch a basketball game, not necessarily to cheer for the home team. Many are parents that bring their kids
and don't actively root for the Sixers, but instead just watch the action and
chat about a myriad of topics that rarely relate to basketball. Other people
of that type cheer for the game, not the teams. One night, for example, I
sat behind a young man who clapped for each team when they scored,
not taking sides until late in the game, and then cheering for the visitors.

Such a crowd makeup is found in several arenas, usually in cities where
the team is struggling. In the case of Philadelphia, however, several fans
have told me that the Sixers haven't had a solid fan base in a long time,
even when the team was enjoying success in the 1980s after winning the
NBA championship in 1983. One fact clearly illustrates how bad things
are in Philadelphia: The team hasn't played a preseason game in the
Spectrum in seven seasons.

The Sixers hang around with the Cavs in a game that is agonizingly low-
scoring, and at halftime Cleveland leads 42-33. A mere 33 points in the
first half gives me little hope that the Sixers will provide the win I so desperately want to see at the Spectrum, but in the third quarter the Sixers
make a run behind the hot shooting of guard Dana Barros. Philadelphia
pulls to within 52-50, but for the rest of the night play a frustrating game
of catch-up.

The misery reaches a head when the Sixers, still within striking distance, turn the ball over three times in the final minute. Barros finishes
with 30 points, but the rest of the team never heats up, and his effort is
in vain. I'll have to wait until tomorrow night for my chance to see the
Sixers win, but they've played well enough to give me some confidence.
As usual, the Spectrum has been a decent building to see a game, complete with the legacy of some great NBA teams and players, but the
Philadelphia fans don't seem to share my enthusiasm. Final score:
Cavaliers 84, 76ers 80.

The Sixers' game at the Spectrum on Saturday is against the Pistons, so I
rest up in my hotel room during the day and catch up on my NBA reading. The Pistons are 8-12, losers of five straight and only 2-8 on the road,

so I am confident that the Sixers will come through and produce a win for me at the Spectrum.

I should be so lucky. Once again, the game stays close throughout, and near the end of the third quarter the Sixers make a push to put them ahead by seven. Still, the Pistons battle back, and late in the fourth the score is tied.

Crossing my fingers, cheering as loudly as possible, all I can do is watch as Pistons forward Terry Mills hits a three-pointer with a minute left. For the second night in a row, the Sixers can't manage to score in the final moments, and their best chance, an attempted three by Willie Burton, turns out to be an airball. Just like the few Sixers fans in the Spectrum (the attendance is 11,642), for the second time in 24 hours I feel the sting of a young Philadelphia team's inability to execute down the stretch. Final score: Pistons 97, 76ers 92.

Average 1994–95 ticket cost: $26.99 (18th highest in the NBA)

Beer: $3.50 (16 oz.)

Soda: $1.50 (12 oz.—Pepsi products)

Hot Dog: $2.00

Parking: $6.00

Mascot: Big Shot (cartoonish-looking purple guy with a big gold chain around his neck)

Cheerleaders: The Dream Team

Remote-controlled blimp: yes

Other teams that play full-time in the Spectrum: Philadelphia Flyers (National Hockey League), Philadelphia Wings (Major Indoor Lacrosse League), Philadelphia Bulldogs (Roller Hockey International)

What I'd change about the Spectrum: The fans.

What I love about the Spectrum: The functional design and the great tradition.

Statistics from Team Marketing Report, Inc.

In the Swamp of the Dragons

Founded: 1967
1993–94 Record: 45-37
Team Colors: Red, White, Blue

Sunday, December 18

With my dream of seeing a win in each arena dashed, I glumly continued on my voyage. Still using I-95 north, I passed through Philadelphia and began to weave my way through smaller highways into New Jersey. Crossing the state line at 1:30 PM, I made steady progress north, eventually joining up with the notorious New Jersey Turnpike in the center of the state.

From there I made my way to exit 14, an extension of the turnpike that branches east toward New York City. It was a bright afternoon, and as I made my way up the elevated highway I could see the Statue of Liberty ahead of me in New York Harbor. The road curved to the left, while to my right was the Hudson River. The city stood behind it, the glorious group of skyscrapers that make up the world's most famous skyline. Although I dislike life in the Big Apple, I have to admit that the sight of New York City always gives me a thrill.

I followed the signs to the Holland Tunnel, but as I approached its entrance I made a left turn and began to work my way through the streets of Hoboken. The birthplace of baseball and Frank Sinatra, the small New Jersey city is typical for the area. Located between the Lincoln and Holland Tunnels, Hoboken is a congested mass of streets, each lined with parked cars on both sides, with most running only one way. Because of the many parked cars, the roads are extremely claustrophobic, and the numerous double-parked vehicles forced me to hold my breath as I squeezed by them while following the directions my friend Jarel gave me.

Jarel, another former Universal Studios guide, now lives in Hoboken while studying in New York to be an actor. After a few minutes on the crowded streets, I located his building, and three blocks later found a spot for my car. Calling upon my long-lost skill at parallel parking, which is rarely required in Orlando, I was able to squeeze into the space. Twenty minutes later I'd unloaded my stuff and locked up my car, hoping it would be safe on the street.

I joined Jarel and his friends as they watched some afternoon football, then headed out two hours later to see the Nets play the Heat at the Meadowlands, a quick ten-minute trip through the small highways in the area. There I would meet Dan and Christine, two more transplanted friends who had left the sunny Florida climate for life in New Jersey.

> **Previous Nets Games at the Meadowlands Arena:**
>
> **1992-93 season:** Atlanta (Nets 114-93)

In my experience, New Jersey is the subject of more jokes than any other state, and driving down the Turnpike you can see why. The highway runs through the middle of the state, and much of the scenery is a mass of industrial developments. Yet most of Jersey's landscape is no more or less pretty than any other northeastern state (they do call it the Garden State, after all).

When it comes to reputation, Jersey's proximity to New York City is a blessing and a curse. There are many benefits to being located near America's largest metropolis, especially when it comes to sports. Given its small size, New Jersians must feel fortunate to have two football teams, a hockey club and an NBA team playing in their state.

Yet all the professional action in Jersey takes place at the Meadowlands Sports Complex, which is basically an extension of the New York City metropolitan area. Located only a few miles from the river that separates Jersey from the Big Apple, the Meadowlands contains a football stadium, racetrack, and the Brendan Byrne Arena, home of the New Jersey Nets.

Much of the area around the Meadowlands is relatively barren, with several major highways crisscrossing nearby. The location will definitely not be featured on any travel brochures produced by the New Jersey Department of Tourism, as the Meadowlands is in the heart of the industrialized areas around the turnpike. The three facilities are a fair distance from each other, divided by acres of parking lots, and the Meadowlands Arena isn't dwarfed by its larger neighbors.

The arena is a modern white building, with a square design that includes indents on each side that show the outline of the upper bowl. Each of the four sides has the same pattern, with stairs and rampways built at each corner to allow access to the concourse level.

Several large entry roads give easy access to the facility, especially on the nights when the arena has a less-than-capacity crowd. During a normal winter, namely one without a work-stoppage in the NHL, the Meadowlands is an extremely busy complex, with Nets and Devils games at the arena, Jets or Giants games each weekend at the stadium, and racing for much of the season at the track. Even so, I've usually found that the traffic in and out of the complex moves pretty smoothly. If you're not bothered by the fact that the Meadowlands is in the middle of nowhere, you can easily have a good time at any of the various events held there.

The problem is, not many people want to go, at least not to see the Nets. Although a trip to the Meadowlands from suburban New Jersey involves only a drive on the highways, unlike the many obstacles present when trying to see a Knicks game in the city, Jersians have always treated the Nets as the black sheep of the New York basketball family. Much of the disdain comes from the suburban aura that surrounds the team, which is definitely not the case with the Knicks and their Manhattan arena. Yet the Nets are also one of the NBA's most troubled franchises, a club that can't shake a negative image despite All-Star talent and competitive rosters in the last few seasons. Like the Los Angeles Clippers out west, the Nets struggle to find a fan base in an area where it's all too easy to root for a different local team with a rich tradition and bigger commitment to winning. After my stops in Washington and Philadelphia, the Nets would be the third team in a row I visited that relied on the visiting team to draw fans.

In some ways I felt sorry for the Nets. When I first visited the Meadowlands in March 1993, the team had two young superstars in Derrick Coleman and Kenny Anderson, one of the league's best guards in Drazen Petrovic, and a quality head coach in Chuck Daly, who had led the Nets to a 36-26 record on the night I saw them beat the Hawks. When I returned to the Meadowlands less than two years later, things were dramatically different. Petrovic was gone, the victim of a fatal car accident in the summer of 1993, Daly had resigned, and Coleman had begun to express dissatisfaction with the team. Even Anderson, not known for causing problems, had begun to show signs of strain as well.

On the other hand, the 1994–95 Nets were making it harder for me to muster much sympathy. My biggest objection was the widely reported rumor that the team hoped to change their name, abandoning the nickname they've had for more than twenty-five years to become—get this—the "New Jersey Swamp Dragons." The team has a simple, dignified name that has a nicely lyrical quality and pays tribute to an important part of the game. Yet the team's front office hoped to clutter things up with a new moniker that they obviously felt would make the club more trendy, thus selling a great deal of merchandise to impressionable eight-year-olds. After years of growth toward becoming a respectable franchise, the Nets looked to a quick-fix solution to impress some superficial basketball fans.

To make matter worse, the Nets actually tried to go through with the idea. A few weeks after I visited, New Jersey officially asked the NBA for permission to become the Fire Dragons (horribly redundant and nonsensical, the name was even dumber than their first choice). Thankfully, the league showed the common sense to turn them down. Even though they were unsuccessful, the Nets' attempt to make the change showed a disheartening lack of respect for tradition, and gave the team an unflattering air of desperation.

It was probably understandable, then, that the Nets treated me differently during the planning of my two trips. The first time, New Jersey's media director left me a comp single, but when I called the second time he asked me to pay. Still, their front office was relatively courteous and helpful, and certainly no more difficult to deal with than most other teams.

✪ **THE MEADOWLANDS ARENA**
Opened: 1981
Capacity: 20,049
East Rutherford,
New Jersey

Sunday, December 18, 1994—7:30 PM

NEW JERSEY NETS (9-15) VS. MIAMI HEAT (6-14)

It's a clear night, cold but not frigid, and the nearly full moon casts a bright light across the Jersey landscape. Illuminated by floodlights that highlight its design, the Meadowlands Arena looks stunning, a classically symmetrical oasis of white that seems to beckon in the darkness. On the first night I saw a game in New Jersey, there was a raging snowstorm blanketing the area, and as I stand in front of the Meadowlands Arena tonight I realize that I missed out on one of the nicer elements of a Nets game: the view from outside the building.

I meet my friends Dan and Christine near the ticket window in the first-floor lobby, and we take the escalator up to the concourse level. We haven't seen each other in a while, and the three of us spend a lot of our time together just catching up on things. Although Christine grew up in Jersey, she follows the trend of most of the NBA fans in her state and roots for the Knicks. Actually, none of us are especially thrilled to be seeing the Nets play, especially against a disappointing Miami Heat team still struggling to blend together.

The Meadowlands Arena is a relatively new facility, and the concourse and seats are clean and well-designed. It's a big building, holding just over 20,000 for basketball, and although the capacity would allow plenty of fans to see the game, the stands are only half full. The building design is typical, with the upper bowl overhanging the lower, and with luxury boxes built above the lower sections. The number of rows in the upper bowl shrinks on the ends, and running behind the last row upstairs is a concrete walkway about five feet wide. The walkway is somewhat like a track, complete with stairs in each corner where the design dips down. On every night I've visited, I've seen kids running around the walkway during the game, circling the arena as if they were entered in some kind of spectator's track meet high above the court.

After an opening that is typically high-tech, the Nets continue the theme and offer a full array of glitzy touches to their game. To the usual items (mascot, dance team, remote-controlled blimp), the Nets add some interesting activities. Just like Washington, they have a host who does remote segments in the crowd, and one involves a "fan of the game" contest. On this night, the winner is a ten-year-old boy, and one of his prizes is a pound of coffee from a local supermarket chain, giving the three of us an amusing image of the kid developing an addiction to caffeine at an early age.

There are a total of eight giant video screens, four on a center hanging scoreboard and one mounted in each corner above the upper bowl. The player boards are built into the top of the arena on both ends, each using a mixture of colors to create an easy-to-read display. The funny thing is, the player boards use a different design than any other arena. The standard format lists the numbers, fouls, and points of each player on the floor, but in the Meadowlands Arena the visitors' board switches the order, listing fouls, points, and players. On my first visit, I couldn't fathom why the Nets used this confusing design, but on this night Dan and I figure out the reason: The player board was designed to display hockey penalties, and the fouls have to be listed first because that column has space for only one digit.

Things look pretty bad for the Nets in the early stages of the game, as the Heat build an 8-point lead at the end of the first quarter. Just as the home team begins to battle back near the end of the first half, Coleman goes up to try to block a dunk and catches his shooting hand on the rim, slicing it open. The injury, which will require twelve stitches, forces Coleman to leave the game, and will keep him out of action for the entire week I'm in the area.

In the experience of seeing a Nets game, some touches are completely original, not found at any other arena. One is the "Nets Playball Program," a small booklet printed by the team and designed to look like the Playbill programs handed out at Broadway productions. Ushers give the programs to fans as they enter the arena, and the free publication contains the kinds of stats and information normally found in the game programs for sale at other NBA venues. Although the Playball programs are free, the Nets still sell a regular program containing general information about the team's players and front office.

In a tradition that Dan finds particularly amusing, the Nets add a little punch to the national anthem. When the performer reaches the lines "And the rockets' red glare/the bombs bursting in air," the team provides a little pyrotechnical accompaniment. On the word "rockets," a pair of sparklers is released from the ceiling, followed by a small explosion to go with, you guessed it, the mention of "bombs."

My favorite touch is the recorded voice that is heard a couple of times a game. Many arenas use different sound effects (often excessively, in my opinion), but one of the Nets' is truly unforgettable. A demonic voice, electronically lowered and laden with bass, will suddenly boom across the crowd. "I say go, you say Nets," it will command, followed by "Go!" The few of us in attendance shout "Nets!" on cue, and the ritual is repeated several times. We can't help it—it feels like some evil demon is ordering us to obey his wicked commands, and we're powerless to resist.

With their top player missing, I expect the Nets to fold under the pressure, but to my surprise they continue their comeback after halftime and tie the score midway through the third quarter. Things stay close the rest of the way, as the Heat build back their lead only to see the Nets score eleven straight points. New Jersey continues to dominate, and with four minutes left go ahead 98-89.

That should seal the victory, but Miami refuses to give up, and several key turnovers by the Nets give the visitors the chance to pull it out. When Nets center Benoit Benjamin throws away a pass with 30 seconds left, the Heat get the ball back down only 100-99. Despite two shots at the basket, Miami can't get the score they need, and have to foul Armon Gilliam after he grabs the second rebound. Gilliam makes only one of the two free throws, and the Heat call a timeout once again. Rather than attacking inside on the next play, Glen Rice takes a three that can win the game, but just like in the Heat–Kings game I saw in Miami, his shot finds the iron and bounces off.

After a Miami foul, Benjamin makes both free throws for the win, but as the fans begin to stream for the exits the Heat inbound the ball to Kevin Gamble, who turns and hits a shot from beyond midcourt as time expires, making the final a one-point victory and reinforcing my belief that you should never leave an NBA game until after the final buzzer.

It turns out to be a pretty good game, especially considering Coleman's early departure, but in all honesty I spend most of the evening chatting with Dan and Christine about everything but basketball. In some arenas such behavior would be a mortal sin, but nobody in the stands at the Meadowlands seemed to mind. Although there appeared to be more loyal fans in East Rutherford than in Philly, any arena that is half-empty and mostly quiet has an atmosphere more conducive to conversation than cheering. Perhaps that's why so many people don't pay much attention at Nets and Sixers games—the environment just doesn't encourage them to become involved with the action. Final score: Nets 103, Heat 102.

Average 1994–95 ticket cost: $32.06 (11th highest in the NBA)

Beer: $4.25 (12 oz.)

Soda: $2.25 (20 oz.—Coca-Cola products)

Hot Dog: $2.75

Parking: $6.00

Mascot: SuperDunk (big blue character with a superhero-style costume)

Cheerleaders: The Jersey Girls

Remote-controlled blimp: yes

Other teams that play full-time in the Meadowlands Arena: New Jersey Devils (National Hockey League), New Jersey Rockin Rollers (Roller Hockey International).

What I'd change about the Meadowlands Arena: Find some fans, have the team play more consistently, and figure out a way to get the Knicks to move a little further away—say, to New Orleans.

What I love about the Meadowlands Arena: The simple but attractive exterior design.

Statistics from Team Marketing Report, Inc.

Tough Town, Tough Team

NEW YORK KNICKERBOCKERS

Founded: 1946
1993–94 Record: 57-25
Team Colors: Orange, White, Blue

Monday, December 19–Thursday, December 22

On the one night without a game during the killer Washington–Philadelphia–New Jersey–New York–Boston leg of my trip, I made my way into Manhattan to have dinner with my agent, Bobbe. Braving both the cold and the New York public transit system, I took a bus from Hoboken through the Lincoln Tunnel into Manhattan, then caught the subway to the Upper West Side.

After an eight-month business relationship conducted entirely by telephone, I finally met the woman who had arranged for this book's publication. As we chatted during the meal, I was struck by the fact that Bobbe, with twenty years of experience as a literary agent after a career in publishing, would have been interested in an NBA book. She's not a basketball fan, but she liked the idea, and as a result I found myself at the first business dinner of my life. As an unpublished writer, I suppose I should have felt pretty cocky, but my unfamiliarity with many of the items on the menu kept me properly humbled. Still, there are worse things to do than spend a night in Manhattan being treated like a big shot.

By Tuesday morning I had decided to move from Jarel's apartment to a Day's Inn in nearby East Bergen. I didn't mind sleeping on a couch in someone's living room, or having little space to spread out all my things.

Instead, what bothered me was the cold—even though I was born and raised in the Northeast, I can't stand staying at a place that isn't at least 70 degrees. Although Jarel's apartment probably reached that level during the day, at night it chilled just a little too much for me to be comfortable.

I settled in the hotel soon after noon, then spent the afternoon at the movies with Dan and Christine. As the sun set for the day, I drove back to Jarel's neighborhood and met him just after six. Although he and I had seen Magic games together in Orlando, it was the first time we'd be experiencing NBA action in his native city.

> **Previous Knicks Games at Madison Square Garden:**
>
> **1992–93 season:** Milwaukee (Knicks 102-99)

New York is the busiest, most crowded metropolis in the United States, and Manhattan is the heart of it all. Mixed among the landmarks of the city—south of Central Park, west of the Empire State Building, north of the World Trade Center—you'll find Madison Square Garden at 33rd Street and Eighth Avenue. They call it "the world's most famous arena," although I would think that Bostonians could argue that claim, at least until the fall of 1995. In any case, I was under the impression that only stadiums and ballparks were really famous, not arenas, but my guess is that New Yorkers feel the need to claim that they have the best of everything, sports arenas included. Opened in 1968, Madison Square Garden is actually the fourth building to have the name, and the third home of the Knicks, one of the original members of the league. Whether it is the world's most famous arena can be argued, but it is certainly one of the most memorable I've ever seen.

Several things about MSG (as the locals call it) surprised me on my first visit. One was that it's round, not square—even though I knew the name referred to a location, not a shape, I'd still always pictured it as rectangular, like most downtown buildings. Another surprise was that it is located on top of Pennsylvania Station, and as a result the pedestrian traffic around the facility on game nights is only partially made up of NBA fans. Mixed in the crowd you'll find commuters, scalpers, religious zealots, vendors, and just about any kind of person that has a reason to walk the streets of Manhattan. The area is packed with people, dense on the sidewalks and inside the structures in the area. New Yorkers are accustomed to it, but I always find it fascinating whenever I visit. The mad crunch of humanity is a marvel to me, especially since practically none of these scores of people are talking to one another.

Yet what surprised me most was that Madison Square Garden is gorgeous. Inside, outside, in all the touches and elements that go into the experience of seeing an NBA game, MSG does it all well. During the '94–95 season, there were only seven arenas older than MSG in the league (two of which were in their final seasons), yet many of the more recently constructed buildings can't measure up to New York's facility. If I were more enamored of the city and its team, MSG might be my favorite place to see a game.

Madison Square Garden is an oval building, constructed with cement blocks and accented with lighted grooves up each side and glass "towers" built into each corner. The towers contain seven levels of escalators, which carry fans to their proper locations in the arena. The base of the building is decorated in black marble, and between the different materials and various lights the arena blends well with the mixture of modern and traditional skyscrapers that surround it. Although there are entrances at the base of each tower, the main ticket office is on the third floor, at the end of a large walkway that connects the east side of the arena with an annex building. Madison Square Garden's big billboard, with a color screen that announces current and upcoming events, is found in front of this building, rather than the arena itself. Watching the colorful displays on the board as the Manhattan traffic goes by is a memorable experience, one that New Yorkers probably take for granted but that a yokel like me can't help but enjoy.

Tuesday, December 20, 1994—8:00 PM

NEW YORK KNICKS (12-9) VS. NEW JERSEY NETS (10-15)

Jarel and I are talking about New York sports teams as we ride the small subway system that runs from Hoboken to Manhattan.

✪ MADISON SQUARE
GARDEN
Opened: 1968
Capacity: 19,763
New York City, New York

He grew up in the area and can't understand why I don't like the local teams. I explain to him that there are two main reasons: First, I grew up in Boston, a city that has several intense sports rivalries with New York teams; and second, I hate the fact that the Big Apple is represented by two teams in every sport. To me, having two clubs gives fans an unfair advantage, because they can just choose to follow whichever one is having a better year.

Jarel doesn't accept my logic, telling me that nearly all the New York sports fans he knows root for only one local team in each sport. And even though I try to explain about the sports rivalries, he doesn't seem to find that argument very strong either, but as a Magic fan I know what I'm talking about.

If the Magic have a rival, it's the Knicks. When Patrick Ewing and the big, bad New Yorkers face Shaquille O'Neal and the clean-cut boys from the land of Disney, it's easy to see that they are two teams that don't like each other. And with the Magic's improvement in recent years, the odds are good that the battle for the Atlantic Division will be waged between them, at least for the next couple of seasons.

I also explain to Jarel that I'm not a fan of the Knicks' grind-it-out, defensive style. I know that the team has a tradition as hard-nosed competitors, but their theme of "Tough Town, Tough Team" doesn't make for exciting basketball, especially when you're used to a fast-break offensive style like that of the Magic.

Still, I have to admit that the Knicks have been very kind to me during my second trip. Although I had a difficult time getting a reply to my ticket request the first time I traveled the NBA, eventually asking Dan and Christine to buy tickets for us to use, this time around New York's media director has graciously given me a pair of tickets for each of their two home games this week. So it's nothing personal—I just don't like the team on the court.

After walking the few blocks from the Port Authority, we arrive to find Madison Square Garden as crowded as usual, especially since the game is going to be on national television on TNT. The Knicks have had decent attendance in recent seasons, but 1993–94 was the first year that the team sold out every game, and tonight will mark the team's ninety-first consecutive full house at MSG.

We enter the arena on the third-floor level into the main ticket lobby, walking through the adjacent building past the main sign and the Paramount Theater, and from there head up to the concourse on the corner escalators. I gawk at the view outside the windows as we make our way up, knowing that I look like a tourist and thankful that only Jarel is around to see me.

The arena has several concourses, and we make our way to the top one, which gives access to the higher sections. The concourses are wide in the middle of the arena, packed with concessions, souvenir stands, and restrooms, but at each end they narrow and have no such amenities. As I expected, the Knicks have a large team store on a lower concourse, but we decided to pick up our souvenirs later. First thing we want to see is where the Knicks have put us.

MSG is laid out in a stadium design, with many of the lower sections surrounded by horizontal rails around the rows of seats. There are four distinct seating sections, with each of the lower three having their own walkways in the arena. The highest level has separate entrances and only runs around three-quarters of the building, with the remaining space at that level used for luxury boxes. In addition, a level of luxury boxes runs around the whole arena at the top of the building.

The design makes the upper seats seem pretty far from the court, but the sightlines are decent, and the other details about the arena are top-notch. For example, the center hanging scoreboard is multi-sided, and alternates between video screens and message boards. The display is exceptional, with bright, clear images, and for most of the game the center message boards show the player and team stats in an efficient fashion. The sound system is high quality as well, and as we enter the building the speakers are blaring a mix of rap and pop music that is well suited to a basketball game.

The Knicks have put us at an upper press table on the north side of the arena. The good news is that we're at center court, but the bad news is that the floor is a long way below us, as the press row is at the top of the third section of seats. With only the last level of seats above us, Jarel is disappointed, as he thought that the team would have set us up with a better pair. After my experiences with some teams, however, I've got no complaints. If nothing else, we're at a table, the first one I've had on this trip, which means we have a place to rest our food, drinks, and elbows during the game.

The table seats are unreserved, so an usher leads us to an empty spot, and as we take off our coats he stands nearby, saying, "Good seats, huh?" Jarel, being a native New Yorker, realizes what's happening and asks me for a dollar. I give him one, and he tips the usher with it. The usher, an older gentleman probably in his fifties, thanks us and leaves, promising to get us a copy of the game notes printed up for the members of the media.

I pull my chair out from under the table and sit down, turning to Jarel slightly as I do. "You know, this is the only arena I've ever visited where the ushers expect a tip," I say, trying to make a point about New York.

"Do you think a dollar was enough?" he asks, missing my meaning entirely.

Still, I've heard stories of ushers returning any kindness the fans extend to them. The most obvious way is to allow generous fans to move to better seats that are unoccupied after the first quarter of the game. I don't expect that a sold-out Knicks game will offer such an opportunity, but we do get some payback: The guy returns a few minutes later with the game notes, just as he promised.

After a typical opening for a modern arena, the crowd seems to fidget in their seats with anxious energy as the game begins. It is the Knicks' first home game after two blowout losses out west to the Suns and Blazers, and the players and fans are anxious for the team to break out of their mini-slump. With Derrick Coleman missing due to the hand injury he sustained two nights ago against the Heat, the Nets appear to be just the cure that the Knicks need to find their way back into the win column.

At first, things go according to script. The Knicks lead 25-22 after one quarter, then with just under four minutes left in the second Patrick Ewing and Nets center Benoit Benjamin begin a shoving match that results in double technicals. For Ewing, it's no big deal, but for Benjamin it's his second technical, and so he's ejected, still shouting at Ewing as Patrick calmly walks away, pleased with the way things have worked out.

Even with two of their key power players missing, however, the Nets continue to hang around. Halftime finds them down 49-44, and Knicks fans have to wonder why their guys can't put them away.

A major part of the experience of visiting Madison Square Garden is the details: the music, the scoreboards and message boards, the food, and the dancers. Not only is the center hanging scoreboard an excellent display, but the end boards are also exceptional, showing out-of-town scores, quarter-by-quarter breakdowns of the other games, and selected bits of the day's sports news. In addition, the more standard scoreboards on the ends of the arena have a space that displays different in-depth statistics about the game on a rotating basis, including field goal and free throw percentage, as well as offensive and defensive rebound totals. The Garden's food is very tasty, although certainly expensive. The Knicks even manage to incorporate a live organ as part of the music during the games.

But the most enjoyable element of seeing a game at MSG is looking for the celebrities in the crowd. On my only other visit to the Garden, my friends and I saw the ubiquitous Spike Lee in his courtside seat, as well football great Reggie White, being courted by the Jets at the time. Other famous faces were Rob and Fav, the former members of Milli Vanilli, in town to promote their big comeback album (the one where they actually did their own singing).

At the Nets game, Jarel and I spot a bonanza of celebrities. First is Spike, of course, but he is upstaged by perhaps the world's most beautiful couple, Alec Baldwin and Kim Basinger, at courtside on the opposite side of the media table. Two rows behind them is Ed Bradley, veteran TV reporter of 60 Minutes fame. For a while they are the only four we can see. Only after scanning the crowd with my tiny binoculars do I spot actors Peter Boyle, Howard Hesseman, and Christopher Reeve, grouped together in the first row behind the basket to our left, all rooting for the Knicks and signing the occasional autograph. One great advantage to a New York game is that any time the action slows down, you can pass the time by checking out what the big shots in the stands are doing.

But this game won't have many dull stretches. The Nets refuse to quit, and after the Knicks go through one of their customary offensive dry spells, their lead is down to two points by the end of the third, 69-67.

Still, the Nets don't go ahead as the fourth quarter begins, and things appear to be going smoothly for the home team, with a six-point lead and only three and a half minutes remaining.

In all the excitement, Jarel and I still have time to notice that a cockroach has begun to slowly cross the table in front of us. In this nice, clean arena, with so many modern amenities, I'm disappointed to see the bug make an appearance. I watch it for a little while, the first insect I can recall seeing inside an arena, until it disappears over the rail.

Meanwhile, the Nets finally put together the run they've been looking for all night, using a Chris Morris tap-in to go ahead 81-80 with 1:26 left. The fans begin to vent their frustration, and can only watch as each possession becomes crucial with the game on the line.

The Knicks miss a driving shot, but Jersey knocks the ball out of bounds. Knicks guard John Starks then rushes a three, but Derek Harper is able to grab the rebound. Finally, Ewing takes control, hitting a 12-foot turnaround from the baseline to put the Knicks up 82-81 with 43 seconds left.

It's the Nets' turn, and for most of the duration of the shot clock they can't find a decent shot. Kenny Anderson has the ball as the clock winds down, and suddenly he dribbles off his foot as he begins to make his move. The crowd gasps, Anderson rushes to the ball, and in all the confusion Armon Gilliam is left alone. Anderson reaches the ball first and bullets a pass to Gilliam, who quickly squares to the basket and buries a 14-footer. Nets 83-82, 20.5 seconds left.

The Knicks call a timeout. The tension is thick as they come out of the huddle, and after a couple of passes Starks drives the lane with eleven seconds left. He collides with Nets forward Jayson Williams, and the ball squirts to Morris. The crowd explodes around me as the officials make no call on the play, and the Knicks foul Morris with 9.7 seconds left. Although later several local members of the media will agree with the non-call, few fans in the arena do in the moments after the play.

Morris makes one of two, putting the Nets ahead 84-82. (During the free throws, we can see Alec Baldwin and Spike Lee literally on the edge of their seats. Baldwin goes so far as to make a "whammy" sign in Morris' direction.) This time, the Knicks work the ball to Ewing, and as he misses his shot the officials call a foul on the Nets with seven seconds to go. Ewing calmly makes the first, the crowd erupts again, but his second free throw bounces off the rim, and the Knicks knock the rebound out of bounds. After fouling Gilliam with 4.1 seconds left, the Knicks watch him make one of two, then hurry the ball upcourt, only to miss a desperation shot at the buzzer.

The Knicks have been backed into a corner in a game that offered little chance of redemption for their recent poor play. A home victory would have been a hollow one against a diminished Nets team, but even that small pleasure has failed to materialize. It has been an exciting finish, but the flaws in the Knicks' roster have been exposed. As I leave the arena after the game, it occurs to me that I am probably the only person in the building not furious with the defending conference champions. Final score: Nets 85, Knicks 83.

It is a busy week for basketball in the New York City area, and so I stay in town for two more days. I see the Nets play the Pistons at the Meadowlands on Wednesday—a strange and frightening day in New York. In mid-afternoon a firebomb explosion rips through a subway car, injuring more than forty people. I watch the news reports from the safety of my Jersey hotel room, glad that my schedule had kept me outside the city.

There are no disruptions to the NBA schedule, and so I drive to the Meadowlands just after 7 PM. The Pistons' previous game was the win over the Sixers that I saw at the Spectrum four nights ago, giving Detroit a 9-12 record. The Nets had improved to 11-15 after their Herculean win over the Knicks, and despite Derrick Coleman's absence the Nets are clearly on a roll. The Pistons, who are also hampered by several injuries, simply can't keep up with New Jersey, who take advantage of Detroit's misfortunes to post their first easy victory after the close games against the Heat and Knicks.

Although it is hard for me to get excited about the matchup, I have to admit that the Nets are growing on me. The experience of seeing a team play a stretch of games both at home and on the road in a short period of time leads to a certain familiarity, and although I've never been a big Nets fan it is difficult not to be impressed with their stretch of three wins in four days. Sure, the two home victories were against sub-par teams, but the victory over the Knicks made them my sentimental favorite, at least for a little while. Final score: Nets 117, Pistons 99.

There is another game at Madison Square Garden during my visit, so on Thursday I head back into Manhattan to see the Knicks play the Cavaliers. Cleveland comes in at 15-8, only a half-game out of first place in the

Central Division, and with their newfound defensive style I dread to imagine how a game between the Cavs and Knicks might go. After their loss to the Nets, the Knicks are clearly on the ropes, with the New York media and fans predicting their team's demise as the favorite to win the Eastern Conference. As my beloved Magic continue to post the best record in the league, I can't help but enjoy my taste of the Knicks' misfortune. Still, I have no illusions about Thursday's game—the Knicks are hungry, and with forward Charles Oakley back in the lineup I expect them to take out their frustration on a Cavs team that many people think are over-achieving.

Joining me for the game is Traci, my editor at Macmillan Books. As with my agent, I'd never met the folks publishing my book in person, and so for the second time in four nights I allow myself to be wined and dined in Manhattan. We go to an Irish pub a couple of blocks from the Garden, an experience made all the more enjoyable when we are joined by Kenny, editor of Macmillan's *The Baseball Encyclopedia*.

After dinner, Traci and I head over to MSG. For the Cavs game, the Knicks' media director gets us seats at a press table in the corner of the lower bowl, a much better location than the upper press row where Jarel and I had sat two night ago. A quick check for celebrities reveals only four: Spike (of course—when does he have time to make movies?), the sportscasting duo of Ahmad Rashad and Bryant Gumbel, and rock singer Meatloaf, all sitting courtside opposite us, although not near each other. Traci is dying to see how much food Meatloaf orders during the game, but he must have eaten ahead of time, because we never see him enjoying so much as a diet soda.

In the beginning, the game follows the pattern I expected, as Oakley returns to provide a big inside presence and pace the Knicks to a 16-point first-half lead. Although the Cavs begin to climb back into it, guard Mark Price seems to be off his game, and New York builds their lead back to 14 in the third quarter. Once again, the Cavs cut into the lead, and by the end of three periods the Knicks are up only 67-62.

In the fourth, Price begins to play at his usual All-Star level, creating basket after basket. Eventually scoring 14 points in the final quarter, Price hits four 3-pointers and sets up several other key shots, and the Knicks lose control of the game. Cavs center John Williams makes a twisting shot off the glass to give Cleveland a 91-90 lead with only 8.9 seconds left. The Knicks call time, then inbound the ball to guard Derek Harper, who drives the lane and runs into Cleveland's Chris Mills. Harper collapses over Mills, the whistle blows, and the ref emphatically points downcourt, signaling an offensive foul. The crowd roars their displeasure with the officials, but to no avail. The two subsequent free throws ice the game for the Cavs, and when the Knicks miss a frantic three at the buzzer they find themselves losers at home for the second time in three nights. In both games it appeared that the Knicks were in control, and in both they lost in the final seconds, in part due to two controversial decisions by the officials late in the contests.

I keep my satisfaction to myself and make my way out of the city that night for the final time during my stay. After taking the bus back to Hoboken, I pick up my car and drive back to my hotel, all the while reflecting back on my five days in the area. I had survived my visit without any mishaps, and the results couldn't have been better. Despite some guilty feelings over my delight with the Knicks' losses, the simple truth is that things had played out better than I could have hoped. I'm a basketball fan, after all, and the next best thing to seeing my favorite team win is watching their biggest rivals lose. Perhaps I wasn't the most gracious visitor to the Big Apple, but the New York stretch would turn out to be one of the most exciting and enjoyable of the trip. Final score: Cavaliers 93, Knicks 90.

Average 1994–95 ticket cost: $43.90 (highest in the NBA)

Beer: $4.50 (16 oz.)

Soda: $2.30 (20 oz.—Coca-Cola products)

Hot Dog: $3.00

Parking: $18.75

Mascot: none

Cheerleaders: Knicks City Dancers

Remote-controlled blimp: none

Other teams that play full-time in Madison Square Garden: New York Rangers (National Hockey League)

What I'd change about Madison Square Garden: Figure out a way to get the upper seats a little closer to the court.

What I love about Madison Square Garden: The big-city atmosphere, the celebrities, and the way it blends into the most exciting city in the NBA.

Statistics from Team Marketing Report, Inc.

Storm Over the Gah-den

Founded: 1946
1993–94 Record: 32-50
Team Colors: Green, White

Friday, December 23

There was no time for me to bask in my good feelings about the Knicks' losses, because I had to drive to Boston for a game the next night. Friday morning was overcast and windy, and I had to cover a distance of 220 miles to Boston. In the early afternoon, I worked my way north through New York and Connecticut as the sky began to darken. Some unforeseen delays put me in Massachusetts very late, and it was almost 5 PM before I crossed into my home state. Fortunately, my familiarity with the area helped me make up some lost time, but there were several tense moments as the skies opened up and a cold rain began to fall on the turnpike. I passed by my hometown of Lexington with barely a glance, heading instead to Belmont, where I was to meet my friend Sally at her apartment. We'd met while working together at a summer job at Boston University, and had stayed friends in the eight years since.

Cutting it very, very close to game time, I finally pulled up to Sally's building just after six. The rain had stopped for the moment, and after the quickest of greetings we hustled off to the bus stop and made our way into the city. The final game of my killer stretch had been difficult for me to reach on time, but once we were on the subway it looked like I was going to pull it off.

Previous Celtics Games at Boston Garden:

Before 1989: about ten, starting in the early 1980s

1992–93: Charlotte (Hornets 96-93)

I hope the young fans of today, with the Magic hats and the Raptor jackets, who think that the NBA began with Jordan and Barkley, are aware of the achievements of the Boston Celtics, the greatest team in league history. Granted, the Lakers have a grand tradition as well, and with a couple of different bounces of the ball they might have raised as many banners over the years as their rivals from Beantown. But the bottom line is, the Celtics have won sixteen NBA championships, had twenty-two members in the Hall of Fame (with at least a couple more to come in the next few years), have won fifteen regular-season or playoff MVP awards, and have retired the numbers of twenty players. The Lakers have won eleven titles, while the Pistons have the next-highest total with four.

Eight of the current teams were founded in the 1940s (the next after them was the Bullets in 1961), and of those only the Celtics and Knicks have remained in their original cities. Once you get past the Celtics, Lakers, and Pistons, the other five teams from that group (the Hawks, Warriors, Knicks, Sixers, and Kings) have a combined total of ten championships between them.

But the collection of titles isn't the only thing that defines the Celtics. The details of their history also make them special: the players and the coaches, the great games, and their tradition of excellence. And along with everything else, it is Boston Garden, the senior building in the NBA, the legendary, rat-infested sweatbox that was the site of many of the NBA's finest moments, that gives Celtics fans reason to feel that their team is the greatest the league has known.

Yet after all the complaints from opposing teams and visiting fans, after legendary tales of the dead spots on the parquet floor and the leprechaun protecting the Celtics' fortunes, after years of rumors that its days were numbered, the time had finally come for Boston Garden to finish its run. All the details for a new, state-of-the-art arena had been finalized by the time I reached Boston on my first trip, and during my next visit construction was in full swing on the new facility, called the Fleet Center, in the lot behind the current Garden.

The new building should be impressive. Budgeted at $160 million, the Fleet Center will be located above a parking garage that will expand the North Station terminal. Rising 162 feet, or ten stories, the completed Fleet Center will sit only inches from Boston Garden when completed— at least, until the Garden is taken down.

The thought of that day depresses me, as it would any fan who grew up in Boston, but I don't go to forty basketball games a year in a building that is almost seventy years old. Tradition has to give way to progress, and after visiting so many modern arenas designed to maximize the fans' comfort and enjoyment of the game, I can't say that a new building in Boston is a bad idea. If nothing else, it will provide 3,500 more seats for each game, while still having a much smaller capacity than most of the arenas built in recent years.

The Garden was almost twenty years old even before the Celtics moved in. The building opened in 1928, but the first Celtics game at Boston Garden was on November 16, 1946, a Saturday night tip-off against the Toronto Huskies. The team didn't win a championship in their first ten years, and their domination began only after their initial title in 1957. Boston won it all again in '59, the first of an amazing string of eight straight NBA championships. Two more followed in the late sixties, two in the mid-seventies, and then three more in the Larry Bird era of the eighties. Through all those years, the Garden was the Celtics' only full-time home. It sat on Causeway Street near Boston's North End without undergoing any major changes, almost as much of a landmark as the sites on the nearby Freedom Trail.

One great thing about the Garden is its location in the heart of the city, not isolated or surrounded by acres of parking lots. The building is rectangular, with walls of dirty tan brick that reflect the years since its opening. On the ground level are several businesses, including a record store, pastry shop, sports bar, and the Bruins' team shop, which also carries Celtics merchandise.

The back side of the building is a train station, complete with traditional wooden benches for waiting passengers in a lobby area on the first floor. Although the station inside the Garden is for commuter trains, a stop across the street from the building on the south side is part of the subway system. The trains run underground through most of the city, but near the Garden they are elevated above the street, masking the front of the building from the ground level and shading the street from the elements. It's hard to see from the street level because of the tracks, but the top of the building has the bright yellow sign that designates the building as Boston Garden. On game nights for almost fifty years, the street in front of the building has become a mass of fans, vendors, and scalpers, all gathered under the tracks in an atmosphere of pre-game excitement.

Friday, December 23, 1994—7:30 PM

BOSTON CELTICS (10-14) VS. PHILADELPHIA 76ERS (8-16)

Sally and I arrive at North Station only 20 minutes before tip-off. We have plenty of time to make our way into the Garden, but the biggest problem is that the rain has started again in full force, and we are soaked the moment we dash out from under the cover of the train tracks above the street. I had hoped to get a look at the site of the new arena, to see how far the construction has progressed, but there's no way I'm spending an extra second outside on this night, as the cold rain drives down on us in the darkness. We head into the press entrance, located in an attached building adjacent to the Garden, and from there we wind through old hallways and up creaking staircases into the Garden.

The inside of the building is functional but old, with cinderblock entrance ramps and large stairwells in each corner. The lower level consists of the promenade, which is closest to the court, and the loge, which is above the promenade. The upper seats are in the balcony, which also contains several boxes above the general seating (although I don't know if it would be accurate to call them "luxury boxes"). There are no padded seats, as each is made of wood in the flip-up design. Most of the building is decorated in yellow, including the rails that are found between each row of seats in the balcony.

✪ BOSTON GARDEN

Opened: 1928
Capacity: 14,890
Boston, Massachusetts

The building has more to offer than just great tradition. For one thing, the Garden's capacity of less than 15,000 means that most of the seats are relatively near the court. On the other hand, the majority of the balcony seats are located on the ends, and there are quite a few obstructed view seats that are located partially or completely behind the pillars that support the structure.

Even after seeing a dozen Celtics games at the Garden, and probably a half-dozen nights watching the Bruins as well, I find myself headed to a place I've never sat before. The Celtics have reserved us a couple of seats on the upper press row, which is located above the balcony but below the boxes. To reach the seats, we need to climb up a small stairwell near the top of the balcony, ducking under a doorway that is perhaps four feet tall. The compact aisle at the table gives only the slightest amount of space for moving around, but once we find our seats I realize that it will be an exciting place to see the game. While we're high above the court, the design of the balcony has us almost over the players, giving a terrific view of the spacing and positional play of the two teams. In addition, we're up among the rafters, high enough that it seems like we could almost reach up and brush our fingers against the famous collection of banners.

I'm thrilled that I'll be enjoying this new angle of the action for tonight's game, but the kindness of the Celtics doesn't surprise me. From the start, Boston's media director has been very helpful, going so far as to give me a seat on the press table along the baseline for the Celtics game I saw on my first trip. Given the demand for tickets—the Garden has been sold out for fourteen years—and the lionization of the team in Boston, I thought that the Celtics would be one of the more snobbish teams, but nothing could be further from the truth.

One of the banners hanging near us displays a special commemorative logo that features a picture of the Garden with the slogan "Honor The Tradition: 1946–1995." As the opening announcements are made, I look at the banner and realize that this is a night better suited to tradition than reality. There was a time when a game between the Celtics and the Sixers would be the hottest ticket in town, and I can remember many crucial battles between the two clubs during my schooldays. It was at a Celtics–Sixers game in the Garden in 1982, the seventh game of the Conference Finals, when the crowd began to chant "Beat L.A.!" to the visitors after it was clear that they would defeat Boston and face the Lakers in the Finals. But the Boston and Philadelphia teams of 1994–95 are mere shadows of their predecessors, as the game quickly demonstrates. To make matters worse, Sixer Willie Burton, he of the 53-point game, is missing tonight due to an illness in his family.

Still, the Celtics start slowly, but eventually make a late run in the quarter to lead 26-17 at the end of the first period. The game of basketball is the centerpiece in Boston Garden, as there is no dance team, no mascot, no video monitors, and no flashy message boards. A center hanging scoreboard displays only the score, time, timeouts remaining, team fouls, and the number and foul total of the last player on each team to get called for an infraction. The scoreboard is so archaic that the numbers change one at a time—when a player scores the first basket, it reads "0...1...2." The score and time are displayed in the corners of the lower level, and there is a message board at each end that shows basic information (although not from the current game). Finally, the only music is provided by an organ, which plays traditional songs and marches during breaks in the action. That's all there is in Boston, the only arena in the league where you can't look to a board and see the current stats for the players on the floor. As a result, it's easy to squint your eyes and imagine that you're watching a game from years past.

By halftime, most of the fans in the Garden are probably doing just that. The Celtics are leading 43-36, the two teams are both shooting in the mid-30 percent range, and the gloom of a cold and rainy night has carried into the Garden like a fog.

Each game of the final season in Boston Garden is dedicated to a Celtics personality, most of whom take advantage of the halftime break to share their memories of Boston's grand old building. Tonight it's Jim Loscutoff, a banger from the old days, and he takes a seat on the court and chats about his fondest moments of the Garden. (His nickname is "Loscy," and it's printed on one of the banners of retired numbers. The reason? Loscutoff wore number 18, the same as Dave Cowens, and the club wanted to honor them both by retiring their numbers. The 18 is for Cowens, and the nickname is for Loscutoff.)

The halftime ceremony is great, but the game just gets worse and worse, with sloppy and uninspired play from both teams. By the end of three, the lead is down to 62-61, and the only positive thing is that the Celtics are still ahead.

In the fourth quarter, the success of the past crashes headfirst into the adversities of the present. Although the Celtics still lead by a point with less than four minutes left, Sixers guard Dana Barros, he of the Spectrum heroics a week before, keys a Philadelphia run that buries the home team. To make matters worse, the crowd has spotted Larry Bird sitting in the stands, watching the mess that his team has become. As the Celtics call their timeouts near the end, trying to win the game, the crowd begins to chant "Larry! Larry!" in recognition of their retired superstar, and Bird can only sit in helpless embarrassment. The crowd will have none of the present Celtics tonight, and for this game, at least, the memory of the glory days is the only thing for them to enjoy.

After the mess of a game is over, Sally and I head into the spitting rain, and I find myself thinking that it might be time to go after all, to say goodbye to Boston Garden in a period when Celtics pride isn't as strong as in the past. Bring the parquet floor, carefully transplant the banners, and begin a new tradition in the Fleet Center, as the team clearly needs to do some building of its own. Final score: 76ers 85, Celtics 77.

Average 1994–95 ticket cost: $34.68 (seventh highest in the NBA)

Beer: $3.25 (14 oz.)

Soda: $1.75 (14 oz.—Coca-Cola products)

Hot Dog: $2.25

Parking: $16.00

Mascot: none

Cheerleaders: none

Remote-controlled blimp: none

Other teams that play full-time in the Boston Garden: Boston Bruins (National Hockey League)

What I'd change about the Boston Garden: In its final season? Nothing.

What I love about the Boston Garden: The great memories, not only of the team's history, but also of my first NBA games— Boston Garden was the place where I was introduced to the league, and I can think of no better arena to first experience the sport.

Statistics from Team Marketing Report, Inc.

NBA standings as of Sunday, December 25, 1994:

EASTERN CONFERENCE
Atlantic Division

	W	L	Pct	GB	Home	Away
Orlando Magic	20	5	.800	—	11-0	9-5
New York Knicks	12	11	.522	7	7-4	5-7
New Jersey Nets	12	16	.429	9.5	8-6	4-10
Boston Celtics	10	15	.400	10	5-7	5-8
Philadelphia 76ers	9	16	.360	11	5-9	4-7
Miami Heat	8	15	.348	11	6-6	2-9
Washington Bullets	7	16	.304	12	3-6	4-10

Central Division

	W	L	Pct	GB	Home	Away
Cleveland Cavaliers	17	8	.680	—	8-4	9-4
Indiana Pacers	15	8	.652	1	9-1	6-7
Charlotte Hornets	14	11	.560	3	8-3	6-8
Chicago Bulls	12	12	.500	4.5	6-6	6-6
Atlanta Hawks	11	15	.423	6.5	6-7	5-8
Detroit Pistons	9	14	.391	7	6-5	3-9
Milwaukee Bucks	7	17	.292	9.5	4-6	3-11

WESTERN CONFERENCE
Midwest Division

	W	L	Pct	GB	Home	Away
Utah Jazz	18	8	.692	—	8-4	10-4
Houston Rockets	14	9	.609	2.5	7-5	7-4
San Antonio Spurs	13	9	.591	3	9-5	4-4
Dallas Mavericks	12	10	.545	4	6-6	6-4
Denver Nuggets	12	11	.522	4.5	7-5	5-6
Minnesota Timberwolves	5	19	.208	12	1-10	4-9

Pacific Division

	W	L	Pct	GB	Home	Away
Phoenix Suns	19	6	.760	—	13-0	6-6
Seattle SuperSonics	16	7	.696	2	12-1	4-6
L.A. Lakers	15	8	.652	3	6-3	9-5
Portland Trail Blazers	12	10	.545	5.5	9-5	3-5
Sacramento Kings	13	11	.542	5.5	9-4	4-7
Golden State Warriors	9	15	.375	9.5	6-6	3-9
L.A. Clippers	3	22	.120	16	2-13	1-9

Out of the woods

Founded: 1970
1993–94 Record: 47-35
Team Colors: Blue, Black, Orange

Saturday, December 24–Wednesday, December 28

Boston was a quick stop, as I arrived on Friday evening and left the next morning after spending the night on a friend's couch. The rain continued to fall on Saturday as I drove to my sister's house in Groton, a town in a thickly wooded part of Massachusetts about a half-hour west of the city. It was Christmas Eve, and as I hummed along with the Yuletide music on the radio I realized that I'd almost completely ignored the holiday season. Some greetings by p.a. announcers and the occasional glimpse of a Santa suit at arenas were about the only things that reminded me of the time of year.

I stopped briefly to greet my sister and her family, and then drove to a fancy hotel in nearby Westwood and waited for my grandmother and parents, who were coming from Rhode Island. They had retired to Maine in the spring of 1993 only a few months after my first tour of the NBA, making my weekend stop in Lexington during that trip my last visit to my childhood home.

In the early evening, the four of us headed to dinner with my cousin Kathy and aunt Martha, who lived in nearby Concord. The meal was a nice family gathering, but my sister and her family were nowhere to be seen, and my parents filled me in on the reason for their absence. Ellen had caught the flu around Thanksgiving, and my father, after seeing her during that holiday weekend, had developed a similar illness that had plagued him for nearly three weeks. As a result, he didn't want to get anywhere near her unless she was in decent health, which wasn't the case:

She and her family were battling nasty colds. I immediately echoed his sentiments, not wanting an illness to slow me down as I began the journey to the Midwest.

For that reason, on Sunday morning my father and I returned to Aunt Martha's house while my mother, grandmother, aunt, and cousin all went to spend Christmas at my sister's place. There were no hard feelings involved in the arrangement, it was just the way things turned out. So after juggling my schedule to be in Massachusetts for the holiday, I spent Christmas day hanging out with my father at my aunt's house, doing laundry and nibbling on leftovers from the night before.

Eventually the other four returned, and we exchanged a few gifts and ate more food before returning to the hotel, where I was sharing a room with my grandmother. It wasn't exactly a storybook Christmas, but I had missed several holiday seasons with my family after my move to Florida, so we enjoyed the time together, no matter how bizarre the circumstances.

The sky was brilliant on Monday, a glorious, cloudless morning after the miserable weekend. After packing up, I said good-bye to my parents and grandmother and drove south to the Massachusetts Turnpike. Reaching it before noon, I turned west toward Cleveland.

It was a great day. I was happy to be done with the East Coast cities, the nasty weather, and the general insanity of the holiday season. It felt comfortable to be on my own once more, ready to drive as long as I wanted before I quit and settled down for the night in a room all to myself.

My good mood led me to drive all day and far into the evening, re-entering New York at 2:45 PM and continuing on until I'd nearly crossed the entire state. After a whopping 510 miles on the road, I finally pulled off the highway in Fredonia, only a half-hour shy of the Pennsylvania border.

On Tuesday I continued west, crossing back into Pennsylvania just after noon and entering Ohio about 45 minutes later. With only 160 miles to travel to Cleveland, I arrived in the city in the early afternoon, and took the highway south to the suburb of Independence, stopping at a hotel about ten miles past the downtown area and the brand-new Gund Arena.

> **Previous Cavaliers Games at Richfield Coliseum:**
>
> **1992–93 season:** Charlotte (Cavaliers 118-99)

The '94–95 Cavaliers had moved back into their namesake city after twenty years of playing in Richfield Coliseum, located about thirty miles south of Cleveland. The Coliseum hadn't been a highlight of my previous trip—a huge concrete box built in the middle of deep woods near some major highways, it was the NBA's most rural arena. Although a couple of the league's current venues are located far outside any downtown area, Richfield's isolation bordered on the absurd. As a basketball facility, the Coliseum was functional if unexceptional, although its isolation led to the frequent traffic jams typical of outlying NBA arenas. I would have thought that the NBA fans of Cleveland would be happy to move out of the suburbs into a modern building, but my visit to their city proved that not everybody was thrilled with the change.

When it came to the '94–95 Cavs, one question was on everybody's mind: What's the deal with those uniforms? A quick look at Gund Arena provides at least part of the answer. Cleveland's front office had decided that their team was going to be one of the most stylish in the league, and it shows in the design of their new building.

Located on the southern side of downtown Cleveland, Gund Arena looks somewhat conventional on three of its four sides, appearing to be a light-colored rectangular building with ground-floor entrances and large windows opening on an upper concourse level. It is the north side of the arena, however, where the designers of The Gund really went nuts. The building has a top roof of a simple design with a slight curve that abruptly ends near the north side. That is the front of the arena, and it is there that the building mixes a variety of features in an architectural potpourri. There is a major section that curves outward in a circular design, next to which is a small sloping roof that begins halfway down the side of the building. But the centerpiece of the arena is a huge overhanging bay window that extends from the front of the building toward the northwest corner of the block. Supported above the steps to the main entrance by a series of columns, this annex includes a large square window with the team name inscribed in stone above it and the arena name marked below. In the plaza near the window, there is a series of stone benches carved into the shape of letters that spell "MEET ME HERE."

It's all just too hip for words, and inside the pattern continues. The Cavs' new uniform and logo are featured on all kinds of merchandise in Cavstown, a team store on the east side that is one of the more impressive in the NBA. There's a 350-seat restaurant, a sports bar, and two food courts. The main concourse has video walls and interactive displays where fans can access information or play trivia games about the team.

Normally, I eat this stuff up. New arenas are like playpens for NBA fans who can afford to pay the high price for a ticket, and most of the time I love visiting the outlandishly modern arenas that seem to be arriving every year. In addition, I like Gund Arena's location, with roads on the north and west sides, and a courtyard on its south side that has two spi-raling sculptures rising in the air. A short distance to the west are railroad tracks and a downtown river bank, which add to the atmosphere. The arena also has ample parking, including two large garages on the east and north sides that are connected to the building with elevated walkways.

In addition to its attractive location, The Gund has a pretty impressive neighbor only a few feet away on its south side: Jacobs Field, the new ballpark built for the Indians. The people of Cleveland found themselves with two ultramodern sports facilities opening in the same year, and once construction was completed the fans of northern Ohio could rest assured that they had one of the most attractive sports complexes in the entire country.

But the location and exterior design are only part of the experience of seeing a game. What goes on inside is much more important, and that's where the controversy in Cleveland began.

✪ GUND ARENA
Opened: 1994
Capacity: 20,562
Cleveland, Ohio

Wednesday, December 28, 1994—7:30 PM

CLEVELAND CAVALIERS (18-8) VS. WASHINGTON BULLETS (7-17)

My first glimpse of The Gund is still several hours away, but as I have my lunch on Wednesday the arena's reputation begins to tarnish. I'm quietly eating a cheeseburger in a lounge near my hotel, facing the back wall as I read a paperback novel. A small group of businessmen at the bar behind me, local guys on an extended lunch hour, are shooting the breeze instead of pushing papers around a desk.

I mostly ignore them, but suddenly one begins to talk about the Cavaliers and their new arena. I stop reading and listen as his disembodied voice editorializes behind me.

"You been to the new arena yet?" he starts. "It's a joke. It's backed up against these parking garages, so it's almost impossible to see from the outside. They put in all these damn suites, and they're right in the best parts of the building. We went the other night, sat in these lousy $75 seats, and we paid all that extra money pretty much just to get waitress service. And not good service, either—it took us a half an hour to get our drink order, and when they brought my gin and tonic it had no ice. The place is a dump."

He stays on the theme a little more, but with his main point made he soon switches to another topic of conversation. I'm intrigued by his comments: Is The Gund really that bad?

Seven hours later, during the second quarter of the game, I'm walking through The Gund's plush luxury suite concourse with David, telling him what the guy at the bar said.

"I saw the arena for the first time a little while ago, and I don't think there's anything wrong with the outside design," I tell him. "The inside is another story, though."

David, a lawyer, is in his business attire tonight, as his firm is entertaining clients in one of the luxury suites. I sat next to him at the Richfield Coliseum on my first trip, and since meeting at that game we have stayed in touch after my return to Orlando. For my first visit, the Cavaliers had sold me a ticket behind the basket about halfway up the lower bowl, a height that made it one of the worst seats for the price in the building. Between my seat location and what I perceived to be a somewhat haughty attitude, I wasn't very happy with the Cavs, especially considering that I'd arranged for the ticket six months before the game. During that first game, I explained to David my beef with his team, and to his credit he agreed that the Cavs had somewhat shortchanged me. When the time came for the second trip, the Cavs said they'd sell me another ticket, but rather than take the chance that Cleveland might sell me a lousy seat a second time, I called David, and he agreed to let me use one of his tickets.

"I don't have a problem with the outside of the arena either," David says. "You've already seen what I have a problem with."

I knew what he was talking about the minute I first sat down. David's season-tickets are in the club level, which is a middle section located between the two rows of luxury suites. Because the Cavs wanted to have the lower suites close to the floor, the bottom section of regular seats has very little slope. Although I wasn't sitting there, David later confirmed what I suspected: The view of the court from the lower sections isn't very good, because the rows seem packed together, without the incline needed for a decent perspective of the action.

At the start of the season, David's seats were located in the lower corner in the new arena, but after he complained about the view the team offered him seats in the club level. Those sections have decent sightlines, but because they are located in the middle they don't feel very close to the action. On top of the club sections is another row of luxury boxes, and above them is a third level of seats.

David pays $48 each for his seats, the same as in the middle lower sections, but his is a special deal because he has been a season-ticket holder. The normal cost for the club seats is $75, which explains the businessman's complaints at lunch. Even the upper level seats between the baskets run a hefty $30, the lowest price you can pay to sit in the middle at Gund Arena.

That's not to say that The Gund is the NBA's most expensive arena, but considering that it holds more than 20,000 fans, both David and I agree that it's an unfortunate pricing plan. The lower $48 seats have drawn criticism for their sightlines, while the $75 seats fail to offer enough amenities to justify their cost.

David has invited me to do something I've never done before: visit a luxury box during an NBA game. His firm has access to a suite on the upper of the two rows for about ten games a year, and they use those nights to entertain clients, which appears to be the primary purpose for the suites.

The corridor running behind the doors to the suites is nicely carpeted, slender due to a lack of concession stands, as each box is fully stocked with food and beverages as part of the hefty rental cost. We walk past door after door, hearing the crowd but unable to see the court, as the walls have no windows into the suites.

Eventually we reach our destination. David opens a door, and as we step into the suite I take in the luxuries of corporate living: A table of food is on my right, refrigerator and wet bar on my left. The side of the suite opposite the door opens toward the court, and a few of the people inside are sitting at a counter on that side, either following the action live or watching the two video monitors that are mounted on the ceiling. In front of the counter and facing the court are two rows of six seats each, separated from the neighboring suites on either side by small panes of Plexiglas.

Although I'm wearing a sweatshirt and jeans, everyone else is properly dressed for a business function, and for a few moments I feel out of place. But David has brought me to the gathering to show off his traveling NBA friend, and the other folks welcome me with a warm graciousness that I've come to expect from Cavaliers fans. They may be the butt of almost as many jokes as the folks from New Jersey, but the people of Cleveland have been some of the nicest I've met in my travels.

We arrive at the suite near the end of the second quarter, and I hang around after halftime for another half-hour. I'd watched the first few minutes of the game closely, but I really had little interest in seeing the whole thing. Once I got a good look at the arena, the thought of seeing the slow-down Cavs and the injury-depleted Bullets play basketball was much less attractive than hanging out with some nice people and drinking free beer. Cleveland is leading the Central Division, winners of nine in a row, and the Bullets are still every bit as bad as when they lost to the Jazz in Landover. And even though Washington hasn't played very well with Chris Webber in the lineup, tonight he's not even available for their first game at The Gund, as a dislocated shoulder has stranded him on the injured list for nearly a week.

One thing I did see in my brief time in my seat, however, was more evidence of the Cavs' effort to be hip. The opening of the game was based on their theme for the season—"Cavs! You've Got to be There!"—complete with original song and video. The introductions were extremely high-tech, using a computer graphic, lasers, and thumping music. The court is decorated with colorful streaks, and the arena boasts clear video screens over the court and a powerful sound system. The Gund also has four extensive message boards in the corners over the upper sections, which provide nicely detailed statistics about the game, including a full box score that appears frequently and is updated instantly throughout the evening. After seeing all the other touches, I can understand why the Cavs wanted to have hip uniforms, although their final choice of a design still confounds me.

I'm standing in the suite, eating a turkey sandwich, when David explains his theory about NBA fans to me. "It's gotten to a point where most of the people in the crowd are corporate types who buy their seats and luxury boxes just to entertain clients and to be seen at the games. They come because the NBA is trendy, and they're not real fans. Some of us were down in Richfield when the team was terrible, and we would cheer and support the Cavs like a fan should. They built the new arena with the corporations in mind, but there's going to come a time when the team has to rebuild, and are the people going to keep coming? Are there really going to be any true fans left, people who come to support the team, rather than just to network and promote their businesses?"

Several of the other folks in the suite echo David's sentiments about the modern basketball fan. It's a little ironic that they voice their complaints while surrounded by the opulent decor of the luxury box, but they are sincere in their comments, and I think they have a point. I certainly can understand their concerns, given the design of their team's new building.

I say my good-byes late in the third quarter, then make my way to the team store, which is big enough to keep me shopping for a fair amount of time. I get back to my seat in the stands with ten minutes left in the game, but there's really not much to see.

The Cavs win by sixteen, even though they score only ten points in the fourth quarter. My hunch about the outcome proves correct, and I don't miss much during my wandering. Final score: Cavaliers 91, Bullets 75.

Average 1994–95 ticket cost: $36.34 (fourth highest in the NBA)

Beer: $3.50 (16 oz.)

Soda: $1.50 (12 oz.—Coca-Cola products)

Hot Dog: $2.00

Parking: $6.00

Mascot: none

Cheerleaders: Cavs Dance Team

Remote-controlled blimp: none

Other teams that play full-time in Gund Arena: Cleveland Lumberjacks (International Hockey League)

What I'd change about Gund Arena: Fix up the problems with the lower seats, and lower the prices a little.

What I love about Gund Arena: The exterior design might be a little too stylish, but I think it's pretty nice. I'm glad the team is downtown once again. Having Jacobs Field across the courtyard is a neat touch.

Statistics from Team Marketing Report, Inc.

Palatial Estate

Founded: 1948
1993–94 Record: 20-62
Team Colors: Red, White, Blue

Thursday, December 29–Friday, December 30
After spending most of the afternoon visiting The Gund and Jacobs Field, I left Cleveland late on Thursday. Heading toward the setting sun, I settled in for a 215-mile drive that would last a little less than four hours.

I'd been amazingly lucky with the weather, only seeing snow once—a brief glimpse of white powder from the highway in upstate New York. The afternoon was bright and clear in the Midwest, but the mercury was falling, and when I stopped to refill my car's gas tank I found myself in the winter climate I'd expected. The warm temperatures were a thing of the past, and as I crossed into Michigan at 6:20 PM I wondered if the winter would turn harsh during my stop in Auburn Hills.

With my book deal firmly in place, I was living a little better on my second trip than I had the first time around, and in Auburn Hills I chose a room at a nicely furnished Hampton Inn located next to the Motel 6 where I had stayed two years earlier. My first visit had been extremely quick—I'd arrived at 5:30 PM on a Tuesday afternoon, seen the Pistons play that night, and left by eleven the following morning. This time, I took my first real break from the road in Auburn Hills, settling in for a full four days as the year came to a close and the NBA took a breather from its crowded schedule.

> **Previous Pistons Games at The Palace:**
>
> **1992–93 season:** L.A. Lakers (Lakers 121-119)

The Pistons play far north of the city they represent. Located only a few miles from the Pontiac Silverdome, the home of the NFL's Detroit Lions, The Palace is about thirty miles from downtown Detroit. As a result, my stop in Auburn Hills would be a pleasant break from some of the challenges that many cities and arenas present. Still, I don't know if the commute to Auburn Hills is as pleasant for Pistons fans.

If they do make the drive, they are rewarded with one of the nicest arenas in the NBA. The Palace of Auburn Hills opened in 1988, a time when the Pistons were among the NBA's elite teams, and the Bad Boys christened the arena by winning championships in their first two seasons in their new home. After such a spectacular opening, Detroit fans probably barely noticed their half-hour commute to the games from the city (on a good night), especially since the Pistons had played in the suburban Silverdome for the previous ten years.

Auburn Hills really is a small town, and in one of the less-developed areas The Palace sits in a slight recess in the landscape, flanked by highway access roads and a small scattering of buildings. Unlike the isolated arenas in Charlotte and Sacramento, The Palace doesn't dominate the area around it, mostly because it occupies low ground in the slightly rolling terrain. It is a round building made of light-brown brick, accented with tan bricks used to create a pattern of crisscrossing ×'s around the exterior walls. Windows open to the concourse level, which is about a quarter of the way up the building, and also near the top of the arena, showing part of the roof structure. Surrounding The Palace are acres of parking spots, just as with every other isolated arena.

It's difficult to get much of a view either inside or outside the arena, depending on where you're located, as the designers of The Palace decided not to include as many windows as most other NBA buildings. Given the rural surrounding area, I guess their decision makes sense.

The brick walls extend up on two sides of the roof, and a blue structure is visible between the gaps at the top of the arena. Overall, it's an odd combination of colors and styles that I'm not too sure I appreciate. But once I got inside The Palace, I learned that the strengths of the Pistons' arena are found in its interior.

The Pistons' VP of Public Relations was nearly impossible to reach by phone, but his assistant was always very nice to me, and even though the team had charged me for a ticket on the first trip, they gave me one for my second visit. Their generosity helped strengthen my feelings about the team, because I'd never been a Pistons fan, especially while they were the "Bad Boys" of basketball. But like most NBA followers, I appreciated the exciting style of play of rookie forward Grant Hill, and so I was pretty neutral toward the team at the time of my second trip. Still, I had reason to be rooting extra hard for them against the Celtics: The Palace was the second arena I would visit where I hadn't seen the home team win a game. Even though the Sixers had failed to post a victory, I felt pretty confident that Detroit could beat the Celtics team that I'd seen lose at Boston Garden a week before.

Friday, December 30, 1994—8:00 PM

DETROIT PISTONS (9-16) VS. BOSTON CELTICS (10-17)

There are a couple of gaps in the NBA schedule each season, and one is at New Year's. It is the final Friday of 1994, and the league is playing a full slate of thirteen games, the last NBA action before a three-day hiatus. As I make the short drive to The Palace from my hotel, I find myself picturing the scene at the various arenas across the country, as every team in the league except the Sonics is playing tonight.

Despite a loss last night in Charlotte, my beloved Magic are 22-6, still the best record in the league, a half-game ahead of the 21-6 Phoenix Suns. Orlando will face the Clippers tonight at the O'rena, and even though it should be a blowout, I'm still a little sad to be a thousand miles north, watching yet another game between two formerly great Eastern Conference teams that are struggling through difficult seasons.

Unlike the Celtics and Sixers, however, the Pistons have found a young stud to rebuild their team around. Grant Hill, the third pick in the '94 draft, has arrived to not only help the team win but also to keep the fans jumping on the highway to make the drive to the league's most sub-urban arena. Although the first few seasons in The Palace's history saw nothing but sellouts, the Pistons' struggles in recent years have created an

✪ THE PALACE OF
AUBURN HILLS
Opened: 1988
Capacity: 21,454
Auburn Hills, Michigan

understandable decline in attendance. Even so, The Palace is the fourth biggest arena in the league, and with an average attendance of 19,674 in '93–94, the Pistons drew the fifth-highest number of fans last year.

After parking on the west side, I make my way to the nearest entrance. The doors on the ground floor open up to a huge lobby, with staircases on both sides leading up to the concourse level. Straight ahead is a display case that contains an impressive tableau: the Pistons' two NBA championship trophies, flanked by uniforms, shoes, and other apparel worn by key members of the winning teams. It's a neat display, the most prominent homage to past excellence found in any NBA arena's concourse.

The concourse is impressive as well. The area above the walkway stretches to the top of the building, a space filled with pipes and tubes like something from the movie Brazil. But the most noteworthy part of the building is the design of its seating sections.

The Palace was the first of the modern arenas to go all out in accentuating its luxury boxes, but unlike The Gund the design is unobtrusive and completely functional. The bottom suites are built right into the middle of the lower bowl, plushly detailed boxes that each include two rows of seats in front of a long table. The middle row of suites is located at the top of the lower bowl, while a third row is built above the upper bowl. Although some fans hate the idea of the suites, they are an important part of a team's revenue, and I have to admit that I admire the way The Palace's design manages to include so many in such good locations, without denying fans access to plenty of other decent seats as well.

Make no mistake about it, The Palace is a big arena, but the upper bowl appears smaller than the lower, so that only a few seats cause eyestrain. In short, Detroit's arena is a terrific place to watch a game, sacrificing very little to pack in a ton of fans and a bunch of luxury boxes.

There was a time when The Palace was kind of like a modern Boston Garden, with very little hoopla surrounding the game. You wouldn't find mascots, dancers, remote-controlled blimps, or an excess of fan contests. But things have changed as 1995 dawns.

Right before the Pistons' p.a. announcer reads the starting lineups, he says something curious: "And now, let's meet some of the greatest athletes in the world!" It strikes me as the ultimate example of hyping the game of basketball and the visiting team, rather than the Pistons themselves.

After the introduction of the entire visiting team, a fancy computer graphic shows a futuristic car flying in from space and blasting a Celtics logo with a flaming basketball. After that bit of fluff, the Pistons are introduced with slick graphics and thunderous music, a moment that brings more excitement than the team will generate for most of the evening.

Still, for a while it appears that the Pistons might be the lesser of two evils. After a tight first quarter, Detroit leads 32-31, but they are getting beaten badly on the boards, and I begin to sense that something is wrong. Things remain close in the second, but in the last two and a half minutes of the quarter the Celtics go on a 13-0 run to lead 62-50 at halftime. The Pistons are shooting well, but rebounds continue to haunt them, and for a while the Celtics have more offensive boards than Detroit's total rebounds for the game.

The Pistons have added more than extra-flashy graphics. I've only seen one other game, but I don't remember nearly as many fan contests. My favorite on this night happens during halftime, when a guy attempts to catch small parachutes dropped from the rafters in a shopping cart that he wheels around the court. The problem is, a dance team scheduled to perform during the break has made its way onto the floor too early, and the dancers are widely scattered across the court. In what will be the most entertaining moment of the evening, the first parachute lands squarely on a dancer's head, blanketing the surprised teenager as she stands innocently in her starting position. The dance team learns its lesson, and wisely moves aside to give the guy room.

But the thing that must grate on the true Pistons fan's nerves, the change that disappoints almost as much as the team's recent losses, is the addition of a mascot. After almost twenty years without one, the Pistons have Sir Slamalot, a medieval knight in a Detroit uniform (I believe he's also referred to as "The Palace Guard"). In addition, a group modeled after the Sports Magic Team in Orlando is running around the stands and interacting with the crowd, just another indication that the time when basketball was the show in Detroit may have come to a close, at least for now.

The Pistons can't cut into the Celtics' 10-point lead, and the primary reason continues to be rebounding. Both teams are shooting well, but the Celtics continue to pluck down offensive boards with alarming ease, and as a result the game is difficult for the crowd to watch. This is too bad, really, because the Pistons have a terrific set of replay screens on the hanging scoreboard over the court, as well as a bunch of message boards hanging on the base of the lower bowl. The biggest drawback tonight is that the abundance of scoreboards allows us to monitor the rebound totals at all times, a depressing reminder of why the Pistons are going to lose on their home court for the fifth straight time.

Nothing changes in the final quarter, as the Pistons make a brief come-back bid but never really pull close. Detroit totals 21 rebounds, one more than the all-time NBA record for fewest in a game, and loses by 17 on a night when they shoot 56.5% and have the same number of turnovers as their opponents.

As I drive back to the hotel, I have to wonder: Am I some sort of terri-ble jinx for the Eastern Conference teams at home? Two weeks ago, I saw the Pistons beat the Sixers in Philadelphia. Last week, I was in the Garden to watch the Sixers top the Celtics. Tonight, the cycle was completed when the Celtics destroyed the Pistons at The Palace.

I'm beginning to think that I might not be getting any more free tick-ets in those cities. Final score: Celtics 124, Pistons 107.

Average 1994–95 ticket cost: $29.41 (14th highest in the NBA)

Beer: $4.00 (14 oz.)

Soda: $1.50 (12 oz.—Coca-Cola products)

Hot Dog: $1.75

Parking: $5.00

Mascot: Sir Slamalot (The Palace Guard—a medieval knight)

Cheerleaders: none

Remote-controlled blimp: none

Other teams that play full-time in The Palace: Detroit Vipers (International Hockey League), Detroit Neon (Continental Indoor Soccer League)

What I'd change about The Palace: Maybe move it a little closer to Detroit—although not too much closer.

What I love about The Palace: It's a great example of a big arena with a lot of luxury boxes that still offers a decent view of the game.

Statistics from Team Marketing Report, Inc.

Elevation

INDIANA PACERS

Founded: 1967
1993–94 Record: 47-35
Team Colors: Navy Blue, Yellow

Saturday, December 31–Wednesday, January 4

The end of 1994 and the start of the new year found me resting up in Auburn Hills. My New Year's Eve was pretty lonely, of course, but the Hampton Inn was stuffed with young people for the night, and I took advantage of the false sense of community created by television and watched the festivities from New York's Times Square. After three weeks on the road, the final night of the year brought the first appearance of snow on my trip, and on Sunday morning my car was blanketed under four inches of fresh powder.

On Sunday and Monday I holed up in my room, dividing my time between watching college and pro football and writing about my trip through the Eastern Conference. In fact, there would be many days when I would resist the temptation to act like a tourist, and barricade myself in my hotel room to work instead.

My short break was over by Tuesday, and I packed my car in the overcast morning before bidding farewell to Auburn Hills and beginning the complicated trip to Indianapolis. I followed small highways to work my way west, then south, then west, then south again.

Just before four that afternoon I crossed the state line into Indiana on I-69, and early that evening I arrived in Indianapolis, a day's drive of 340 miles. It had been pretty cold since I left Cleveland, but by the time I reached Indianapolis it was downright nasty. I unloaded my gear and cranked up the heater in my room, settling in until the game the following night.

> **Previous Pacers Games at Market Square Arena:**
>
> **1992–93 season:** Seattle (Pacers 105-99)

The people of Indiana are known for their love of basketball, a sport in which the best players often demonstrate an uncanny ability to elevate into the air. It is perhaps fitting, then, that the Pacers play in an elevated arena, the only one in the NBA that stands lifted off the ground.

Market Square Arena, or MSA, is located directly above Market Street, one of the downtown area's major thoroughfares. On the north and south sides of the street are huge parking garages that support the arena between them. The building itself is topped by a large white dome, with brown walls supported by pillars at its base. Mounted directly over the street on the sides of the arena are exterior message boards, which display information about upcoming events to passing motorists.

Located at the eastern end of the downtown area, MSA blends well with the local skyline, and its elevated design is unique to the NBA. According to the Pacers' media guide, their team name was chosen to reflect the owners' desire to set the pace in professional basketball, and their arena's design is certainly unparalleled.

Once the Pacers reached the NBA after nine years in the American Basketball Association, however, they took a long time to live up to their name on the court. The people of Indiana express their love of basketball more with the high school and college game, and for years attendance for their professional franchise was mediocre. But the '93–94 club had overcome their lukewarm tradition to be the surprise team of the season. After failing to win a playoff series in their history, the Pacers rode a second-half surge to storm into the playoffs and sweep the Magic in the first round. They weren't finished there, either, going on to beat the top-seeded Hawks before bowing out in seven games to the Knicks in the conference finals.

Even though they inflicted the two most heartbreaking losses in Magic history, I still had a soft spot for Indiana's team. The Pacers' front office was one of the nicest I encountered in my travels, although it was annoying to call them and be put on hold, only to hear the radio broadcast of Byron Scott's game-winning 3-pointer against the Magic in the first game

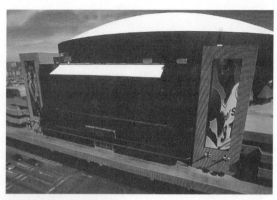

✪ MARKET SQUARE
ARENA
Opened: 1974
Capacity: 16,530
Indianapolis, Indiana

of the 1994 playoffs. I also enjoyed seeing how Market Square Arena blends in with the downtown area. Unfortunately, MSA is one of those buildings where the best views are from the outside.

Wednesday, January 4, 1995—7:30 PM

INDIANA PACERS (17-10) VS. WASHINGTON BULLETS (7-20)

Winter has arrived in Indiana in full force. Although the skies have been beautifully bright, the day's high temperature topped out at nine degrees, and the wind chill has dropped as low as 23 degrees below zero. My car struggles to start as I leave the hotel for the game, but eventually it turns over and I'm on my way.

The radio pregame show warns of a nasty accident on the highway to the arena, so I turn off and make my way there through small streets.

It is another case where my previous trip has given me the experience to be able to improvise, and by using the downtown skyscrapers as landmarks I reach a parking lot a block north of the arena without losing too much time. I bundle up in my Warriors jacket, a souvenir from the first trip, and hurry to the base of the building.

Speaking of the Warriors, their former star Chris Webber is still injured as Washington comes to town, and with Rex Chapman and Don MacLean also out the team is just as understaffed as when I saw them in Cleveland a week ago. Although the Pacers have been disappointing on the road, they've won nine in a row at home, and the Bullets squad they are facing has lost 12 of its last 13 games. It's going to be a blowout, no doubt about it.

The Pacers have left me a ticket low in the corner, almost exactly the same place they put me the first time I visited. Some things are different, however, including a new jazzed-up opening that rivals the best of them, with a fancy computer graphic and lots of spotlights and music in the darkened arena.

The other big excitement is provided by two special guests, who will spend the evening sheepishly taking part in several lame little sketches and activities during breaks in the action. Yes, it's Jerry Mathers and Ken Osmond, better known as Beaver Cleaver and Eddie Haskell, as I find myself in Indianapolis on *Leave It to Beaver* night. I guess they've got to do something to keep fans coming to see these great Eastern Conference games.

Despite my low expectations of the game, I'm pleased to look around and see a near-sellout. The crowd is just under 16,000, a great improvement over my last visit, when the Pacers drew about 10,000 against the Sonics—a dream matchup compared to tonight.

The crowd is packed into Market Square Arena, which is not only the NBA's sole elevated arena but also the only league building with a domed roof. Although domes can sometimes hurt an arena's acoustics, they also provide a distinct look to the building's design, giving the action a more dramatic atmosphere.

The seating layout is perfectly round, and the number of rows is highest in the middle and gradually shrinks down to only a few on each end. Overlooking the west side basket is a restaurant called Market Square Gardens (not to be confused with Madison Square Garden), which is built above the small seating sections on that side of the building. On the opposite side is the only player board, a big multicolored screen that shows assists and rebounds in addition to the points and fouls for the players on the floor. There are video monitors mounted in each of the four corners above the seats, and a traditional four-sided scoreboard hangs over the court, with message boards on each face.

One other element of the arena deserves mentioning. The building has a stadium design, where the seats are laid out on one level, rather than two or three. In the case of MSA, however, the arena is like one big section, as the slope from the first row to the last is perfectly uniform. The only thing interrupting the rows of seats is a walkway about halfway up that circles the building.

Although it's a relative small arena, the layout puts the upper seats far from the action, and in general Market Square Arena doesn't hide the fact that it's almost thirty years old. In short, even though I'm a fan of some parts of its design, MSA isn't one of my favorite arenas.

Amazingly, the Bullets actually lead by two after the first quarter, but in the second the Pacers begin to play as expected and open up a 9-point halftime advantage. Indiana is an exciting team to watch when they play well, and Washington can only stay competitive for brief segments of the game.

Some things are just as I remember them from my first visit. I've decided that MSA has the toughest ushers in the NBA. During both games, I saw plenty of examples of the Pacers' employees demonstrating that they are strict but fair, and heaven help anyone trying to move to better seats or even walk across a row to another area.

Much like the ushers, the people around me seem to have a no-nonsense attitude. Of all the arenas I visited alone, MSA was the only one where I sat with people on both sides of me and never got into a conversation. I don't try to force such a dialog, but very often one would happen naturally, especially if a person next to me was curious as to why I was taking notes during games.

Not in Indiana. While none of the people sitting near me were especially rude, they also were perfect examples of stereotypically stubborn Midwesterners. The few times I would make any comments to someone around me, I would be met with either a curt answer or a blank stare. After my experience on the road, I've found a curious pattern: Whenever a team was really nice to me, its fans weren't, and vice versa. I have no idea why that would be, but Indiana was a perfect example.

The Pacers pour it on in the third quarter, leading 85-68 by the end. I wish that I could head off to a luxury box for some free food and beer like I did in Cleveland, but Indiana has no such amenities, and even if they did I wouldn't know anyone who could get me into one.

With 6:25 to go, the Pacers lead 90-76, and I'm pretty sure that the officials must share my feeling: Let's get this over with. Little could I know that the Pacers have just scored their final basket of the game.

The Bullets score a few points here and there, and the Pacers do not. In four and a half minutes, the home team hits only three free throws, while Scott Skiles nails a couple of 3-pointers to help the Bullets score 14. Suddenly it's 93-90 with 2:03 left, and the fans begin the kind of grumbling that is understandable in such a situation. The Pacers keep forcing shots, and it is only a couple of solid defensive plays by center Rik Smits that prevent Washington from tying the score. Still, the win is far from satisfying, as Indiana scores 1 point in the final 3:20, and only 9 in the fourth quarter, an all-time franchise record for fewest points in that period.

I suppose I should be happy that the final score was close, and that the result really wasn't decided until the final seconds. Even so, the Pacers' collapse has been so embarrassing, and the Bullets' comeback such a tease, that the game leaves a sour taste in my mouth.

After it's all over, I walk to my car and thank the stars above that I won't see the Bullets again for the rest of my trip. I'm fooling myself, though—the L.A. Clippers are the Bullets of the West, and I will see them four times. Still, maybe they can make a decent effort, something Washington has failed to do at home or on the road. Final score: Pacers 94, Bullets 90.

Average 1994–95 ticket cost: $27.82 (16th highest in the NBA)

Beer: $3.00 (12 oz.)

Soda: $1.75 (16 oz.—Coca-Cola products)

Hot Dog: $2.00

Parking: $4.00

Mascot: Boomer (panther wearing a Pacers uniform)

Cheerleaders: The Pacemates

Remote-controlled blimp: none

Other teams that play full-time in Market Square Arena:
Indianapolis Ice (International Hockey League)

What I'd change about Market Square Arena: Modify the slope
of the seats to improve the sightlines and bring the back seats
closer to the court.

What I love about Market Square Arena: The elevated design and
the unique atmosphere under the domed roof.

Statistics from Team Marketing Report, Inc.

Playground of the Rich

CHICAGO BULLS

Founded: 1966
1993–94 Record: 55-27
Team Colors: Red, White, Black

Thursday, January 5–Tuesday, January 10

I stayed in Indianapolis the day after the Pacers game, hanging out and hoping that the temperature would rise before I had to leave. Sure enough, the air was a little warmer on Thursday, and my car had no trouble starting when I went out to turn it over and let it run for a few minutes.

The two days I spent in Indiana's capital had been clear, so I was disappointed to see that the skies had clouded over by Friday morning. Worse still, there was a light snow as I loaded my car just before noon, and it was of the heavy, slushy kind that forced me to scrape my windows thoroughly before I could leave.

The weather slowed my progress in places, but mostly I was able to make pretty good time. The trip took much of the afternoon, and at 4:30 PM I made it to Illinois, where I immediately gained an hour by crossing into the Central time zone. Even so, it took me a while to work my way to the north side of the city, where my friend Todd keeps an apartment while attending graduate school at Northwestern University in nearby Evanston.

Todd is not only one of my closest friends from Orlando, he's also among my favorite NBA fans. His great appreciation of basketball is strengthened by his wry sense of humor, and we both have a similarly irreverent view of the NBA game. As a result, Chicago was a special stop for me: Not only did I have someone to do most of the driving in the challenging traffic of the Windy City, I also got to enjoy some terrific company at the Bulls games.

Previous Bulls Games at Chicago Stadium:

1992-93 season: San Antonio (Spurs 107-102 in OT)

Lean in close, and I'll tell you a secret. It's blasphemy to many Bulls fans, the kind of statement that could end my fledgling career as a sports-writer, but I've got to be honest: I never liked Chicago Stadium.

Starting with the '94–95 season, the brand-new United Center became the home of the Bulls and Blackhawks, and the Stadium was obsolete. As a result, the tributes and reminiscences were in full swing when I returned to Chicago, as both the local and national media waxed poetically about the grand old building that was in its final days of existence.

In my opinion, such accolades made sense in Boston, but not Chicago. The Bruins began playing in Boston Garden in the 1920s, winning five championships, one each in the twenties, thirties, forties, sixties, and seventies. The Blackhawks also began play in that era, but won only three titles in Chicago: two in the thirties and one in the sixties. In basketball, the Celtics had occupied the Garden for almost fifty years, winning sixteen championships as far back as the mid-1950s. The Bulls, meanwhile, didn't even begin play until 1966, and were a mediocre team with no great history until a rookie named Michael Jordan showed up in 1984. The Bulls did win three championships in a row in the early 1990s, but that's not exactly ancient history.

Boston Garden was notorious for some terrible seats, but for the most part it was an intimate place to see a game. Chicago Stadium, meanwhile, was a barn, with three levels of fans stuffed to the rafters in every direction. Both had ancient facilities, but Boston maintained their tradition by showcasing the game and its players, which made it easier to plant one's behind in the uncomfortable confines of a wooden chair. The Bulls, meanwhile, added details such as cheerleaders, a mascot, colorful message boards, and a flashy opening, all of which belong in a modern facility, not a building meant to evoke fond memories of yesteryear.

And this stuff about the Bulls having the best fans in the NBA—maybe, but if Jordan had played for the Sixers, I bet they would have had pretty decent crowds too. Chicago is a great sports town, but I don't remember many people bragging about the Bulls fans at the Stadium when Artis Gilmore was the big star of the team.

The bottom line is, I will miss Boston Garden, but not Chicago Stadium. Whatever the popular opinion among Bulls fans, the days of the older facility were numbered, and although it stood like a silent ghost when I returned to Chicago, less than a month later the wrecking ball would begin to take down the Stadium for good.

Although I was never enamoured of Chicago Stadium, I can't complain about the team, as the Bulls have been helpful in my planning, especially considering their popularity in recent seasons. Both times that I requested tickets, the team allowed me to buy them through their front office, and even though the seat locations were never very memorable, all three Bulls games that I saw were high-profile enough to keep me from complaining. I must admit, though, that I wouldn't mind seeing a game from a seat in the lower bowl someday—Chicago is the only city in the NBA where I've never sat in the lowest section of the arena.

Friday, January 6, 1995—7:00 PM

CHICAGO BULLS (16-13) VS. SEATTLE SUPERSONICS (20-9)

Soon after I arrive at Todd's apartment it's time for us to go. The game is on national television, and as a result tip-off will be a half-hour earlier than usual. The snow has quit falling, and after clearing off Todd's car we begin the drive to Chicago's new arena.

We weave through the city and park a couple of blocks east of the United Center, hustled into a lot by a group of energetic young men. Their signs say the cost is $7, but the guy directing us to our spot tells us that

✪ THE UNITED
CENTER
Opened: 1994
Capacity: 21,500
Chicago, Illinois

a "preferred" location near the front would be $5 more. Todd tells him that we're not paying any more, and as a result we are packed into a tight spot so close to the other cars that we both have to exit on the passenger's side.

The night is heavy with mist, and as a result I don't get a good look at the United Center until after we walk to the end of the lot and turn left on Madison. Chicago Stadium had been the biggest building in the area, but now the old arena is dwarfed by its replacement across the street. The Stadium is on our right as we draw closer to the new building, and after a quick visual check we decide that you could fit at least three or four Stadiums into the United Center.

Although I've never heard anyone from the Bulls acknowledge it, I think the United Center has a pretty similar design to the old Stadium. They are both big rectangles, with main entrances on the north and south sides and only a limited amount of other decorations. As we get closer to the United Center, however, we see one thing that the Stadium never had: a huge bronze statue of Michael Jordan soaring to dunk over a faceless opponent, which stands outside the east entrance to the new arena.

Looking at the statue, I can't help but think that Jordan built this house, that if it weren't for his contribution to Chicago sports there would be no United Center, and yet he has never played a game here. But who knows? Maybe someday he will.

The extra space in the United Center is apparent in the huge concourses, the many staircases, and the convenient escalators that are found throughout the building. As we travel up to our seats, I'm not surprised to see the dozens of concession and souvenir stands, or to learn that the arena has a snazzy team shop (you can even buy a seat or brick from the Stadium). I also anticipated the full-service restaurant and the lounge, but one thing I didn't expect was the extras included on the main and upper concourses.

The Bulls have created—what do I call it?—an interactive museum unlike anything I've seen in any other NBA arena. Throughout the concourses are displays and exhibits devoted to basketball, giving fans the chance to get an idea of some of the inner workings of the game. On the main level, one stand-alone wall has basketballs with the imbedded handprints of a dozen past and present players, both from the Bulls and many other teams around the league. Another wall has shoes, including a display of how a player's signature shoe is created, as well as a nearby low platform with the footprints of many of the same stars. Vivid cutouts demonstrate the height and armspan of a variety of notable players, and there are numerous photo opportunities at several other displays.

The main exhibits are a terrific demonstration of the physical scale of the NBA, but upstairs Todd and I have the chance to test our own muscles. A tribute to vertical leap, the display shows the ability of various stars, and allows fans to gauge their own prowess with mounted targets at various heights above the floor. Wearing a camera, binoculars and my winter clothes, I can only elevate to touch the target hanging at the 9-foot level, but hell, I'm paid to write about basketball, not play it.

Is it all cheesy, like a playground for people rich enough to afford a ticket to the game? Sure. If I were a Bulls season-ticket holder, would I quickly tire of the displays, completely ignoring them after a couple of games? I'm certain I would. But on this night I'm a sucker for my newly-discovered delights, and I have Todd take pictures of me in front of several displays. I even convince him to join me in a couple of shots, which is no small feat, considering that most people from Orlando hate acting like tourists, and Todd is no exception.

Just like every other game we would see in Chicago, our seats are upstairs on the end. At least we get a good view of the layout: a lower level of seats, then a row of luxury boxes around the arena, then the club level seats, then more luxury boxes, a third level of seats, and a final group of boxes above everything else. Unlike Cleveland, the sightlines are good, but a great many seats are pretty far from the action.

The Bulls are playing the SuperSonics, and although both Todd and I are disillusioned with Chicago's '94–95 team, we agree that we despise Seattle even more. There are many teams that we would root for against the Bulls, but fortunately we've come on a night when that isn't the case.

The Bulls had a splashy opening before they moved to their new arena, so it's no surprise that their current version turns out to involve computer graphics, laser signatures on the court, and crystal-clear photos of both teams' players.

In the first half, the Bulls play as if they don't need that Jordan guy after all. Shooting 70 percent, they lead by 3 at the end of the first quarter, and twice build 8-point leads. But Seattle is one of the league's best, and they keep pace with the home team before pushing out to a 58-51 lead at half-time.

As Seattle builds its lead to 14 in the third quarter, the state-of-the-art video and sound systems begin to draw my attention from the game. The center scoreboard is eight-sided, with half the screens showing video of the game while the other boards display full player stats, including points, rebounds, assists, steals, blocks, and personal fouls. Many other scoreboards and message boards are built around the upper levels, including a board that shows detailed statistics that even surpass the similar board in Cleveland in their insight. If you want to see the current shooting percentages broken down by quarter, or the points in the paint, or even the number of points from 9–15 foot shots, you're in luck in the United Center. Todd and I also keep a close eye on the out-of-town scoreboard, not only to see how the Magic are doing but also to learn if Atlanta coach Lenny Wilkins will get the win that would put him past Red Auerbach on the all-time list (he will, by the way).

The on-court entertainment is pretty decent as well. In addition to a mascot and cheerleaders, the Bulls have a sports team running around the stands, a splinter group from the Sports Magic Team in Orlando. With the Bulls Brothers, however, Chicago has an original production found nowhere else in the NBA. Based on the Blues Brothers, the Bulls Brothers do a variety of routines, usually big production numbers based on the characters and their songs. On one memorable night, the duo finished a song, then the Jake look-alike got down on all fours under a basket, only to have Elwood make a running start before vaulting off his back and dunking a ball. Painful to watch, but certainly memorable.

One other bit of entertainment is unique to Chicago: fan limbo, where cameras take shots of the crowd while a graphic of a limbo stick is projected on the big screens. The idea is that any fan the camera catches is supposed to mimic doing the limbo under the on-screen stick, which often produces hilarious results.

With all these distractions, I only start to pay attention to the game again when the Bulls pull back within 7 by the end of the third quarter. The comeback continues in the fourth, helped by six technical fouls on Seattle, three for arguing with the officials (is it any wonder I love them so?). The Bulls manage to tie the score at 93 with 4:29 to play, which brings loud cheers from the Chicago faithful, demonstrating both their continued loyalty and the new arena's acoustics, which are certainly impressive given its size. But the Sonics can be very, very strong on both ends of the floor, and they settle the issue with an 8-2 run over the next two minutes. Seattle gets the late baskets they need to seal the win, and the result is pretty much as everyone expected. Perhaps the best news is that the Bulls made a good showing, but as I leave the United Center I find myself thinking that it would have been nice to see Jordan play at least one season in the new arena. Such a sparkling facility deserves a solid team, and it's unfortunate that it opened a couple of years too late.

For three days after the game I hang out with friends, but the real highlight of my stop in Chicago is the night the Magic come to town to face the Bulls. This game will mark two important firsts: the first time that I see my hometown team play outside of Florida, and the first game where forward Horace Grant will face his former team as a member of the Magic. With the expected dose of hype from the local media, I find myself barely able to contain my excitement. For me, this is the most anticipated game of both my trips.

The Magic are 26-6, still the best record in the league, while the Bulls had lost in Cleveland on Saturday night to drop to 16-15. Todd and I go down to the arena early, and by the time the opening lineups are announced we are settled in our customary upper-level seats behind the basket. I am curious to see the Chicago fans' reaction to Grant's return and am surprised when almost all greet him warmly when he is introduced. In what I think is a test of their level of class, Bulls fans respond highly—I'd expected catcalls from almost every seat.

The Bulls come out shooting well, just like they had against the Sonics, and the Magic fail to keep up. In the first few minutes, Chicago takes smart shots, while the Magic fail to put the ball in the basket. Suddenly it is 11-0, and before I get a chance to settle into the action the Magic are in deep trouble. The agony continues through the first quarter, as my boys go down 35-15 at the first break. In the second quarter they begin to climb back into it, cutting the lead to thirteen by halftime. Things are still precarious for the Magic, but at least they are well within striking distance, so I try to keep my hopes up.

After spending halftime being guardedly optimistic, I am stunned by the start of the second half. It is like a replay of the opening of the game, as the Bulls begin to pound my poor team incessantly, driving the lead back to twenty with relative ease. Yet Chicago isn't finished yet, pouring it on to go up by a horrifying 30 *points* at the end of the third quarter, 89-59. The Magic, who had scored only 15 points in the first quarter, post only 13 in the third. Coming after their deceiving comeback at the end of the first half, the collapse is like a nightmare, the second one I am forced to experience tonight.

The reserves play most of the fourth quarter, and in the end the Magic score 77 points, one more than their all-time record for fewest in a game. Hell, the Bulls could have gone scoreless in the fourth and still won by twelve. It is humiliating, to say the least, and as it is the first Magic game I've seen in person in more than a month, I couldn't be more disappointed. The people back home can talk about championships all they want, but after what I see in Chicago I'm keeping my own expectations a little lower, at least for the time being. Final score: Bulls 109, Magic 77.

Average 1994–95 ticket cost: $36.00 (fifth highest in the NBA)

Beer: $4.00 (16 oz.)

Soda: $2.50 (16 oz.—Coca-Cola products)

Hot Dog: $2.50

Parking: $10.00

Mascot: Benny the Bull (big, goofy-looking animal)

Cheerleaders: The LuvaBulls

Remote-controlled blimp: yes (enormous, menacing-looking bull)

Other teams that play full-time in the United Center: Chicago Blackhawks (National Hockey League)

What I'd change about the United Center: It would be nice if it wasn't so big—the upper seats are quite a distance from the court.

What I love about the United Center: The interactive displays, the Jordan statue, and the plush new concourses.

Statistics from Team Marketing Report, Inc.

The Bucks Stop Here

Founded: 1968
1993–94 Record: 20-62
Team Colors: Hunter Green, Purple, Silver

Wednesday, January 11
Milwaukee is blissfully close to Chicago, so I took advantage of the fact to run a few errands, including changing the oil in my car, before heading out on Wednesday. But a strong batch of fog, which was blanketing the area when I entered Wisconsin at three that afternoon, made the supposedly easy drive a little more challenging. Visibility was incredibly poor by the time I reached Milwaukee a little later, and I would soon learn that the airport had been shut down for the day. Even so, the Sacramento Kings had managed to arrive for their game against the Bucks, and soon after I unpacked I got a call from Keith, my contact in Milwaukee. Drained after the horrendous Magic loss the night before, I was ready to see a game in which I had no real emotional involvement.

> **Previous Bucks Games at the Bradley Center:**
>
> **1992–93 season:** Dallas (Bucks 120-86)

After the Nets moved into the Meadowlands Arena in 1981, there was a seven-year period with no new NBA buildings. The league's rise in popularity during that time not only produced four expansion teams in the late 1980s, but also led to the opening of five new arenas in 1988. While the expansion teams in Miami and Charlotte dedicated their new buildings, three established clubs also christened new venues: The Palace in Detroit, ARCO Arena in Sacramento, and the Bradley Center in Milwaukee. With new buildings opening every year since then, by the start of the '95–96 season more than half of the NBA teams will be playing in arenas built during the construction boom of the past decade.

Among all these glorious new venues across the country, it was easy for me to overlook Milwaukee's arena, but the first time I visited the Brew City to see a Bucks game I realized that the Bradley Center deserves a place among the league's nicer buildings. Even though the team has struggled in recent years, Milwaukee fans still enjoy the benefits that only a modern arena can offer.

For one thing, the Bradley Center is nicely incorporated into the downtown area, a huge building constructed with blocks of dark tan stone and a jet-black roof that occupies an entire city block. With only one garage nearby, the arena isn't isolated in a sea of parking lots, yet there are still plenty of available spots in the nearby area for fans to leave their cars.

But the best part of the arena's design is the huge atrium that extends on the east side, a marvelous glass front that rises roughly six stories. Fans entering the arena get to enjoy the sensation of walking through the NBA's largest lobby, with a variety of ramps, stairways, and escalators there to take them to their seats. There is a similar atrium on the west side, but since it faces another structure it's not as impressive.

In short, the Bradley Center is clean, spacious, and modern, and provides very pleasant surroundings at a Bucks game.

When I contacted all the NBA teams about my first trip, most were very helpful. I had trouble getting a straight answer out of the Knicks, but virtually every other club agreed to either sell or give me a ticket to a game, usually in a friendly manner. There was only one team that flat-out refused to help me in any way, and that team was the Bucks.

Of all the media directors in the NBA, Milwaukee's has held the job the longest, and perhaps the years have made him extra surly. Whatever

✪ THE BRADLEY
CENTER
Opened: 1988
Capacity: 18,633
Milwaukee, Wisconsin

the reason, when I called him a couple of weeks after I sent my first letter, he coolly gave me the local number for Ticketmaster and told me to call them. I tried another time after I'd arranged my schedule, figuring that he might be more helpful if he knew I was planning to see a Tuesday night game against the Mavericks. It made no difference, as during my second attempt I couldn't even get past the switchboard operator.

Later I told people on the first trip of my troubles with the Bucks, including folks from other front offices, and was surprised to find that Milwaukee had a reputation around the league for such behavior. Needless to say, this gave me a prejudice against the team. But I must admit that their media director gave me a comp for my second visit— after I signed my book contract.

Wednesday, January 11, 1995—7:30 PM

MILWAUKEE BUCKS (10-22) VS. SACRAMENTO KINGS (18-13)

Keith picks me up at my hotel a couple of hours before the game, just as he did two years ago. Once the Bucks had made their position clear while I was planning my first trip, I'd posted a message on a computer bulletin board explaining my situation, and Keith had responded. A Bucks season-ticket holder in his mid-thirties, he'd offered to sell me one of his seats for the Mavericks game, and I'd taken him up on it. During my first visit to Milwaukee, I'd been battling a nasty cold, and Keith came to my rescue by driving me to and from the game. We hung out before the game that night at the Safe House, a local bar with an espionage theme located a short walk from the arena. Later, we were joined by Jan, his longtime girlfriend, and her coworker Rose, and the four of us had seen the Bucks destroy the Mavericks. When the time came to visit Milwaukee again, I'd given him another call and we had made similar arrangements, although this time Keith suggested that we visit a downtown sports bar.

Rose had stolen my heart—I can be somewhat of a wise guy, and she proved to be every bit as irreverent as I am. Yet as helpful and enjoyable as my three Wisconsin friends are, the biggest thrill for me in Milwaukee is hanging out with Keith, because he's the greatest NBA fan I've ever met. Although his job is running a grocery store, Keith has found the time to do a little traveling: In the past few years, he's been to games in twenty NBA arenas, usually during short trips that involve only a couple of cities at a time. As a result, we spend much of our time in the bar comparing our reactions to the different buildings.

But even more impressive is Keith's loyalty to the Bucks. As I mentioned earlier, I saw the Magic's first 141 home games, a streak broken only when I left on my first trip. Even so, I've still never missed a game held while I was in Orlando. I've had to rearrange travel plans every once in a while, but it's never been too difficult for me, and I thought I had a pretty good attendance record. Once I met Keith, however, I realized that I was a total amateur in that respect.

Keith has seen every Bucks home game dating back to the early 1980s, a streak that he guesses is around ten or twelve years long. That's in the neighborhood of *five hundred* games without an absence. He's my kindred spirit, and while he's told me that he will never take a trip around the NBA like I have (too much driving for his taste), he's compensated with an iron-man fan streak that has to be one of the longest in the country.

Yet what some people might find most surprising is that he's an average guy. Not an overzealous sports junkie who uses the local team as some sort of strange emotional outlet, but a normal, well-adjusted, and gracious man who has been fortunate enough to avoid any potential conflicts that might make him miss a game. It meant a great deal to me to meet someone who shared my fan profile and yet wasn't drooling at the mouth or cackling like a mad scientist. He's a nice guy, I'm a nice guy, and we're both normal. And so, by the happy chance of meeting Keith, Jan, and Rose, Milwaukee became for me a city where the Bucks took second place to a nice trio of people.

The ladies meet us at the bar, and after drinks and appetizers the four of us walk over to the nearby Bradley Center. Entering through the towering lobby, we head up to the main concourse, which is fashioned out of stone and tile. The concourse area is remarkably clean and spacious, and Jan comments that it reminds her of an airport.

Keith's seats are about halfway up the lower bowl, roughly even with the baseline. Although the Bradley Center has a traditional lower bowl/upper bowl design, with luxury boxes in between the two sections, there are distinctive touches that are found in several recently constructed arenas. For example, the entire layout is very linear, much like The Omni in Atlanta, without the traditional oval shape that follows the contours of a hockey rink. Also, while the lower bowl has a typical slope, the upper level is very steep, creating a somewhat dramatic climb for fans in the higher rows.

As we settle in our seats, Jan explains that the arena was really designed for hockey, not basketball, something I'd never heard before. It seems that the owners built the arena with the goal of bringing an NHL team to the city. I'm not an expert in arena design, whether for hockey or basketball, so Keith explains to me that the differences in the preferred layout for the two sports have to do with how the seats are positioned and where most are located. Since many hockey fans feel the best seats should be some-what elevated, he explains, the Bradley Center actually has more upstairs than in the lower level.

I love this kind of insight, although I can't help but wonder why I've never heard Milwaukee mentioned in the national media as one of the cities pursuing an existing or expansion NHL franchise. In any case, that's about all the idle chitchat I'm going to get out of Keith this evening, because once the game begins he's totally engrossed in the action, as any great fan would be. We exchange a few comments now and then, but most of the time I talk to Rose and Jan.

The Bucks employ certain rare touches at their games, beginning with the opening announcements: They are one of the few teams that announce the entire visitors' roster before the game. Although they only do it dur-ing a team's first visit to Milwaukee, I think it's a classy gesture. The rest of the announcements are pretty standard, although their computer graphic, depicting a sleek-looking buck running through the woods, is especially nice (but the sheer number of computer-graphic openings during the '94–95 season is beginning to numb my brain). After that, another relatively rare detail is added to the atmosphere: a live band. Known as StreetLife, and complete with both a male and female singer, the group is a Bradley Center staple. I have to admit that the band sounds pretty good, but I still hate them. For me, live music just doesn't belong at NBA games.

Even though the Kings are having a better season, it's clear from the start that the Bucks are in much stronger form on this night. Although the arena is only about two-thirds full, the relatively small crowd has plenty to cheer about, as Milwaukee builds a 10-point lead by the end of the first quarter. A bizarre thought occurs to me: If I'd seen these two teams play each other during my first trip, there wouldn't have been a hint of pur-ple on the court, but since that time both have switched to new uniforms that include the fashionable color. The Bucks' game program has an exten-sive article detailing the artistic reasons behind the new design, and I'm amused to read the pretentious explanation. No matter what fancy reasons the Bucks give, it's well known that sports apparel that is purple, black, or silver sells, and that more than anything explains their switch to green and purple. The Kings are no dummies either, changing from blue, red, and white to the big three I just mentioned, and I'm sure that during my upcoming visit to ARCO Arena I'll see one of the busiest team shops in the league.

Slick uniforms or not, the Kings are losing by 11 at the break. Rose and I take an extended walk through the arena, including shopping for my customary souvenir hat, and when we get back the third quarter is almost over. The Bucks, who have built a 75-55 lead, would have to pull an amazing, Pacer-esque disappearing act to lose the game, and for a while almost do. If not for the timely scoring of journeyman sub Marty Conlon, the Kings might have pulled off the big comeback, but in the end Milwaukee hangs on for the victory.

Although the arena's exterior and concourse are exceptional, the interior design is merely average, and with so many empty seats the experience of seeing a Bucks game is less than inspiring. Perhaps things would be different with a full crowd and an exciting matchup, but for now my visits to the Bradley Center are merely average basketball memories. For me, the highlight of Milwaukee had to be my three friends, who proved that the kindness of fellow fans can more than compensate for the bad attitude of a team's front office.

Which, by the way, once again proves my theory—the worse the team, the better the fans. Final score: Bucks 97, Kings 88.

Average 1994–95 ticket cost: $22.56 (25th highest in the NBA)

Beer: $3.25 (16 oz.)

Soda: $2.00 (20 oz.—Coca-Cola products)

Hot Dog: $1.75

Parking: $5.00

Mascot: Bango (big, sleek deer wearing uniform)

Cheerleaders: The Energee! Dance Team (scheduled to perform at 28 games during '94–95 season, but I've never seen them)

Remote-controlled blimp: none

Other teams that play full-time in the Bradley Center: Milwaukee Admirals (International Hockey League), Milwaukee Mustangs (Arena Football League), Milwaukee Wave (National Professional Soccer League)

What I'd change about the Bradley Center: Add some energetic fans, and turn up the contrast on the video screens—they're far too dark to see clearly.

What I love about the Bradley Center: The entrances, and the beautiful concourse level.

Statistics from Team Marketing Report, Inc.

Howling Winds, Howling Fans

MINNESOTA TIMBERWOLVES

Founded: 1989
1993–94 Record: 20-62
Team Colors: Royal Blue, Kelly Green, Silver

Thursday, January 12–Friday, January 13

Thursday morning was overcast in Milwaukee, but at least the heavy fog had cleared, and by noon I was headed west on the interstate. After about an hour on the road the highway turned to the northwest, heading straight for the Twin Cities. I was in a good mood, feeling rested and looking forward to returning to Target Center.

No, that's not a misprint—I enjoyed my first visit to see the Timberwolves. During my travels, there were several factors that made certain stops enjoyable. It was always nice to feel safe, for example, while staying somewhere with easy access to the games. It helped if the team had friendly people who made me feel like a welcomed visitor. If the arena was appealing, with a decent atmosphere and loyal fans, that was another plus. And perhaps most important, if the game was a good matchup, what NBA fan wouldn't look forward to a visit?

Minneapolis fit the bill in virtually every way, and since the Wolves were playing the Pistons, who had five of their top eight players injured, the game would feature two evenly matched teams. The fact that they were two of the worst teams in the league didn't bother me at all.

Due to an unscheduled stop at a casino, I covered only 195 miles on Thursday, so on Friday I had a full three hours of driving left, crossing into Minnesota at 1:30 PM. It was only a few hours before the Wolves game, but I had one more pressing errand, so I found a laundromat near my hotel, which was just west of the city and only a few miles from Target Center. For the rest of the afternoon I did laundry and repacked my duffel bags, finishing only 45 minutes before the game.

Previous Timberwolves Games at Target Center:

1992–93 season: Seattle (SuperSonics 89-77)/Dallas (Timberwolves 99-89)

This is how dumb I am: I always thought it was neat that several western arenas had such cool names, like Target Center, America West Arena, the Delta Center, the Great Western Forum, and ARCO Arena. I had no clue that all those buildings were named after corporations; after all, Orlando, Miami, and Boston had no such sponsorship. I learned the truth pretty quickly during my travels, especially because all the corporate-sponsored arenas have the logos of their parent companies prominently displayed, like the bull's-eye design that is found outside every Target store and, of course, on the home of the Timberwolves.

Target Center stands on the north side of the city, located near the Mall of America and the downtown skyscrapers. Even among so many buildings, the arena boasts an impressive design, rising high in the air while occupying an entire city block.

One of the great design details is the connecting walkways that link the arena with several nearby structures, including a half-dozen huge parking garages. By using the walkways, fans can park a fair distance from the arena and still have a pleasant stroll to the game, enjoying a nice view in heated comfort.

Target Center is a striking combination of light colors, a mixture of brown, orange, purple, and yellow sections, all of which together create a stylish exterior. In addition, the building isn't a rectangle, but instead has eight walls that follow the contours of the city streets that surround it. The south side is considered the front of the arena, and has a pleasant facade that includes an overhang and pillars made of brick. At night, the building is lit up with bright neon strips in various colors, adding to its distinctive appearance.

Struggling through their sixth NBA season, the Timberwolves were still trying to develop into a decent team, but appeared to be heading the route of the Nets, Clippers, and Kings toward consistent futility. Adding to the trouble was an ongoing uncertainty about the ownership of the team and the arena, which led to talk during the summer of 1994 of the Wolves moving to New Orleans or Memphis. Things were still unsettled at the time I visited, but it appeared that the team was secure in Minneapolis, at least for the immediate future. I was glad, for even though the Wolves have been a disappointment, it would be a shame if an arena as nice as Target Center didn't have an NBA team as a tenant. If only they could win a few more games. . .

Friday, January 13, 1995—7:00 PM

MINNESOTA TIMBERWOLVES (6-26) VS. DETROIT PISTONS (10-21)

The Timberwolves have always been very helpful, so I'm not surprised to find that the seat they've left for me is down low, a few rows behind one of the baskets. I pick up the ticket at the will-call window, which is in the NBA's most beautiful ticket lobby, including a gigantic sculpture of neon lights in the ceiling that is constantly shifting patterns.

While the opening announcements are relatively average, everything else in the experience of seeing a game at Target Center is exceptional. The center scoreboard has video screens and player boards on each of its four sides, and the Wolves' graphics have won awards as the best in the league.

As the game begins, it looks as if the graphics will be far better than the action. On the first play, Pistons guard Allan Houston works free for a shot on the basket right in front of me. He's about twenty feet out, and

✪ TARGET CENTER
Opened: 1990
Capacity: 19,006
Minneapolis, Minnesota

his shot misses everything. As if following Houston's lead, both teams are sluggish at the start, unable to convert easy opportunities, and at the end of the first quarter the Pistons hold a sloppy 18-17 lead. Thankfully, the level of play improves in the second, and the Wolves begin to execute. The scoring picks up, and at the half Minnesota leads 45-42.

Inside, Target Center is very similar to the Bradley Center, with a square design that has a lower level, a row of luxury boxes, and a steep upper level that begins above the suites. Although both arenas offer decent sight-lines, the upper seats are far from the action, and I can understand why I have yet to see the higher seats filled at a game in Target Center.

Those fans who do show up have their rituals. Prompted by urging message boards, they often howl during opposing free throws. The wolf theme continues in other ways, especially when the loudspeakers blare "Werewolves of London" during a couple of timeouts.

In addition to the center scoreboard, the Wolves' arena has scoreboards and message boards mounted at the base of the upper level, but in an unusual move they are found on the ends of the building, rather than the center.

If there's one thing that Wolves fans want to see on those scoreboards tonight, it's a number with three digits under their team's name. Minnesota hasn't scored a hundred points for 16 straight games, a streak that has lasted almost six weeks and is the second-longest in league history since the introduction of the shot clock in 1954. With 45 points at halftime, maybe there's hope.

With the double pressure on them to win the game and score a hundred points, the Wolves respond by posting 30 in the third quarter, giving them a 75-68 lead and putting them right on pace for the century mark. Wonder of wonders, they continue to take good shots, and before long it becomes clear that they're going to win, only their third victory in 16 games at Target Center. The excitement doesn't come to a head, however, until Christian Laettner hits a jumper with 1:31 left, giving the Wolves a 100-84 lead, and effectively ending both the Pistons and the streak in one smooth stroke.

When the final buzzer sounds, the crowd cheers their team as multicolored streamers are released from the ceiling. These may be tough times in Minneapolis, but tonight the Wolves have celebrated Friday the 13th by playing like a quality NBA team. Final score: Timberwolves 104, Pistons 92.

Average 1994–95 ticket cost: $27.58 (17th highest in the NBA)

Beer: $3.25 (16 oz.)

Soda: $2.00 (16 oz.—Coca-Cola products)

Hot Dog: $2.25

Parking: $4.00

Mascot: CRUNCH (silver-gray wolf wearing Timberwolves uniform)

Cheerleaders: Timberwolves Performance Team

Remote-controlled blimp: yes

Other teams that play full-time in Target Center: none

What I'd change about Target Center: Take out some of the upper level seats, so the top rows aren't as far from the court. And maybe do something to make the team play a little better.

What I love about Target Center: The stylish exterior design, the interconnecting walkways through the downtown area, and the howling of the fans during opponents' free throws.

Statistics from Team Marketing Report, Inc.

NBA standings as of Saturday, January 14, 1995:

EASTERN CONFERENCE
Atlantic Division

	W	L	Pct	GB	Home	Away
Orlando Magic	28	7	.800	—	16-0	12-7
New York Knicks	20	12	.625	6.5	11-4	9-8
Boston Celtics	14	20	.412	13.5	8-10	6-10
New Jersey Nets	14	23	.378	15	9-8	5-15
Miami Heat	10	23	.303	17	5-11	5-12
Philadelphia 76ers	10	23	.303	17	8-7	2-16
Washington Bullets	7	26	.212	20	3-12	4-14

Central Division

	W	L	Pct	GB	Home	Away
Cleveland Cavaliers	22	11	.667	—	12-7	10-4
Charlotte Hornets	21	12	.625	1	12-3	9-9
Indiana Pacers	20	13	.606	2	11-1	9-12
Chicago Bulls	18	16	.529	4.5	10-9	8-7
Atlanta Hawks	15	20	.429	8	9-9	6-11
Milwaukee Bucks	11	23	.324	11.5	6-8	5-15
Detroit Pistons	10	22	.313	11.5	7-8	3-14

WESTERN CONFERENCE
Midwest Division

	W	L	Pct	GB	Home	Away
Utah Jazz	24	10	.706	—	13-6	11-4
Houston Rockets	22	10	.688	1	12-6	10-4
San Antonio Spurs	20	11	.645	2.5	12-5	8-6
Denver Nuggets	17	16	.515	6.5	11-7	6-9
Dallas Mavericks	15	16	.484	7.5	9-8	6-8
Minnesota Timberwolves	7	26	.212	16.5	3-13	4-13

Pacific Division

	W	L	Pct	GB	Home	Away
Phoenix Suns	26	8	.765	—	16-2	10-6
Seattle SuperSonics	23	9	.719	2	15-1	8-8
L.A. Lakers	21	11	.656	4	11-4	10-7
Sacramento Kings	19	14	.576	6.5	13-5	6-9
Portland Trail Blazers	18	14	.563	7	12-6	6-8
Golden State Warriors	10	22	.312	15	7-9	3-13
L.A. Clippers	5	29	.147	20.5	3-14	2-15

The Evil Leaper

PORTLAND TRAIL BLAZERS

Founded: 1970
1993–94 Record: 47-35
Team Colors: Scarlet, Black, White

Saturday, January 14–Sunday, January 22

My visit to Minneapolis had been extremely quick—I'd arrived on Friday afternoon, and by Saturday morning I was once again headed west. While the Timberwolves game had been a pleasant distraction, my mind had been focused all week on the killer stretch of road I faced when I left the Twin Cities.

You have no idea how big Montana is until you have to drive across it. Not to mention Minnesota, North Dakota, Oregon—you get the idea. It was the longest leg of my trip, a mere five days to drive the 1,750 miles from Minneapolis to Portland. To give you an idea of how far I had to go, think about this: If I had decided that I wanted to see the Magic play instead of the Blazers, the trip south to Orlando would have been about 200 miles shorter. It was a long, daunting journey.

On Saturday I covered 535 miles, crossing into North Dakota just after 4 PM before stopping in Dickinson late in the evening. Hoping to drive a similar distance on Sunday, I entered Montana around 1 PM, continuing through Billings as the sun set hours later. As I neared the 400-mile mark that night, I suddenly found myself in the middle of an unexpected snowstorm, and after a scary hour in the heavy precipitation I was able to find shelter in the town of Big Timber. The skies had cleared by Monday morning, and I made a light day of it by driving the relatively quick 275 miles to Missoula.

Tuesday found me heading into the mountains before crossing into the Idaho panhandle at 1:45 PM. An hour later I was in Washington, where I turned south towards Oregon. I reached my fourth state that day just after six, and stopped in Boardman that night after 390 miles on the road. The last stretch was a 165-mile trip to Portland on a rainy Wednesday afternoon.

With the biggest leg of the trip behind me, I settled into my hotel near Memorial Coliseum, glad that the seemingly endless days of driving across the Plains were over.

A break in the SuperSonics' home schedule forced me to make Portland my first stop on the West Coast, but it was a change I welcomed. After my first trip, I found Portland much more enjoyable than Seattle, both in terms of the cities and the teams.

Previous Trail Blazers Games at Memorial Coliseum:

1992–93 season: L.A. Clippers (Clippers 96-86)

I'd never been to Portland before my first trip, and I was surprised to learn that the Rose City is dominated by a pair of rivers. The Columbia River marks the city's north side, while the Willamette River runs right through the downtown area.

Memorial Coliseum is located on the east side, at the top of the small hill that slopes down to the river. As you might expect from a 35-year-old building, the arena's design is extremely basic: It is a square structure with glass walls on all four sides that reach about three-quarters of the way up the building. The outline of the stands can be seen from the outside through the metal grids of the walls.

The Coliseum was the smallest arena in the NBA during the '94–95 season, and with a capacity of 12,888 it had two thousand less seats than Boston Garden, the next-smallest building. But just like the Garden, the Coliseum was in its final season as the home of the Trail Blazers. A massive new arena was well on its way to being completed. The Rose Garden, as it will be called, is located next to the Coliseum, and during the time of my visit construction was in full swing on both the new arena and the parking garages and courtyard areas around it. Unlike Chicago Stadium, the Coliseum will remain standing, and the two facilities will make up a new sports and entertainment complex known as the Rose Quarter.

The two games on my schedule in Portland would be the 787th and 788th consecutive sellouts for the Blazers, a streak that is not only the longest in the NBA but also in the history of professional sports, at least if the Blazers' media guide is to be believed. Portland has sold out every regular-season and playoff game in their tiny arena since 1977, the year they won their only NBA championship, and one advantage to the new building is that it will increase capacity by a whopping 7,500 fans. The plans certainly are impressive, and the finished product should be one of the NBA's showcases for years to come, although I have to wonder if the sellout streak might be in jeopardy.

I never liked the Trail Blazers before I traveled. I didn't care for any of their players, their uniform design was one of my least-favorite in the league, and they were really good, which bothered me immensely. But the Blazers turned out to have a nice front office, and Portland proved to be a beautiful city, so by the end of my first visit I had a newfound respect for the team. But one of the big advantages of traveling a second time was that I got to double-check my opinions, to see what things were consistent at NBA arenas, and when I returned to the Coliseum I felt my respect for the Blazers turn to downright admiration.

Portland was also the city where a situation I'd half-expected for the last couple of years finally occurred, and in the most dramatic way possible.

Thursday, January 19, 1995—7:00 PM

PORTLAND TRAIL BLAZERS (18-16) VS. PHOENIX SUNS (28-8)

The TV show *Quantum Leap* was about a scientist who found himself traveling through time to temporarily replace people and change the course of history for the better. After spending several years at this pursuit, he suddenly came face to face with another person in the same situation. Shocked and delighted to find out that he wasn't the only one in his

✪ MEMORIAL
COLISEUM
Opened: 1960
Capacity: 12,888
Portland, Oregon

predicament, he soon discovered that the other leaper was actually trying to change history in a negative way, which naturally dampened his enthusiasm about their meeting.

I mention this because in Portland I found out that I was the evil leaper.

I am booked into a motel located across the street from the arena, so I don't leave my room until about twenty minutes before tip-off. On paper, Phoenix at Portland sounds like a good matchup, but the Blazers have found themselves with the dubious honor of being the first team to violate a new league rule that dictates that any player leaving the bench area during an altercation automatically must be suspended for a game. Two nights ago, a brief scuffle broke out between Portland's Rod Strickland and Sacramento's Olden Polynice after they tangled under a basket during a game at ARCO Arena. Although no punches were thrown, nearly the entire Blazers bench went to the fight to protect Strickland, and as a result six players will face a one-game suspension. To be able to dress at least eight players for each contest, the Blazers will lose three players for tonight, including Strickland and Clyde Drexler, and three for tomorrow night's game in L.A. against the Clippers. To make matters worse, only two of the eight players available for tonight's game are guards—James Robinson and Tracy Murray. The bottom line is, it's pretty clear that the Blazers are going to get mauled, playing so shorthanded against the team with the best record in the Western Conference.

It has been surprisingly warm and clear in Portland all day, and I don't even need a jacket for the short walk to the Coliseum's will-call window. The slope of the hill makes the west side of the arena much bigger than the east, where the ticket windows are located, and I need to climb some stairs to reach my destination.

I'm surprised to find that the Blazers have left me a media pass, as they didn't issue me credentials during the first trip. I go through the turnstiles onto the concourse, which is level with the hill on that side of the building and offers some nice views of the nearby area through the glass walls.

With the pass hanging around my neck, I make my way down to the media room. There I find the Blazers' director of basketball information, who has been my contact for both visits. We shake hands, then he leads me to the floor and points up toward my seat, which is at a press table at the top of one of the end sections of the lower bowl.

"You'll be sitting next to Walter," he tells me. "He's doing the same thing you are."

Excuse me?

I make my way to the press table to find that in the seat next to mine is a dark-haired young man dressed in slacks, a nice collared shirt, and a blazer. He's taking notes on a pad, and my guess is that he's in his mid-twenties. I'm dressed in my typical fashion for the trip: sneakers, jeans, and a sweatshirt. Soon after I sit down, I make a casual comment about the game, which has just gotten underway, and he responds. With the ice broken, I ask him the important question: Is he traveling around the NBA? Sure enough, he is, and after I tell him that I'm doing the same thing, for the second time no less, we sit for a few seconds in stunned silence.

I'd always thought that there was a good possibility that other people had toured the NBA without my knowing about it. Most sports fans have heard about people traveling to baseball stadiums, so it only made sense that someone would try it for basketball. In fact, I'd spent some anxious moments in the last couple of years checking out bookstores, half-expecting to find that a fan had beaten me to the shelves with his or her own story of an NBA trip.

I knew that I'd been lucky, but until tonight I had no idea how much. Not only have I learned of another person doing the same thing, I've found myself sitting next to him at a Blazers game. He's Walter from Denver, a recent college graduate who is in the third city of a trip around the league that will last for the rest of the regular season. He's got a bag with him, and from it he produces a stack of paperwork that outlines his plans, much like the information I prepared before each of my trips. As I press him for details, it becomes obvious that he has followed a similar method in planning his travels as I have. And yes, Walter intends to write a book as well, although he doesn't have a publisher yet.

So not only do we suddenly discover that our ideas aren't exclusive, but I have to tell Walter that I have a contract, and my book will be on the shelves in a few months. It's not like the moment is some great triumph for me—I had enjoyed thinking that I might be the only person who had ever done such a trip—and I feel terrible that I'm interfering with his plans. I know I would've been devastated if I had run into someone on my first trip who had gotten a two-year head start on virtually the same project.

At least Walter is doing a few things differently, and as we talk I'm encouraged by some of the variations. For example, he's requesting media credentials in each city, and plans that a major portion of his book will involve interviewing players. I tell him that I'm trying to experience things more as a fan, rather than a journalist, and we're both heartened by the fact that we didn't go about traveling in exactly the same manner. And Walter turns out to be polite and gracious, which is commendable considering the circumstances. (Actually, it's widely known that people who travel the NBA display tremendous depth of character.)

But still, I know I'm disappointed, and I realize that Walter must be doubly so. I can no longer fool myself into thinking I'm the only NBA traveler, and Walter has to adjust to that and the fact that my book will almost certainly be released long before his. My mind wanders back to that *Quantum Leap* episode, and I feel like I'm the evil leaper, sent to destroy Walter's best-laid plans.

Perhaps the NBA gods are making it up to us by giving us a pretty good game to watch. The Portland–Phoenix game is the only one that both we NBA travelers will be seeing, and the shorthanded Blazers are surprisingly competitive. With James "Hollywood" Robinson leading the way at point guard, they keep pace with the Suns for the entire first half, and by intermission manage to cling to a 61-59 lead. Robinson has played all 24 minutes, which is two minutes more than his average playing time per game. Tracy Murray, another little-used reserve, has risen to the occasion as well, hitting 7 of 8 baskets to score 17 points in 22 minutes.

Even more interesting than the unexpectedly solid play of Portland's depleted backcourt is the flow of the game: Both teams are running the break, shooting from long range, and not grinding down the tempo with intense defensive play. Basically, it's a Western Conference–style game, and that alone makes the long drive from Minnesota seem worth it.

Although Portland's arena was built a decade before the 25-year-old team came into existence, it's still not a bad place to see a game. For one thing, any building this small is going to be pretty intimate, with no fans too far from the action. The Coliseum has a stadium design, with the upper-level seats beginning behind rather than above the lower sections. As might be expected in a square building, the sections begin to slope down towards the ends of the arena, eventually shrinking to only ten rows, compared to twenty-one rows in the middle sections.

Although the building is old, the high-tech additions in the years since it opened are top-notch, some of the best in the NBA. The center hanging scoreboard has crystal-clear video screens on each side, which show quick replays of the action. In addition to a variety of other boards, each end has a player board hanging in one corner, which shows the stats for seven players on each team, not just the five on the court.

Yet the most impressive statistics are found in the corners opposite the player boards. Although both Cleveland and Chicago have tried to duplicate it on a smaller scale, the Blazers have a separate stats board not to be believed. Both of the two boards hanging on opposite ends contain three slots which have spots for numbers from each quarter as well as a total for the game. The incredibly varied and detailed stats displayed in each of the positions switch throughout the game, including score totals, shooting percentages from both the floor and the line, turnovers, offensive and defensive rebounds, points off the bench, points in the paint, assists, fast-break points, dunks, layups, and shooting percentages from in the paint, 9–15 feet, and 15-plus feet. It's a dream situation for basketball fans: to be able to study the stats in remarkable detail without missing any of the action. I'm sure that they'll have similar statistic boards in the Rose Garden, and I hope that Blazers fans realize how fortunate they are to be able to enjoy them.

The stat boards begin to display bad news, however, as the Suns take the lead in the third quarter behind the typically stellar play of Charles Barkley and Dan Majerle. Although Barkley is his usual dominating self, Majerle is also contributing on both ends, both by draining his trademark 3-pointers and by closely guarding Murray, who manages only two points in the second half. By the end of the third, the Suns have regained the lead at 85-80, and although both James and Cliff Robinson continue to play well for the Blazers they can't lead Portland over the top. The heroic effort of the undermanned Blazers falls short, largely because Majerle hits five of eight attempts from beyond the arc in the second half.

Portland's fans are disappointed, grumbling about what they feel were undeserved suspensions, but I can't complain. It's my first game between two Western Conference teams, and it has reminded me of what I love about the league: the beauty of wide-open basketball, with the NBA players' remarkable skills on full display. Final score: Suns 122, Trail Blazers 115.

For three days I stay in Portland, enjoying beautiful warm weather in one of my favorite cities. Sunday night promises more excitement, as the Blazers will host Sacramento, and I'm hungry to see a victory. Although my two previous visits to Memorial Coliseum ended in disappointing Portland losses, I figure that the Blazers will make a better showing against the Kings, especially after the donnybrook between the two teams earlier in the week. Although the Kings are 22-15, better than Portland's 19-17 record, I have a feeling that the Blazers will have revenge on their minds, especially since they have completed their suspensions and will have a full roster for the first time in three games.

My prediction turns out to be accurate, as Portland takes control early and leads for the entire game. It is a sloppy effort on both sides, with each team shooting less than 40 percent, and both Clyde Drexler and Sacramento's Mitch Richmond have an off-night. Still, I enjoy another chance to savor the atmosphere of a Blazers game, and by the time I leave the Coliseum for the final time I am daydreaming of returning to see the Blazers in their new arena. Final score: Trail Blazers 103, Kings 87.

People want absolutes in this world, and I came back from my first trip shorthanded. Nearly everyone would quiz me: What was your favorite arena? Who has the loudest fans? Which arena serves the best food? More often than not, I would have no concrete answers and that was one reason I wanted to tour the NBA a second time. Once I'd been to every arena for at least two games (and usually three or more), I would have a better understanding of the nuances that make the experience different in each city.

Now that I've made my additional visits, however, I'm more inclined to make a few bold statements. Although I've left most of them for the final chapter of this book, I thought I should make one of them here:

The Portland Trail Blazers have the best fans in the NBA.

When I saw my first game at Memorial Coliseum, a late afternoon matchup against the Clippers on Valentine's Day 1993, I thought that it might have been a fluke, but after three visits I'm convinced. The evidence is all around.

For one thing, the concourse is practically deserted as the game begins, because everybody is in their seats. Once things start up, the fans are completely engrossed in the game. Looking around the stands, you see virtually every head turned to the action, and almost every conversation you hear relates to the game.

During the Blazers' free throw attempts, it's as quiet as a library, so much so that if someone does make a comment it can be heard throughout the stands. When the Blazers are in action, however, the crowd responds with deafening enthusiasm, their noise level keyed to the game as if controlled with a switch. And the fans themselves are among the most knowledgeable and dedicated I've encountered.

In short, being in the stands in Portland is an experience that few other arenas can match, and no others can exceed.

Things may change when the Portland faithful move to their big, spacious new arena, complete with luxury boxes and all the other amenities. But still, there's more to having an exceptional group of fans than just the design of the building they occupy, and I suspect that most of the things I've described will remain the same in the Rose Garden. By the time I'd seen three games, each against opponents of different quality, I was convinced: I'll stack the Blazers fans against any in the NBA.

Although I guess I'm not the smartest guy in the world—here I am praising a team located all the way across the country from where I live. How am I going to use all those free tickets they send me?

Average 1994–95 ticket cost: $34.61 (eighth highest in the NBA)

Beer: $3.50 (14 oz.)

Soda: $1.50 (14 oz.—Coca-Cola products)

Hot Dog: $2.00

Parking: $7.50

Mascot: none

Cheerleaders: Blazer Dancers

Remote-controlled blimp: none

Other teams that play full-time in Memorial Coliseum: Portland Winter Hawks (Western Hockey League), Portland Pride (Continental Indoor Soccer League)

What I'd change about Memorial Coliseum: It is awfully small, and some elements of the design betray the arena's age.

What I love about Memorial Coliseum: The detailed stats boards (best in the NBA), and the fans (ditto).

Statistics from Team Marketing Report, Inc.

Roaming to Tacoma

SEATTLE SUPERSONICS

Founded: 1967
1993–94 Record: 63-19
Team Colors: Green, Yellow

Monday, January 23–Thursday, January 26

The Blazers–Kings game was on Sunday, but I was enjoying myself so much in Portland that I stayed one more night before continuing on. Relaxed after five full days without any driving, I felt refreshed and ready to go by Tuesday, especially since Tacoma is only 145 miles north of Portland. At 1:30 that afternoon I crossed the Columbia River into Washington, then spent a couple of hours on I-5 before reaching Tacoma.

Tacoma Dome is located next to the highway, and I was able to find a reasonably priced hotel across the street from the arena. Although I had little desire to see the Sonics again, at least their temporary move to Tacoma would allow me to avoid venturing into downtown Seattle.

> **Previous SuperSonics Games at Seattle Coliseum:**
>
> **1992–93 season:** Washington (SuperSonics 112-102)

For several seasons, Portland's Memorial Coliseum had been the smallest arena in the league, but the Seattle Center Coliseum's capacity of just over 14,000 was next in line, followed by Boston Garden's nightly total of 14,890. You've already heard about Portland and Boston's moves to new arenas, but Seattle was making a less-publicized change as well. After years of debate, the team and the city had decided that the best way to improve the Sonics' arena was to put their money into a massive upgrade of the Coliseum, rather than construct a new building in a different location.

To me, it sounded like a good plan. Although the Coliseum was an intimate place to watch a game, it had faced much criticism for being outdated, especially since it had undergone few changes since it opened in 1962. The plan called for the building to be completely gutted, to be followed by the construction of a new interior that would run much deeper than the previous design. The new seating layout would be of the basic oval design, with lower and upper levels separated by a row of 58 luxury boxes. The new facility, to be called the Key Arena, will have a capacity of roughly 17,100 fans, and the only parts of the old building remaining will be the roof and the four distinct concrete beams that support it.

The roof was one of the best parts of the old Coliseum, and I'm glad they're keeping it. Each of its four sides slope up to a pointed top, which makes the arena look like a giant tent. (The roof was once used for a ski-jumping competition.) On the inside, a pattern of square panels on the ceiling gave the building a look unlike any other in the NBA, and it would be nice if the designers of the new facility keep that detail as well.

In addition, the arena is in a good location, only steps from the trademark Space Needle in the downtown area known as the Seattle Center. The plans seemed solid, but obviously would require that the Coliseum be unoccupied for a big chunk of time.

With their arena undergoing major renovations, the Sonics needed somewhere to play for the '94–95 season, and decided on the nearby Tacoma Dome as the perfect solution. Even though season-ticket holders would face the kind of commute usually reserved for Pistons fans, the opportunity to draw more people from the Tacoma area could only increase the team's fan base. And with a facility that needed only minor revisions to accommodate 16,000 fans for an NBA game, Seattle's neighbor to the south won itself a team for a year.

On the other hand, the T-Dome (as the locals call it) would become the most primitive arena in the league, sparing the Boston Garden that distinction for the first time in years. Tacoma Dome is as basic as its name, a simple building decorated with a big, checkered paint scheme utilizing different shades of blue. Inside, the venue has four large bleachers under a huge wooden roof, which is big enough to make it one of the largest wood domed structures in the world. The dome is supported by an intricate set of beams, meaning the Sonics moved from one building with a distinctive ceiling to another.

With no real concourse, many bench seats, and major traffic congestion on game nights, it's a good thing that the T-Dome was a temporary NBA arena, but in that capacity it wasn't causing any major problems.

Getting in wouldn't be a problem: I'd had some difficulties with Seattle's front office in the past, but they had agreed to sell me tickets for the games during my stop in Tacoma. Still, I'm not very fond of the organization, and the team on the court didn't help matters. They had one of the most talented collections of players in the league, but to me the roster seemed to be full of the worst kind of modern NBA player: incredibly skilled but terribly immature. In fact, both my visits to Seattle might have been completely forgettable if not for one thing: the chance to hang out with a true basketball fan. I might not like the players, and the organization may have frustrated me, but there always seems to be a quality fan around ready to make me feel welcome.

Tuesday, January 24, 1995—7:00 PM

SEATTLE SUPERSONICS (27-9) VS. DENVER NUGGETS (18-20)

Although I'm not very excited about tonight's game, Sonics fans have reason to be. If there's any team that they've looked forward to hosting, it's the Nuggets.

The Sonics had the best record in the NBA during the '93–94 season, and easily won their first two games against the Nuggets in their best-of-five series that opened the playoffs. But Denver responded by posting two improbable victories on their home court, and set the stage for the single most amazing game of the year—a 98-94 overtime victory over Seattle in the Coliseum, a game that ended with the unforgettable image of Dikembe Mutombo clutching the ball while flat on the court, his face twisted into an expression of pure joy.

✪ TACOMA DOME
Opened: 1983
Capacity: 16,352
Tacoma, Washington

*Above: Interior of
the Tacoma Dome.
Left: Model of the
interior of the new
Key Arena.*

As you can guess, it was a highly enjoyable moment for me, and an agonizing one for Sonics fans. To make matters worse, the Nuggets began this season's series against Seattle by beating them in Denver on Christmas Day.

Yet the Nuggets are struggling through a tough season, especially since Dan Issel resigned as head coach, and I have a feeling that the Sonics are going to vent their frustrations in a big way.

Joining me for the game is Ted, another fan I met through a basketball group on the Internet. As we walk across the street from the hotel to the T-Dome, I fill him in on what I'm doing, and by the time we reach the turnstiles we're exchanging opinions on the game and its players. He's a few years younger than me, but is mature enough not to be bothered by my feelings about his team. Once he offers to buy me a beer, I figure that there will be no hard feelings, and I try not to make a big deal about how much I hate the Sonics.

We arrive a few minutes early and head to our seats, which are located about halfway up a huge bleacher behind one of the baskets. There's no concourse at the T-Dome, only a group of concession and souvenir stands built into the spaces between the four huge seating sections, and fans have to travel alongside the court to get to their seats. The arena is far too basic to attract any visitors on its own, but the game is appealing enough to pack the place on this Tuesday night.

The opening announcements are as bare-boned as the building, but the Sonics provide the spark to the evening by jumping to a 9-0 lead. Still, the Nuggets regroup and go on a 12-2 run, and as a few key Sonics struggle from the floor the game remains close. By the end of the first quarter the Sonics' lead is only 26-25, and it looks like the Nuggets may have come prepared to continue their mastery of Seattle.

But the Nuggets are offering the basketball equivalent of fool's gold, and the Sonics go on a 21-9 run of their own, leading by as many as 12 in the second quarter before settling for a 58-50 edge at halftime.

Just like in the Coliseum, there are no replay boards, and even the usual hanging scoreboard is missing. A message board on one end provides an occasional glimpse of the current players' stats, but even that occurs intermittently. The team has brought their mascot and dancers into their temporary home, and they provide the only real show off the court. Sonics fans probably don't have much reason to complain, however, as games at the aged Coliseum never offered many extras anyway.

The Sonics continue their domination in the third, going on a 10-2 run to pull ahead 71-56. The Nuggets make several attempts to cut into the lead, but a final surge in the fourth ends any doubt that the jinx is over, at least for tonight.

The blowout lets me spend more time talking basketball with Ted without feeling like I'm intruding. The one bad thing about seeing a close game during my travels is that it limits my opportunity to spend time talking to the local fans, as they are usually preoccupied with the game, but happily that's not the case tonight. If nothing else, my conversations with Ted prove that at least one part of the Sonics' franchise isn't all bad— some Seattle fans are pretty cool. I have a better time at the Sonics game than I'd anticipated, mostly because it's the first game I've seen with some company since Milwaukee two weeks ago. Once again, a pleasant experience with an NBA fan has helped offset my negative feelings about a team. Final score: SuperSonics 111, Nuggets 89.

With more than a thousand NBA games every year, basketball fans love to make a big deal about certain streaks and matchups that happen during the regular season, the kind of games that cause a lot of excitement at the time but usually mean little by the end of April. Yet the start of the playoffs is almost three months away, and on Thursday the biggest NBA game in recent memory is going to be held in Tacoma Dome.

The Sonics won their tenth straight game when they beat the Nuggets two days ago, but the Utah Jazz come to town with a 10-game win streak of their own. Not only that, but the Jazz have won their last 14 road games, the second-longest streak in league history, only two less than the Lakers' all-time record of 16. To top it off, the Sonics have won their last 17 home games. It is a matchup that any NBA fan would love to see, even in the stark setting of Tacoma Dome.

The best part is that the game lives up to the hype. I go alone, but my dislike of the Sonics gives me a strong emotional interest, and so I watch with rapt attention and silently root for the Jazz.

Utah stays even with Seattle in the first half, each team executing well and demonstrating how the game should be played. At halftime the score is 56-56, the seventh tie after ten lead changes. Seattle bursts to a 10-point lead by the middle of the third, and it looks as if the Sonics will be the team that protects its winning streaks. But the Jazz roar back again, and by the end of the quarter it is tied once more, this time at 85.

The fourth turns into a nightmare for the Sonics fans and a dream for me. Utah dominates the boards and begins to pick apart Seattle's defense, opening up the floor to create high-percentage shots. Suddenly the Sonics are down by 8 with six minutes to play, and their best efforts to make a comeback fall short. The Jazz increase their lead, and at the final buzzer the Sonics find themselves losers of only their second home game of the season.

Tacoma is the farthest from Orlando I will be on my trip, but the chance to see a game like the Sonics–Jazz makes all the miles worthwhile. Final score: Jazz 120, SuperSonics 108.

Average 1994–95 ticket cost: $34.58 (ninth highest in the NBA)

Beer: $3.00 (14 oz.)

Soda: $2.50 (16 oz.—Coca-Cola products)

Hot Dog: $2.00

Parking: $5.00

Mascot: Squatch (Bigfoot-creature in Sonics uniform)

Cheerleaders: Sonics Dance Team

Remote-controlled blimp: yes—two (one green, one yellow)

Other teams that play full-time in Tacoma Dome: Tacoma Rockies (Western Hockey League)

Other teams that will play in the Key Arena: Seattle Sea Dogs (Continental Indoor Soccer League)

What I'd change about Tacoma Dome: Nothing—I just wouldn't play NBA games in it.

What I love about Tacoma Dome: The fact that it's a temporary facility.

Statistics from Team Marketing Report, Inc.

Where the Kings Hold Court

Founded: 1948
1993–94 Record: 28-54
Team Colors: Purple, Silver, Black

Friday, January 27–Thursday, February 2

The day after the matchup between Seattle and Utah, I began the long trip to Sacramento. It was an exciting afternoon, because for the rest of my travels I would be heading home. Over the next six weeks almost every leg of my journey would bring me closer to Orlando, starting with my drive south that Friday afternoon. Even though I was confident that some of the best basketball was still ahead, the prospect of making my way home certainly was appealing.

The first day I drove almost 400 miles, crossing back into Oregon just before 4 PM before continuing on to Grants Pass, a town in the southern part of the state. I'd planned to drive the rest of the 350 miles to Sacramento on Saturday, but the day was chilly and overcast, and soon after I entered California at 12:15 PM I was in the midst of a heavy downpour. Before long I was sick of the bad weather, so I quit driving earlier than I'd planned and found a hotel room in the town of Redding. Since the Super Bowl was the next day, I booked the room for two nights and planned to finish the last few hours to Sacramento on Monday.

Previous Kings Games at ARCO Arena:
1992-93 season: Atlanta (Kings 116-105)

The term "fan" has its roots in the word "fanatic," which is defined as "a person marked or motivated by an extreme, unreasoning enthusiasm." Of all the NBA cities, in no other arena will you find people who fit that description more closely than in Sacramento.

As I traveled during the 1994–95 season, the Kings were playing in California for their ninth year after moving from Kansas City. In their first season on the West Coast, the Kings finished 37-45 and advanced to the playoffs, where they were swept by the Rockets in three games. Since that time, the team had never won more than 29 games in a season, usually finishing at the bottom of the standings and never qualifying for the play-offs. Yet every single game in Sacramento had been a sellout, a streak that brings the phrase "extreme, unreasoning enthusiasm" to mind.

The Kings have one of the strongest fan bases in the league, a situation that continues despite those years of losing. Between November 21, 1990 and November 22, 1991, the Kings lost a record 43 consecutive road games, yet the '90–91 Kings were 24-17 at home, and in the years since the move the team has played close to .500 ball in Sacramento.

One visit to a Kings game will quickly demonstrate why they play well at home: Unlike other teams that seem to be always struggling, such as the Nets and the Clippers, the Kings have a rowdy, enthusiastic group of fans who expect a decent effort by their club. The stands of ARCO Arena will remain packed as long as the Kings keep working hard, and my first visit reminded me of the early days of the Magic, when the team faced an uphill battle every night but still played in front of a full house of die-hard fans.

ARCO Arena itself is also an incentive for Kings fans to show up for the games. Surrounded by more than a hundred acres of undeveloped land, the building can be seen for miles, yet still is only a short drive up the highway from the downtown area. The arena is made of tan brick, a perfectly square building decorated with an interesting design of ridges and windows. The only interruption to the symmetrical design is on the south corner, where a small rectangular ticket office cuts across the building. Like most of the arenas built in recent years, ARCO has a clean, bright look, especially during the day.

Even though the building looks more like a large corporation's head-quarters than an arena, ARCO is still an attractive facility, and the sight of the arena among the miles of level farmland and parking lots certainly is unique in the NBA. And once you get inside, the distinctive touches of Sacramento really become apparent.

Tuesday, January 31, 1995—7:30 PM

SACRAMENTO KINGS (24-17) VS. SAN ANTONIO SPURS (25-14)

On my way to the game, I'm surprised to see that the outside of ARCO Arena still is poorly lit. During my first visit, the building had been so dark outside that I wasn't sure if I was in the right place. Tonight a few more lights are glowing, but the arena still seems to blend into the night sky. The brightest lights are the signs that mark the building on each side, but even some of these letters are dark; as I park, the nearest sign proclaims "AR O ARENA."

During my first trip, the Kings had left me a complimentary courtside seat on one of the corners for a game against the Hawks. While I was planning the second trip, however, the Kings' media director had been impossible to reach on the phone. Just after my arrival in Sacramento, I convinced the Kings' ticket manager to leave me a seat for tonight's game against the Spurs, only to have the media director call a short time later, finally responding only a few hours before the game.

Though not expecting to be courtside again, I still am surprised at my ticket location. Opening the envelope at will-call, I find the Kings have given me an $8 seat located about three rows from the top of one of the upper-level sections on the end of the arena. Discouraged by the location, I ask at the ticket windows if they have any singles left, and they sell me a $30 seat about halfway up the lower bowl off of one corner.

Each of the four sides has an entrance, and I make my way to the nearest one. The doors open onto the concourse level, which is the arena's weakest feature. Somewhat cramped, the concourse is decorated in a light blue shade that gives the walls a washed-out look. Still, I like the rough cloth that hangs over the portals to the lower-bowl seats, dark blue curtains that appear to be made of burlap.

Passing the team shop, I see that it's packed with people, just as I had predicted. Critics may say that the Kings' new uniforms and colors have

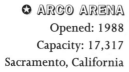
Opened: 1988
Capacity: 17,317
Sacramento, California

been cynically designed for maximum merchandise sales, but if the team is bothered by such accusations, they can console themselves by listening to the ringing of the cash registers.

Passing through a blue curtain, I make my way down to my seat, admiring the best feature of ARCO Arena: the wooden floors. Instead of the usual gray concrete, the seats rest on varnished wood, while metal plates cover the steps in the aisles. Not only do the wood floors give the arena a look unlike any other in the NBA, they also allow fans to make noise when they stomp their feet, which is next to impossible on concrete.

Even though Sacramento and San Antonio have nearly identical records, the Kings are 16-5 at ARCO this year, and so the crowd is slightly stunned when the Spurs jump to a 13-2 lead to start the game. But Sacramento fans are not going to give up, not during the season when the Kings seem to be turning things around, and they keep cheering as their team uses a 13-3 run in the last 3:20 of the period to tie the score at 24.

In the second quarter the game stays close, a wide-open, Western Conference–style of run-and-gun, and the Kings trail by two at the half.

ARCO opened the same year as Milwaukee's Bradley Center, and has a similar layout of seats. The sections are square, with a wide lower level topped by luxury boxes, and an upper level with a steep slope. At the top of the upper level is a wide concourse that runs around the entire arena and includes a full restaurant and nightclub.

Although the Kings' Sacramento history hasn't been very memorable, banners hanging from the rafters honor the players and teams from their pre-California era. The hanging scoreboard has video screens on all four sides, although the image on the screens is a little too washed out for my taste, and message boards line the bottom of the upper level. My favorite part of the displays is found on the corners of the center scoreboard, each of which has a multicolored strip of lights that act as sound meters. As the crowd gets louder, the lights begin to reach towards the top, until the noise level brings the entire strip to life, and a Kings logo built above them lights up as well. Even though Sacramento fans don't need much encouragement to make noise, it's nice that their efforts are rewarded with a colorful display.

The Kings need just such enthusiastic support in the third quarter, as they fall behind 69-59 with a little under five minutes left, yet they manage to make their second big comeback of the game. Led by Mitch Richmond's 12 third-quarter points, Sacramento closes to within two by the end of the period.

Richmond has scored 33 points with 7 minutes left in the game, matching his season high, and Spurs coach Bob Hill sends in Doc Rivers to guard him. Meanwhile, the game remains close as the clock winds down, the action quickly moving from end to end.

With less than a minute to go and the Kings leading 96-95, David Robinson dribbles the ball off his foot and loses it out of bounds. The

Kings come down and run a decent play, but rookie Brian Grant rushes a short shot, and Spurs forward Dennis Rodman grabs the rebound and calls a timeout.

After the huddle, the Spurs work the ball to Robinson, and against a solid Kings defense he has to force a shot as the 24-second clock ticks down. The ball bounces off the iron, the fans roar in approval, but Rodman is in perfect position to elevate and tap it back in, and the crowd falls silent. Sacramento take a timeout of their own, down by a point with 8 seconds left.

Everyone in the building expects the ball to go to Richmond for the last shot, but Mitch has been held scoreless since Rivers checked in to guard him, a stat that proves prophetic. Richmond gets the ball isolated at the 3-point line, but when he makes his move Rivers reaches in to knock the ball away and out of bounds. Suddenly there's only 2.8 seconds left, and on their next attempt Kings guard Spud Webb has the ball tipped away from him as well. With the clock showing only 1.2 remaining, the Kings have one more chance, but the Spurs tip the ball for the third straight play, and Walt Williams can only manage a weak attempt that barely draws iron as the buzzer sounds.

If the Kings had hit their last-second shot, this probably would have been the best game I saw on either of my two trips. Still, Sacramento fans have reason to be optimistic, as their '94–95 Kings have stayed healthy and played well. For once, it looks as if their enthusiasm might not be so unreasoning after all. Final score: Spurs 97, Kings 96.

After a quiet day in Sacramento on Wednesday, I spend Thursday afternoon doing laundry at my hotel, anxious to return to ARCO to see the Kings play the Bulls. Although I'd mentioned to the Kings' ticket manager that I would be in town for both games this week, I hadn't heard from him since Tuesday, so the day of the game I call and leave a message requesting another ticket.

After returning to ARCO Arena, I'm not especially surprised to find that there is no ticket for me at will-call, which I figure is no great loss after the seat two nights earlier. What does surprise me is that the only other tickets left for sale are standing room only—for five bucks I can watch the game while standing on the concourse at the top of the upper level. I can't believe that there had been a bunch of seats available a half-hour before the game against the Spurs, but that the 22-21 Bulls, without Michael Jordan, would make tickets scarce.

So I look for a scalper near the arena, and there aren't any. Although hundreds of people are streaming from the parking lots into ARCO, nobody is buying or selling tickets. I'd heard that the season-ticket holders in Sacramento always use their tickets, but I can't believe that an event drawing 17,000 people would have no market for extra seats.

With $80 in my pocket, I am ready to make a deal, but I feel my blood pressure rise as the Kings fans stream past me for nearly twenty minutes without acknowledging my pleas for a ticket. Just as I am about to give up and go watch Seinfeld back at the hotel, a couple of guys walk up with an extra single, and I sigh with relief. The amazing thing is, it turns out to be a great seat: ARCO's design has the stands running all the way down to the floor on each end, and the location is only a few rows behind the baseline. Not only that, but with a $40 price, the ticket is a decent value, as are most of the seats in Sacramento.

It is a blessing that I was able to get a good seat tonight, because soon after the game begins one of the out-of-town scoreboards shows that the Magic have lost their first home game of the season, to the Sonics no less, after opening with 21 straight wins at the O'rena. Add that news to the Kings' snubbing me for a ticket, and I am in a somewhat foul mood.

But I refuse to let myself get mad at the team. I love seeing the Kings play at ARCO, in part because of the loyal fans, in part because of the stylish arena, and in part because I really like Mitch Richmond. Although most NBA fans know that he's one of the league's premier guards, I also have a personal reason to appreciate the guy.

It was nothing earth-shattering, just a simple moment that I've always remembered. My single seat in Orlando is right above the entranceway that the visiting team uses to get to and from the court, and one night the Kings were coming off the court after losing a tough game to the Magic. Richmond had scored 40 points, single-handedly keeping Sacramento in the game most of the way, and although I don't usually say anything to the visiting players as they leave the court, I decided to make an exception. "Good game, Mitch!" I shouted at him, not really expecting a reaction, but he looked up at me, smiled, and raised his hand in a half-wave. I was surprised—most of the players ignore the fans near the tunnel— and I thought it was a pretty cool thing for him to do. Ever since then, I've been a big fan.

At tonight's game, the action stays close early on, with Sacramento leading 46-44 at halftime. As the second half gets underway, however, the Bulls fall apart offensively, missing shot after shot while scoring a paltry 11 points in the third quarter. Chicago's woes continue in the fourth, as Sacramento puts on a defensive show in the period, and at the buzzer the Bulls, who score only 13 points in the final quarter, have set a team record for fewest points in a half. With such a stifling defense, the Kings could be forgiven for having a slow night on the offensive end, especially since they manage to win by twenty.

And once again, I enjoy the company of some friendly locals who help make up for an unpleasant experience with their team's front office. During a game that might have been somewhat boring if I'd seen it alone, Jerry and Jim (the guys who sold me the ticket) keep me interested by telling me stories about the NBA experience in Sacramento that only the locals would know. Final score: Kings 88, Bulls 68.

Average 1994–95 ticket cost: $23.52 (24th highest in the NBA)

Beer: $3.00 (16 oz.)

Soda: $2.00 (16 oz.—Coca-Cola products)

Hot Dog: $2.25

Parking: $5.00

Mascot: yes (a lion in a Kings uniform—although he has no official name, I've heard him referred to as Slamson and, more simply, The Lion.)

Cheerleaders: Fast Break Dance Team

Remote-controlled blimp: yes—traditional hot-air balloon design

Other teams that play full-time in ARCO Arena: Sacramento Knights (Continental Indoor Soccer League), Sacramento River Rats (Roller Hockey International)

What I'd change about ARCO Arena: It would be nice to avoid the huge traffic jam after nearly every game.

What I love about ARCO Arena: The fans, the relatively low ticket prices, and the wood floors.

Statistics from Team Marketing Report, Inc.

Battered by the Bay

GOLDEN STATE WARRIORS

Founded: 1946
1993–94 Record: 50-32
Team Colors: Gold, Blue

Friday, February 3–Sunday, February 5

On Friday I packed up and headed out to the next arena. The Golden State Warriors had a game that night in Oakland, a quick 95 miles down the highway, and after only an hour and a half of driving through the California farmlands I found myself in the Bay Area. Even though I would visit five cities on the West Coast, the only time I'd see the Pacific Ocean was that afternoon, when it appeared on my right near the end of my drive.

The Coliseum Arena is located on the south side of Oakland, and I passed by the downtown area to the left of the highway a few minutes before I reached the exit I wanted. There were several hotels less than a mile from the arena, and although the area wasn't the safest place I would stay on the trip, I thought I could survive three nights in the neighborhood. It was still slightly unsettling, though, that the hotel where I stayed that weekend was the only one I visited on either trip that had a security guard patrolling the grounds every night.

> **Previous Warriors Games at Oakland Coliseum Arena:**
>
> **1992-93 season:** Atlanta (Hawks 125-114)

It was funny how some things went in cycles. The Warriors had been one of the up-and-comimg teams in the NBA in the years before my first trip, but by the time I visited Oakland Coliseum Arena in early 1993 the team was suffering through a terrible season, brought on by a rash of injuries to several of their key players. I didn't care, though—the Warriors were one of my favorite teams.

During the '89–90 and '90–91 seasons, the first two years that I had season-tickets for the Magic, Golden State was among the most exciting teams in the NBA. They were nicknamed "Run-TMC," which came from a combination of the name of rap group Run-DMC and the first initials of their three star players—Tim Hardaway, Mitch Richmond (before his trade to the Kings), and Chris Mullin. Although Golden State had a weak power game during those two seasons, their brand of run-and-gun basketball was tremendously exciting, and after seeing them in action I was hooked.

Once I began to plan my travels, the Warriors were one of the quickest teams to respond to my initial letter, and that only increased my fondness for the team. When I arrived in Oakland to learn that the ticket they gave me was near center court and only about ten rows off the floor, I knew that I had become a Golden State fan for life. And on top of everything else, I've always found San Francisco and the Bay Area to be one of the most diverse and beautiful urban areas in the country.

My appreciation for the Warriors stemmed from other factors as well. Although I usually don't like arenas that are isolated from downtown areas, the Coliseum Arena is an exception. Located next to one of the city's major highways, the Oakland sports complex has a certain flair, at least from my perspective. Surrounded by close to a hundred acres of parking lots, the complex contains two sports facilities built on top of a small hill. On the west side, closest to the highway, is the arena, while across a courtyard to the east is the Coliseum, home of baseball's Oakland Athletics.

The Coliseum Arena is basically a round version of Portland's Memorial Coliseum, complete with glass walls that provide a view of the concourse and upper bowl from outside the arena. Although the Coliseum Arena appears black from the outside, after dark a series of banners hanging above the main concourse are lit in a variety of colors, including different shades of blue, red, maroon, and orange. Perhaps the most distinctive part of the Coliseum Arena's design is the big gray support beams that cross over the windows, lining the building with a recurring "×" pattern. To me, they make the arena look like a giant birthday cake.

Yet in early February 1995, any hint of a party involving the Warriors ended outside of the arena. The team had recovered from their '92–93 troubles to post 50 wins in '93–94, even though the injury curse continued to sideline several key players. Golden State was supposed to have been saved by the arrival of Chris Webber and Latrell Sprewell, and as the '94–95 season began the Warriors had a collection of talent that could stand up to nearly any other team in the league. But Webber forced the trade to the Bullets, and after that mess was resolved the Warriors had fallen apart. They had come full circle, from being good to bad to good to bad again. Their front office remained one of the friendliest in the league, and their fans kept coming to the games, but that was all that remained consistent about the Bay Area's NBA team.

Friday, February 3, 1995—7:30 PM

GOLDEN STATE WARRIORS (12-29) VS. L.A. CLIPPERS (7-38)

Soon after I finish the drive from Sacramento to the Oakland hotel, I connect my computer to the phone and log on to the Prodigy service to check the latest basketball news. The Warriors play the Clippers in a couple of hours, so I punch up a preview of the game. "There will be plenty of choice seats available for tonight's game between two of the league's worst teams," it begins, as if I need a further reminder of what a blight on my schedule tonight is going to be.

Still, that line about plenty of seats being available just isn't true, unless you count the scalpers. The Warriors have sold out every game for more than five seasons, another reason I enjoy visiting the Coliseum Arena. Oakland may not have the NBA's loudest fans, but there's only so much noise you can be expected to make when your team is struggling through the dog days that settle on every arena sooner or later.

And yet the days of 1995 are even more shaggy than they were in '93. The Warrior team I saw during the first trip was 20-27, which at the time

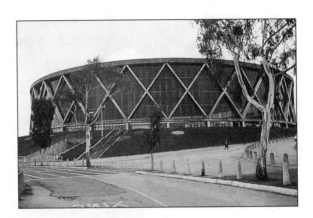

✪ OAKLAND
COLISEUM ARENA
Opened: 1966
Capacity: 15,025
Oakland, California

seemed as bad as it would get for a while, but heading into tonight's game Golden State is 12-29. As I walk the three-quarters of a mile to the arena, my only real consolation is that tonight's opponent is the Clippers, one of the few teams with a worse record.

With the lights on, the Coliseum Arena gains the color that it lacks during the day, becoming much more attractive. Several scalpers approach as I cross the parking lot and climb the small hill to the entrances, and it's clear by their manner that they are struggling in a buyer's market. I consider telling them to drive to Sacramento, where they could control the business outside ARCO Arena, but I doubt that they'd appreciate my sense of humor.

My ticket is close to the floor, although a fair distance back from the court near the corner that has the Clippers' bench. The location is actually a little too low for my taste, making it difficult to see the action on the far end of the floor, but I'm pretty sure that the game won't be that pretty to watch anyway.

The opening is very basic, and I'm a little disappointed that the crowd barely reacts to the announcement of the Warriors' starters. Then again, the Golden State fans have been battered all year, especially considering that only three months ago many had dreams of a championship.

As I mentioned earlier about the Timberwolves–Pistons game, sometimes two bad teams can match up well, but it quickly becomes clear that tonight isn't one of those times. The Warriors jump to an early lead, as the Clippers prove unable to develop any offensive rhythm. Golden State leads 23-18 after the first quarter, then extends to a whopping 58-34 advantage by halftime, as the Clippers clank shots, don't defend, and do a pretty good impression of the worst team in the league. Which, of course, is exactly what they are.

The rest of the game will be garbage time, so I try to relax, hope for a few more exciting plays, and check out my surroundings.

Not just the outside of the Coliseum Arena is similar to Portland's building; the seating layout is as well. The stadium design has the upper level beginning behind the lower. With its circular design, the rows of seats rise high in the middle of the upper level, but drop to only two rows in each section on the dead ends. There are no luxury boxes or other such amenities, but the Coliseum Arena is clean, functional, and offers decent views of the action, in part because of its small capacity.

The four-sided hanging scoreboard has colorful message boards and player stats on each side, but lacks any video monitors. Although there are a small number of message boards and scoreboards in other parts of the building, there is an unfortunate absence of replay screens in the Coliseum Arena. Still, the building has an attractive design, with huge banners hanging on each end that give a striking look to the arena. Also, there is a beautiful series of lights hung under the ceiling that extend outward from the center of the building and resemble an ornate chandelier. If only they could install some video screens, I would have few complaints about the layout, despite the arena's age.

The Warriors actually increase their lead in the third quarter, as the Clippers can't even begin to mount a comeback, and by the end of the period Golden State is ahead 85-56. Although the game should be a joy for the victory-starved fans, it's a sloppy affair that is hard to appreciate, with the Warriors eventually totaling 29 turnovers. That kind of messy play allows the Clippers to make the final score somewhat respectable, but everybody in the building is aware that they've watched an ugly blowout from start to finish.

But as the local media would rather cynically point out later, a win is a win, and at least I've seen the Warriors emerge with a victory—the Coliseum Arena was one of the venues where the home team lost during my first trip. And there are some things that I enjoy in Oakland no matter what the score, like the vendors who travel through the stands hawking their goods. Not only do they have traditional items like beer and soda, they also offer bottled water as well, a subtle reminder of the California setting.

Once the new buildings open in Portland, Seattle, and Boston, Oakland Coliseum Arena will be the NBA's smallest, and only the Clippers' L.A. Memorial Sports Arena will be older. The Warriors' front office is committed to make a change in the future, either by moving to a new arena in a different location (possibly San Francisco), or by extensively renovating the current building. With so many new venues around the country, and with a strong fan base that continues to support the Warriors through the turmoil of recent seasons, I can understand their motivation.

But I don't think that Golden State fans have very many reasons to complain about their current building. I can't say the same about their team's fortunes—for whatever reason, the Warriors have gone through enough drama to fill a soap opera. Final score: Warriors 106, Clippers 89.

Oakland is the fourth city in a row where I'll see a second game. (Actually, my schedule has me seeing two games in eight of the thirteen Western Conference arenas.) The Bulls are still on their West Coast trip, and they come into Oakland to face the Warriors on Sunday afternoon with a 22-23 record.

Although I hate day games that start around noon, I kind of like when they begin in the late afternoon, and so I enjoy my walk to the arena in the waning sunlight a few minutes before the 5:00 PM tip-off. Latrell Sprewell is set to return from an injury, so I think the Warriors might have a chance against a Chicago team that has been hot and cold all season.

At the start it appears that I am terribly mistaken. The Bulls jump to an astounding 28-6 lead in the first quarter, and when the Warriors burn a timeout with 4:34 left the crowd begins to boo mercilessly. Although I rarely approve of dedicated fans booing their team at home, I have to admit that Golden State looks like a team that is simply playing out its schedule, and if I'd paid for my ticket I probably would join in the chorus of catcalls.

The Bulls lead by as many as 24 in the first quarter while shooting 17 for 20, a blistering 85 percent. The score is 38-17 after the first period, but if there's one thing I've learned in my NBA experience, it's that the first quarter means nothing. Unless a player gets hurt or ejected, there is practically no first-quarter score that can't change dramatically by half-time. In every other sport, a big lead early in the game nearly always ends the excitement, but I've seen so many NBA games change tempo after the first quarter that I treat the opening twelve minutes as an extension of the warmups. I respect a twenty-point halftime lead, but before then there's just too much time left for anyone to take the result for granted.

As if to prove my theory, the Warriors begin a long comeback by shaving ten points off the lead in the second quarter, trimming the margin to 59-48 by halftime. This is happening despite a horrible return by Sprewell, who misses all 12 shots he takes in the first three quarters, and despite the departure of Warriors starting forward Carlos Rogers, who was ejected in the second quarter after picking up two technical fouls.

The third quarter is relatively even, but the Warriors are heating up, led by the inside play of forward Chris Gatling. Golden State closes to 82-76 with just over nine minutes left, but Gatling argues a call and is quickly tossed from the game, one of six technicals the officials slap on the Warriors during the game. Even with their inside threat gone, the Warriors manage to tie the score two minutes later, but Scottie Pippen quickly hits a jumper, grabs a rebound of another Sprewell miss, then nails a 3-pointer from the corner.

The Warriors stay close the rest of the way, and with only 19 seconds left guard Keith Jennings grabs a defensive rebound and breaks free in the open floor with a chance to tie the game. Jennings seems to be in the clear as he sails into the lane, but Bulls guard Steve Kerr runs by as he puts up the shot, distracting Jennings just enough to cause him to miss the layup, and the Oakland faithful see their chance at a miracle comeback slip away. It has been an impressive attempt to steal a win, and an exciting game as well, but the technical fouls and missed last shot taint any positive feelings the fans might have taken home from the arena. It is the middle of another disappointing season for Warriors fans, and I can only hope that some day I'll get the chance to see Golden State play at the Coliseum Arena when things are going well for the team. Final score: Bulls 97, Warriors 93.

Average 1994–95 ticket cost: $29.27 (15th highest in the NBA)

Beer: $3.00 (14 oz.)

Soda: $1.50 (14 oz.—Coca-Cola products)

Hot Dog: $2.00

Parking: $6.00

Mascot: none

Cheerleaders: Warrior Girls

Remote-controlled blimp: none

Other teams that play full-time in Oakland Coliseum Arena: Oakland Skates (Roller Hockey International)

What I'd change about Oakland Coliseum Arena: Add some kind of video monitors.

What I love about Oakland Coliseum Arena: The loyal fans, friendly team, and small capacity.

Statistics from Team Marketing Report, Inc.

The Clip Joint

LOS ANGELES CLIPPERS

Founded: 1970
1993–94 Record: 27-55
Team Colors: Red, White, Blue

Monday, February 6—Tuesday, February 7

Monday would bring a long trip on an overcast day through more California farmland. Although I'm sure the drive down the coastline from Oakland to Los Angeles is beautiful, it's also much more time-consuming than the quickest route between the two cities, which is to take I-5 south for almost 400 miles. After traveling so many miles in the previous two months, I definitely wanted to avoid any extra ones, but even with my decision to take the shortest route it still took me all day to reach L.A.

An aunt named Betty from my father's side of the family lives in Agoura Hills, located on the western outskirts of greater Los Angeles, and she let me stay at her house while I made my stop to see the Clippers and Lakers play. Even though Agoura Hills is a sleepy suburb, I was still anxious about my impending trips into the city. Although I had made it safely through other major cities many times, a venture into the City of Angels always promises to be a little unnerving.

Previous Clippers Games at Los Angeles Memorial Sports Arena:

1992-93 season: Sacramento (Clippers 119-110)

About ten years ago, while the superb Celtics and Lakers had fans wondering if they were watching the two greatest teams of all time, the San Diego Clippers quietly moved into Los Angeles and began to play at the facility built in the late 1950s known as the Memorial Sports Arena. The 14-year-old Clippers, who were founded as the Buffalo Braves before moving to San Diego, took on the role as L.A.'s second team in 1984, but as their counterparts from across town continued to dominate the Western Conference, the Clips never could seem to get things started in their new home. After seven years without a trip to the playoffs, most spent near the bottom of the Pacific Division, the Clippers finally began to earn some respect in Tinseltown, and in '91–92 the amazing happened: The Clips finished with a better record than the Lakers.

During '92–93, when I first visited the Sports Arena, the Clippers were on their way to repeating that feat, and the buzz around the league was that the fashion-conscious L.A. fans might switch their allegiance from the purple and gold to the red, white, and blue.

But even with their new-found success, the Clips couldn't get past the first round of the playoffs in those two seasons, and their key players continued what had become a team tradition: They all tried to leave as soon as possible. With departures, injuries, and dissension, the Clippers were back in the cellar in '93–94. As I began my second trip, they looked certain to be the worst team in the league in '94–95, especially after they lost their first 16 games of the season. The Clippers, like the Nets and Kings, are one of the league's snakebitten teams, struggling to be competitive but always making mistakes. Yet the Kings have a great group of fans and the Nets have a modern building, while the Clippers play in front of sparse crowds in an arena that the Lakers abandoned more than twenty-five years ago.

They call it the Clip Joint, but nothing about the arena is as exotic as its nickname. Once the Boston Celtics move to their new building at the start of the '95–96 season, the L.A. Memorial Sports Arena will become the league's oldest—a fact that anyone who visits will have no trouble believing. One of the least-adorned buildings in the league, the arena is found in south-central L.A. near the University of Southern California, in a

neighborhood that is generally considered to be one of the most dangerous in the NBA. Still, one advantage to the low attendance at Clippers
games is that parking can be found in the lots near the arena, and the
security in the immediate area is adequate to keep fans safe.

The building itself is a round structure reminiscent of a grounded flying saucer, with a ridged blue top and a white bottom. Standing in the
middle of concrete lots, the Sports Arena is also surrounded by grass,
trees, and an iron fence, which make it look as if it's part of an urban
park. Still, the neighborhood directly adjacent to the arena is as urban as
any other part of the city, with a variety of stores and buildings lining
every nearby block.

One consequence of the arena's age and the neighborhood's bad reputation is that the Clippers seem to be in constant negotiations to move
to a new location. The '94–95 season provided an interesting development, as the team scheduled six regular-season games at the Pond, the
new arena built for the NHL's expansion Mighty Ducks of Anaheim,
which is found a fair distance down the highway in Orange County. With
the Clips continuing to suffer in downtown L.A., fans can only speculate
how long the team will stay put, but with no concrete plans for a change
any major move is still at least a couple of seasons away. For the immediate future, Clippers fans will watch their team play either in the ancient
Sports Arena, soon to be the NBA's oldest, or in the ultramodern Pond,
which has been described as the most luxurious arena in the NHL.

Tuesday, February 7, 1995—7:30 PM

LOS ANGELES CLIPPERS (7-39) VS. UTAH JAZZ (34-12)

The crime doesn't scare me when I visit L.A. for a game—both the
Clippers and the Lakers have agreed to put my name on their parking lists,
which means I can leave my car near the arenas and only have to exit after
I'm in the secure areas. No, what really makes me tense is the traffic. Los
Angeles is like no other city I've seen, with its vast highways cutting
through the rolling hills that make up the metropolitan area. Although
Agoura Hills appears on my guidebook map of the city, the suburb is still
forty miles from the downtown arenas where L.A.'s NBA teams play.

✪ LOS ANGELES
MEMORIAL SPORTS
ARENA
Opened: 1959
Capacity: 16,021
Los Angeles, California

I try to relax as I begin the journey, but the terrible reputation of the area highways is well deserved, and before long the traffic grinds to a halt. The maddening thing about L.A. is that you never see what's causing the delays, but I try to be patient, listening to the pregame show on the radio as I creep along. Not only are the Clippers still struggling, they have to face the Jazz tonight, one of the best teams in the league in recent weeks, and the announcer has the proper tone of dread in his voice as he previews the matchup.

It's a long, slow trip, and by the time I reach the arena I've spent a full hour and a half on the road. As it turns out, my experience on the congested highways is only the start of an interesting evening.

Tip-off is moments away as I make my way to the will-call window. As the lady in the box office searches for my ticket, a well-dressed man behind me loudly offers a free seat to anyone who wants one. From what

I can tell, he's the brother of Clippers forward Malik Sealy, and he's trying to give away one of the tickets that his sibling has left for him. Perhaps not surprisingly for a Clippers game, nobody takes him up on his offer.

But maybe I should, because there's no ticket for me at will-call, so I walk around the side of the building to the media entrance. Sure enough, I'm on the press list, but the media representative at the door needs to double-check my seating assignment, and uses a radio to contact the Clippers' Director of Communications. As she does, I glance at the press sheet for the evening, and see that my name has an unfamiliar affiliation next to it. A moment later I hear a voice on the radio ask, "Wasn't he here last game?" It's obvious what has happened: Walter was here a few days ago, and the Clippers' staff has confused my trip with his. I can only wonder if there will be other situations where my alter ego from Denver and I will be mistaken for each other.

After the dramatic entrance into the arena, I figure that it would be too much to expect an equally interesting game, but the first half turns out to be pretty exciting. As I make my way to my seat at a press table located at the top of the arena's lower section, the Clippers open the game with a 10-2 run. Even after the Jazz come back to tie the score, the Clippers continue to contain Karl Malone and John Stockton enough to lead 29-23 at the end of the first quarter.

Amazingly, improbably, the trend continues in the second, as L.A. goes up by 10 before settling for a 7-point halftime lead. Could it be? Will the woeful Clippers make my strange evening even more bizarre by pulling off the major upset?

Sure, the Sports Arena is old, but there are some things I like about it. For one thing, it has a unique layout, with the lower section consisting entirely of temporary bleachers built around the floor. A middle level of permanent seats is located above the court, and set behind and above that is a third level as well. The bleacher level, which only connects to the second tier in a handful of places, offers seats that are very close to the court, making them seem all the more exclusive. Overall, the layout gives the Sports Arena the appearance of a big gym, which may not be great for the Clippers' season-ticket holders, but is a nice change of pace for someone traveling to all the NBA arenas.

Just like in Oakland, the Sports Arena has an intimate feel, and the oval design gives fans all over the building a decent view of the action. The first time I visited the arena, the Clippers left me a ticket about halfway up the third level in one corner, but even from such a relatively poor seat I had a terrific view of the game. Still, that was at a time when the Clippers were peaking, and people actually showed up to watch the team play.

Given the Clippers' struggles this season, I'm not surprised that tonight's attendance is terrible. It will be officially announced at just under 7,000 people, but a quick look through the stands makes me think that even the paltry figure might be exaggerated. The bleachers are somewhat full, at least between the baskets, but only a third of the seats in the middle level have fans in them, and the number of people in the upper level could fit on a school bus.

It's the smallest crowd I've ever seen at an NBA game, but the few Clippers faithful in attendance try to keep their boys in the game as the second half begins. The problem is, good teams have a tendency to play sluggishly against bad opponents at the start of a game, only to crush them after halftime, and that's exactly what happens to the poor Clippers at the hands of the Jazz. Karl Malone, held to only 8 points in the first quarter and none in the second, explodes for 15 in the third, and the Clips can only watch as Utah outscores them 31-18 in the period to take a 6-point lead.

It's sad, really, because the Clippers are playing hard, making the kind of effort that might produce a win against a weaker team than the Jazz. Actually, the home team has to work hard at the Sports Arena in order for the crowd to have an enjoyable evening, because the building has little to distract the fans from the action. There's a decent four-sided scoreboard hanging over center court that displays a variety of stats, and a colorful message board mounted on one end of the stands, but there are no video screens and very few ads to be seen.

Although it's tough to watch a game without being able to see replays of the action, I still like the overall feel of the Sports Arena, one of only a few arenas that harken back to the roots of basketball, a traditional building that might be thought of as a poor man's Boston Garden. And although the Sports Arena doesn't boast the tradition of the Garden, it has been maintained better through the years, with a wide concourse, easily accessible food stands, and a nice team shop with a wide selection of merchandise. I don't think that I'd want to have season-tickets in a building like the Sports Arena, but the facility shouldn't keep anyone away who's looking to catch some NBA action.

The Clippers keep things close in the fourth, which surprises me after the blowout loss I saw four nights ago in Oakland, and Stockton and Malone are on the floor right up until the end. But the home team can pull no closer than four points, and in the end the clock just runs out before the Clippers can mount a good charge at the Jazz.

Yet it's been an entertaining evening for me, a change of pace from the crowded arenas I've been visiting, and I can't complain about the Clippers at all. The team played hard on the court, and their staff has been gracious. As I begin the hour-long trip back to Agoura Hills, I look forward to returning in a couple of days for another game. Who knows? Maybe the Clippers can give the Rockets a run for their money on Thursday night. Final score: Jazz 101, Clippers 88.

Average 1994–95 ticket cost: $25.50 (19th highest in the NBA)

Beer: $4.50 (12 oz.)

Soda: $2.00 (16 oz.—Coca-Cola products)

Hot Dog: $2.50

Parking: $7.00

Mascot: none

Cheerleaders: B.U.M. Shakalaka

Remote-controlled blimp: none

Other teams that play full-time in L.A. Memorial Sports Arena: Los Angeles Ice Dogs (International Hockey League)

What I'd change about L.A. Memorial Sports Arena: Add some replay boards, move to a better neighborhood, get some fans in the seats, and find a way to keep the better players and coaches with the team.

What I love about L.A. Memorial Sports Arena: The way it feels like a gym, and the fact that it offers a less-pretentious alternative to the Forum.

Statistics from Team Marketing Report, Inc.

Showtime Revisited

LOS ANGELES LAKERS

Founded: 1948
1993–94 Record: 33-49
Team Colors: Royal Purple, Gold

Wednesday, February 8–Thursday February 9

Although I was born in Boston, from an early age I had a yearning to migrate south, and after moving to Florida I felt completely at home in my new climate. During most of my travels, I made it a habit to crank the heat in my hotel rooms so I could feel at home. It was ironic, then, that I would spend the nights in L.A. bundled in a sleeping bag, but my aunt liked to turn off the heat at night, and even Southern California can get pretty chilly in the winter.

But staying at Betty's house had its advantages. While my aunt went off to work on Wednesday, I had plenty of space to stretch out and relax.

After my day off, I was ready to face another long trip down the L.A. freeways. Even though I was staying in the same place while visiting the City of Angels, the commute into the downtown area on three consecutive nights certainly didn't make me feel very settled. By then, however, I'd had enough practice on the freeways to feel relatively confident in my ability to get downtown and back without any problems.

Previous Lakers Games at the Great Western Forum:

1992–93 season: Utah (Lakers 114-110)

Although the Celtics have the richest history in the league, the Lakers are close behind, and were clearly the dominant team during the 1980s. But like their Boston counterparts, the Lakers suffered a collapse as the new decade began, and during the time of my first visit were playing only .500 ball. Things got worse in '93–94, when the team missed the play-offs for the first time after seventeen straight appearances, a streak that included five championships. The Lakers sold out only four games at the Great Western Forum all year, and it appeared that the city's fondness for the team might be in a serious decline, especially with the Clippers' development into a decent club.

But the tide shifted as '94–95 began, and not only because the Clippers began their season so poorly. The Lakers started strong and played well, led by forward Cedric Ceballos, who had come to the team in a trade with the Phoenix Suns. Although they had yet to demonstrate the kind of consistency they would need to compete for another title, the '94–95 Lakers were certainly the surprise team of the season, and it was exciting to visit an arena with such an air of unexpected good fortune.

The league had recognized Ceballos's accomplishments by naming him as a reserve to the Western Conference All-Star team that would play four days later in Phoenix. Unfortunately, he had been hurt in a collision with Denver's Dikembe Mutombo in a game a few days earlier, so he would not only miss All-Star Weekend but also faced a couple of months on the injured list. (Ironically, Mutombo would replace him on the All-Star team.) Still, I hoped that the Lakers would continue their run of solid play during my visit, especially since they were to face the San Antonio Spurs, winners of eight straight games.

I had extra motivation to hope for a good game because of my dislike for the Lakers' home arena. During the great Lakers–Celtics battles of the 1980s, we fans in Boston could only watch the games from L.A. on television and wonder what the Forum was like. Although it was never regarded in the same historic light as Boston Garden, it was still the site of many of the tremendous battles between the two teams, so I had been looking forward to visiting it.

When I finally arrived years later, I was pretty disappointed. The arena is a big, circular building with blue walls and white detailing, with no

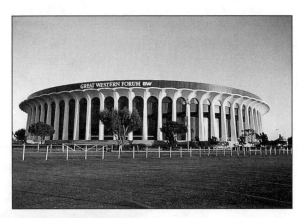

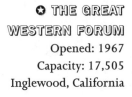

✪ THE GREAT
WESTERN FORUM
Opened: 1967
Capacity: 17,505
Inglewood, California

windows to provide a view into the building from the outside. Located in the middle of a cleared city block, the Forum is surrounded by a vast parking lot on all sides.

Even before I was able to check out the interior, the Forum lost points just for its basic design. If Oakland's Coliseum Arena resembles a big birthday cake, then the Forum might be the box to put it in. To me, it looks like a big Tupperware container, with ribbed blue walls that appear to be made of plastic, and white columns and molding formed into a pattern of ridges around the top of the arena. Although the Forum has a clean appearance, it's also very sterile, and without windows it gives no sense of any activity happening inside.

Instead, the most interesting action outside the arena is on the west side of the building at the entrance to the Forum Club, a canopied stairway where the celebrities arrive in their limousines. Fans pack the spot before the games, hoping to catch a glimpse of the rich and famous, but most of the arriving VIPs are unrecognizable, the movers and shakers who work behind the scenes. Still, the hopefuls wait, and every once in a while they are rewarded with a familiar face. But the pleasures of seeing a Lakers game are found almost solely inside the arena, at least in my experience.

Wednesday, February 8, 1995—7:30 PM

LOS ANGELES LAKERS (28-16) VS. SAN ANTONIO SPURS (30-14)

The traffic runs relatively smoothly into the city, and I reach the Forum in under an hour. Although the Lakers play in a somewhat safer neighborhood than the Clippers, Inglewood isn't the place to take a stroll late at night, and I'm glad to be able to park in the big lot adjacent to the arena.

Everybody loves a winner, and the crowd buzzing outside the Forum is a big one. Still, tonight should be a huge challenge for the home team, for not only are the Lakers missing Ceballos, but key players Sam Bowie and Elden Campbell will be out of action as well. It's hard to imagine that the Lakers have a chance, but hope springs eternal when your team is playing well.

Once inside, I make my way to my seat just above the upper press box. The location reminds me of where I sat for the Knicks–Nets game at Madison Square Garden, a spot in the center of the arena but far from the floor. The Lakers' public relations director has been enthusiastic about my travels and left me a comp ticket for both games at the Forum, although neither of the seats has been in a great location. On my first visit, I sat dead on the end at the top of the lower bowl, which is a difficult place to watch the game, and tonight I'm far away from the court. Still, I am grateful for the free tickets, and I certainly can understand why the team wouldn't comp many lower bowl seats: Most have an astonishingly high face value of close to $100.

Lakers fans have a reputation for arriving late for games, and as I look around the Forum I can see that it is well deserved. Although the game won't be a sellout, most of the decent seats have been purchased, but as the opening announcements are made there are huge blocks of empty rows in the lower bowl.

The Forum has a stadium design, with the upper level shrinking on each end. The lower sections are part of the "colonnade," while the upper areas are the "loges." Typically for such a design, a walkway runs around the building between the levels.

The gaps in the crowd might not be so bad, except that the color design for the seats is pretty hideous. Split right down the middle, one side of the stands is yellow while the other is orange, and neither color is very appealing. Not only that, but the arena is almost thirty years old, and shows its age in several places, especially with the battered seats and dingy walls.

Not all of the Forum is bad, however. Although its design puts some of the higher seats a fair distance from the court, there are no obstructed views, and the center scoreboard has decent video monitors on all four sides, in addition to a small message board. Bigger and more detailed message boards and scoreboards are found in the ends of the arena, which provide a good mix of basic information about the game and out-of-town scores.

Neither of the L.A. arenas has the kind of splashy opening announcements found in many other cities, probably because many fans don't arrive before tip-off.

During the first quarter, the stands slowly begin to fill, but the Lakers don't wait for the latecomers before they start their show. With three key players out, and several others battling injuries and illnesses, the home team still plays evenly with the Spurs, and are helped when David Robinson is called for two early fouls. Near the end of the period, the Lakers provide an unexpected delight: Forward Kurt Rambis, who had retired to become an assistant coach but was added to the roster after the recent rash of injuries to the L.A. front line, comes in to score a couple of baskets and block a shot. Not only do the Lakers lead 28-26 at the end of the quarter, but now I can tell my grandchildren that I saw Rambis play for the Lakers at the Forum, even if it wasn't during the glory days of the 1980s.

Robinson picks up his third foul early in the second quarter, and I take advantage of his absence to make a trip to the concession stands for a soda. Even though the Forum is nearly a decade younger than the Sports Arena, its concourse area is much more cramped, and there is usually a long wait for service at the food stands. Neither L.A. arena has the friendliest employees in the league, but in my experience the people working at the Clippers' building are much more pleasant than those at the Forum.

At least the ushers have an excuse to be cranky, as they're forced to wear one of the most ridiculous outfits I've ever seen: a blue ensemble that includes slacks, a checkered Western shirt, a vest, and a string tie. And as if the cramped concourse and frequently surly employees aren't enough, taking a trip to the facilities is no picnic either. Fans have to travel down a long flight of stairs, only to find that the restrooms are small as well. Still, the men's rooms do offer one interesting touch—they are the only facilities in the NBA where I've seen vending machines that distribute condoms.

The Lakers continue to hang tough in the second, taking advantage of Robinson's foul trouble to challenge the Spurs down low. The score stays close, but the Lakers are able to push their lead to five points by halftime. Although the arena is filled by the end of the quarter, at the break the stands nearly empty once more, and it will be late in the third quarter before many of the deserted seats are occupied again.

During the breaks in the game, the most celebrated entertainment is provided by the Laker Girls, but there are several other distinctive touches at the Forum as well. I'm forced to listen to my first live band since Milwaukee, but at least they play less than I remember they did during my first visit. On the positive side, the Lakers have one of the best p.a. announcers in the league, a guy with a deep bass voice reminiscent of Lou Rawls that perfectly suits the game of basketball.

And then there are the celebrities. Although the Lakers have returned to their competitive form, they're still not hip enough to bring out many famous faces. I spend much of the third quarter glancing through my binoculars, but in the end I can only spot the big one, the ultimate celebrity basketball fan: Jack Nicholson. My memories of Jack's antics during the epic playoff battles of the '80s are as strong as any others from that time, and I'm pleased that he's in his courtside seat near the scorer's table, protected by a personal usher who sits behind him to ward off any autograph hounds.

It makes me happy that he's still coming despite his team's misfortunes, because I like his style. Nicholson stays cool, watching and cheering in a subdued manner, but not intruding on the action like a certain movie director/Knicks fan I could mention. And although Dyan Cannon has a reputation for being almost as big a fan, she's nowhere to be seen tonight (although she was at my first game at the Forum).

Instead, only Jack is constant, and I hope that every time I visit the Forum he will be there. Heck, I think he should arrange to be stuffed and mounted in his seat after he passes away, so he could be an eternal Lakers fan providing supernatural support from beyond the grave.

While I search in vain for other celebrities, the game remains close, but halfway through the third quarter Robinson lands wrong and twists an ankle. The Lakers have been executing well all night, but it's not as if the Spurs lose all their talent when the Admiral leaves the floor, and Dennis Rodman pulls down enough crucial rebounds to keep things close—at the end of the third, the Lakers' lead is 77-74. Suddenly, I realize one of the main reasons I don't like being in the loges at the Forum: The team drops the lights upstairs, and in the aging arena the upper level seems murky and cramped in the darkness. It's far too similar to USAir Arena, where the people upstairs have to peer from the shadows towards the court.

One thing I do like about Lakers games is the balance between the action on and off the court. While many arenas seem to have too many contests and promotions, the Forum offers a near-perfect blend of basketball and frills. There are some fan contests, but not too many. The Lakers offer a great dance team, but no mascot. The ads, replays, and announcements during the breaks are well handled. In short, the Lakers demonstrate a good sense of how to stage a game, even if their arena doesn't measure up.

The Lakers use a makeshift lineup of four guards and a center for much of the fourth, and it works to perfection. Combining decent jump-shooting with quick slashes to the basket, L.A. has built the lead to near double-digits when rookie Eddie Jones drives for a dunk and is flattened by Rodman. It's a hard foul, to be sure, but I'm still surprised when the officials eject the tattooed wild man, who had managed to be a good boy all night before the incident. With their two key players gone and only four minutes left, the Spurs pack it in, and the Lakers are able to run up the score a little and make it look like an easy win. The few fans remaining cheer the effort at the final buzzer, but most made their exits long before Rodman did. Another rumor confirmed: Lakers fans really do leave early, too. Final score: Lakers 115, Spurs 99.

Average 1994–95 ticket cost: $32.64 (10th highest in the NBA)

Beer: $3.75 (14 oz.)

Soda: $1.75 (14 oz.—Coca-Cola products)

Hot Dog: $2.75

Parking: $6.00

Mascot: none

Cheerleaders: The Laker Girls

Remote-controlled blimp: none

Other teams that play full-time in the Forum: Los Angeles Kings (National Hockey League), Los Angeles Blades (Roller Hockey International)

What I'd change about the Forum: Lots of things: the ugly-colored seats, the cramped concourse, the submerged restrooms, the often-rude staff, and the fickle fans, just to start. And couldn't they have put in some windows?

What I love about the Forum: The p.a. announcer, the balance between the game and activities during the breaks, and the sense of history. Also, seeing Jack Nicholson sitting courtside.

Statistics from Team Marketing Report, Inc.

My visit to Los Angeles includes one more game, as the Clippers play the Rockets at the Sports Arena on Thursday, the final night of action before the All-Star break. The defending champions come in at 29-16, a strong indication that the Rockets will hammer the lowly Clips. Call me crazy, but I had taken to the road to see as many games as I could, and what the heck, it wasn't like a crowd of 7,000 fans was going to present many traffic problems. If the Clips were willing to give me a free ticket, who was I to turn it down?

There are no seats in the lower media sections, as a big group of journalists is traveling with the Rockets, but I figure I can find somewhere to sit closer than my assigned spot in the upper press box at the top of the arena. I spend the first quarter in the third level, the only person in my section, and watch the Clippers jump out to another good start, just like they had against the Jazz. The home team leads 26-19 at the end of one, and during the break I move to a decent seat in the middle level to get a better look at what is turning into a pretty good game. The Clippers manage to increase their lead to 9 by the halftime break, and once again I can only wonder: Is it really a close game, or is the league's worst team merely teasing its fans into false hope once again?

Remembering what had happened against the Jazz, I anxiously cross my fingers during the third quarter, but the Clippers don't budge, scoring a season-high 38 points in the period while building their lead to 93-78. It isn't a fluke, either—the Clips are finding the open man, creating decent shots, and working hard on defense.

So I brace myself for the final 12 minutes, as involved in the action as any of the Clippers fans in attendance, and the Rockets begin their big charge back. It is a race against the clock to overcome the sizable lead, but Houston storms within four at 106-102 with almost four and a half minutes left. With plenty of time remaining, the Clippers appear doomed to accept another moral victory.

So what do they do? Merely finish the game with a 16-5 run, outhustling and outshooting the Rockets, playing to the best of their ability and, as a member of the Clippers' media department will remark to me later, probably beyond their ability as well. The building rocks with as much noise as 7,000 people can make, and I feel great for those who showed up.

It reminds me of the occasional games when the struggling Magic would ambush a much better team during their early seasons, nights when a group of average players would put it all together and beat a team made up of the guys who normally get all the publicity. Even though the '94–95 Magic had become one of the powerhouses that lesser teams love to beat, I still could remember the other side of the coin: what it was like to be a fan of a team that wins two or three games out of every ten.

The Clippers shoot an astounding 63 percent for the game, and I am happy that they will be able to savor their victory during the All-Star break. L.A.'s "other" team can spend the long weekend remembering a night when, for once, they were the better team. Final score: Clippers 122, Rockets 107.

NBA standings as of Friday, February 10, 1995:

EASTERN CONFERENCE
Atlantic Division

	W	L	Pct	GB	Home	Away
Orlando Magic	37	10	.787	—	23-1	14-9
New York Knicks	30	16	.652	6.5	16-6	14-10
Boston Celtics	19	27	.413	17.5	12-14	7-13
New Jersey Nets	19	31	.380	19.5	12-10	7-21
Miami Heat	17	29	.370	19.5	12-11	5-18
Philadelphia 76ers	14	34	.292	23.5	7-17	7-17
Washington Bullets	11	34	.244	25	6-15	5-19

Central Division

	W	L	Pct	GB	Home	Away
Charlotte Hornets	31	17	.646	—	18-6	13-11
Cleveland Cavaliers	28	19	.596	2.5	15-9	13-10
Indiana Pacers	27	19	.587	3	17-5	10-14
Chicago Bulls	23	25	.479	8	13-11	10-14
Atlanta Hawks	22	26	.458	9	13-13	9-13
Milwaukee Bucks	19	29	.396	12	10-11	9-18
Detroit Pistons	17	29	.370	13	13-12	4-17

WESTERN CONFERENCE
Midwest Division

	W	L	Pct	GB	Home	Away
Utah Jazz	35	13	.729	—	19-7	16-6
San Antonio Spurs	30	15	.667	3.5	15-6	15-9
Houston Rockets	29	17	.630	5	15-7	14-10
Denver Nuggets	20	26	.435	14	13-11	7-15
Dallas Mavericks	18	28	.391	16	10-16	8-12
Minnesota Timberwolves	11	36	.234	23.5	6-17	5-19

Pacific Division

	W	L	Pct	GB	Home	Away
Phoenix Suns	38	10	.792	—	20-3	18-7
Seattle SuperSonics	33	12	.733	3.5	19-4	14-8
L.A. Lakers	29	16	.644	7.5	14-6	15-10
Portland Trail Blazers	25	20	.556	11.5	15-9	10-11
Sacramento Kings	25	20	.556	11.5	17-7	8-13
Golden State Warriors	14	31	.311	22.5	9-12	5-19
L.A. Clippers	8	40	.167	30	5-19	3-21

Duel in the Desert

ALL-STAR WEEKEND

Friday, February 10–Sunday, February 12

Friday morning was bright and beautiful, perfect weather for a drive through the desert. I was glad I'd spent my last night in my aunt's frigid house, but the few days with my family had been pleasant.

It was the eve of All-Star Weekend in Phoenix, the annual midseason highlight that drew fans and players from all around the league. The NBA had promised to leave me a media pass, giving me backstage access to all the weekend's events, but my excitement was tempered by the fact that I had a drive of more than 400 miles to reach Phoenix, a trip that would last the entire day.

Leaving L.A. around noon, I crossed into Arizona four and a half hours later. It took me another couple of hours to reach Phoenix, and from there I had no problem finding my way to the downtown hotel where I'd made a reservation for the weekend. I tried to relax that night, feeling tired from the drive and slightly stressed by my visit to L.A., but mostly excited about the week to come in one of the NBA's best cities.

The entire weekend was a blur, a mixture of boundless excitement and annoying difficulties, a time when I felt like both a privileged journalist and a fraudulent outsider. Events began late Saturday morning and continued until Sunday evening, a dizzying 36 hours of NBA sights and sounds at the league's midseason showcase held at one of its premiere arenas.

Orlando had hosted the event in 1992, and as a Magic season-ticket holder I'd been able to get my hands on some decent tickets. But the Phoenix weekend was a part of my long NBA journey, which made it all the more exciting. The other difference was that this time I would have a media pass that would let me experience what went on behind the scenes at All-Star Weekend.

Late Saturday morning, I drive to Scottsdale, a suburb northeast of Phoenix, to the resort hotel that serves as media headquarters. I give my name to Evan, a serious and efficient young man on the NBA staff, and after he finds my credentials I explain my situation. The NBA had kept me waiting for a response to my request for the pass until only a week before the event, and even then only promised to get me in the building, not necessarily to assign me a seat. After I describe my status to Evan as politely as I can, he tells me that nearly all the members of the media have been given a seat location, so it should be no problem to find me a spot somewhere in the arena.

Two hours later I walk the half-mile south from my hotel to America West Arena. The downtown area is crowded with excited fans, who move through the city streets amid the vendors and scalpers. There have been big parties every night since Thursday in the downtown clubs and restaurants, and as I walk I pass scalpers who not only have game tickets but are also selling passes to tonight's premiere bash, a league-sponsored affair taking place in a courtyard north of the arena. The view of the busy streets on such a beautiful afternoon in Phoenix is thrilling, with bright All-Star banners hanging from light poles and on several nearby buildings, and I feel a sense of power as I cross the street in front of the arena, knowing that my media pass is safely tucked away in the small Magic duffel bag I've brought from the hotel.

I arrive around 2:30 PM, two hours before All-Star Saturday begins. After making my way into the bowels of the arena to the press area, my first priority is to get a seat for the evening, and when I spot Evan I ask him if he can arrange it. He points out his boss, an NBA vice-president who is standing nearby clutching a seating list and answering the questions of a few media people around him. I patiently wait my turn, only to have the NBA honcho literally look down his nose at my pass and say, "You don't have a seat yet."

"That's right," I reply, feeling horribly underdressed in my jeans and sweatshirt.

"I can't help you now. Talk to me later," he says, and spins away before I can reply.

I feel I might make a better impression in a coat and tie, but I don't have such an outfit in my luggage. Still, most members of the media are dressed like I am, as the league has requested that the people covering the game wear "resort casual" clothing, rather than professional attire. I can easily imagine why: The temporary stands have been removed on all four sides of the court and replaced by numerous rows of press tables, and it's a safe bet that the league doesn't want every person within camera view to be wearing a tie.

The situation is the same as in Orlando three years ago: The league has commandeered the arena for its use, and local season-ticket holders have only limited access to seats in the upper level. At the O'rena, fans could buy a reduced number of tickets for only one of the two weekend events, while at America West a lottery was held to determine which season-ticket holders would get to see the game.

It's customary for teams to provide a meal for the media before each game, and today a large area has been set up near the interview room under the stands on the court level, with dozens of tables and an impressive spread of food. Even though I've been in media rooms in several arenas, I feel swamped by the sheer number of press people in the bowels of America West—according to this morning's newspapers, more than 1,300 press credentials have been issued for the weekend. The huge crowd of media members makes it easier for me to blend in, but certainly reduces the privileged feeling that the pass had given me a few hours ago.

I find a quiet spot away from the groups, and spend a few minutes talking to the only other guy at my table. He's the Suns' timekeeper, and he tells me a few stories about running the game clock. I find his insights fascinating, especially since he has held the job in Phoenix for twenty years, but he seems somewhat aloof, unimpressed by the weekend's festivities.

But why should he be any different? As I look around at the multitude of journalists, I see grim faces, humorless and indifferent. A few are smiling, but they are in the minority—most act as if they're way too cool to be here.

Just before the start of the Schick Rookie Game, I find Evan and ask if there's a seat for me yet. He tells me that he still can't get a straight answer from his boss, but that I can use his seat until he does. He leads me to a spot in the second row behind one of the baskets, and I find myself in the midst of a bevy of NBA celebrities.

Looking to my left, I see that Chuck Daly is a few seats down my row, chatting with some league officials. Behind him are a couple of representatives from the Magic, including Penny Hardaway and Tree Rollins. Next to them is Will Smith, which comes as no surprise—the Fresh Prince has a reputation as a big NBA fan. But the best moment comes a few seconds later, when none other than Shaquille O'Neal makes an appearance. Passing right in front of me, Shaq is dressed in a dapper suit, making a stylish showing the night before starting for the Eastern Conference in the big game. He towers over me for a moment, accompanied by fewer people than I might have expected, before heading down the row to a seat near Daly. I am understandably starstruck, and I enjoy the few minutes I spend among so many famous faces.

Evan soon returns to tell me that there should be a seat for me in the upper press row, located in the center near the top of the lower level. My thanks for his help are sincere—he's tolerated my incessant pestering with exceptional patience.

After being unsure all day whether I would get a seat, I'm both relieved and annoyed to find that the press row is only half-full. As I take a spot in the second row, I'm puzzled that I had to spend so much time fretting.

The Rookie Game is exciting, a nice showcase for the league's first-year players. It's an indication of the NBA's savvy that they replaced the Legends Game, with its frequent injuries and sluggish play, with an exhibition of the most promising newcomers in the league.

Although the Rookie Game is in its second year, the big event during the halftime break is making its debut. It's the Foot Locker Million-Dollar Shot, a chance for a contest winner to hit a 3-pointer and become an instant millionaire. This year's contestant is Mike Hoban, a 16-year-old junior-varsity basketball player from Strongsville, Ohio. As you might expect from such an outlandish contest, the hype surrounding Hoban's shot has been tremendous, including an appearance on *The Late Show with David Letterman*.

Although some people have complained that the contest creates too much pressure for such a young man, I think it's a great event. Still, I'm disheartened when it comes time for the poor kid to make his attempt, because the court is packed with dozens of people, all watching intently as he takes his shot. There's another problem: Hoban is a low-post player, not much of an outside threat, and when the big moment comes the ball arcs on a straight line to the basket but falls far short of the rim. Hoban hangs his head, which is too bad: He's handled the crush of media attention with dignity and seems like a level-headed young man, and I hope the missed shot didn't completely ruin his enjoyment of his fifteen minutes of fame.

Although most of the people in the lower bowl seem restless as the Rookie Game continues, I enjoy it right up to the end, especially when it finishes in a tie and goes into a unique form of overtime—the first team to score 3 points wins. In the end, Milwaukee's Glenn Robinson and the Clippers' Lamond Murray of the White team each score baskets to win the game, spoiling an impressive 16-point comeback by the Green team, led by Dallas' Jason Kidd and the Lakers' Eddie Jones, who is named the MVP.

Next up is the AT&T Long Distance Shootout, which is my personal favorite event of the night—a contest of pure skill, with no judges to influence the outcome.

As I watch the warmups, I exchange a few words with the only person near me on press row, a guy who works for a video production company based in Minneapolis. As we talk, I give him my prediction— Miami's Glen Rice, who is demonstrating perfect form as he takes

ly personal choice is the Magic's Nick Anderson,
e that his style makes him an underdog, as jump-
ncy to tire as the event goes on.
out to be a disappointment, only because the con-
kinds of scores most fans expected in the first event
line at the shorter distance of 22 feet. There is at
though: My prediction is correct, as Rice beats
in the final round.

ampionship follows the Shootout, but I decide to
nt and head down to the interview room. There I
.....sning his comments, and as he walks out of the room he
passes right by me. He politely talks to a couple of people on his way out,
making a nice impression that surprises me; during the Pacers' playoff
series against the Magic last year, I saw footage of him talking to reporters
that made me think he was an immature jerk. I watch Rice for a couple
of minutes, then head back to the upper press row.

The dunk competition is also disappointing, as the lineup is woefully
short of any big stars. Fans have begun to express their displeasure with
the event, and with a group of contestants that includes such generic players as Jamie Watson, Antonio Harvey, Tim Perry, and Tony Dumas, I can
understand the complaints.

In the end, Harold Miner takes his second title in three years, making
the Saturday events a sweep for the Miami Heat. Still, not many of the fans
in America West seem very enthusiastic with the result, and by late in the
evening most of the lower-level seats are empty.

I head back to the interview room to watch a few more players. As
I arrive, Minnesota's Isaiah Rider, who placed second in the dunk
competition, is finishing his interview. By now I've found a good spot to
stand so that the players walk by me on their way out of the room, and as
Rider passes I hear him say to the guy next to him, "Well, at least I got
$10,000."

Miner is next, but by now I'm jaded enough that I leave soon after he
walks by me on his way to the podium. With my head still buzzing after
rubbing elbows with so many NBA stars, I make my way out of the arena
and back to my hotel.

On the morning of the All-Star Game, I'm watching *SportsCenter* on ESPN when I learn that I missed at least one thing yesterday.

Charles Barkley is the Suns' marquee player, and as such most people considered him to be the unofficial host for Phoenix's All-Star Weekend. But Barkley has a habit of creating controversy, and unfortunately this weekend would be no different. A white reporter had asked Barkley a brusque question about NBA groupies, and the Phoenix forward had rolled his eyes, delivered a quick answer, and walked away, saying to another reporter in jest: "Now you know why I hate white people."

An ESPN camera picked up the remark, and the network decided to broadcast the tape. Never mind that Barkley is married to a white woman, or that his best friend on the Suns is white, or that he made the comment to a white guy—the folks at ESPN decided that the remark was newsworthy.

Sir Charles is one of my favorite players, not only a tremendous athlete but a frank and outspoken man who refuses to let the media influence his behavior. Sure, he does things that tick people off, but his overall contribution to the league has been overwhelmingly positive. Barkley is a showman who can back up his mouth with exceptional play, and the fact that he made a politically incorrect joke was no reason to vilify him in the press.

Determined not to let the controversy spoil my day, I walk back to America West through the sunshine of another glorious Phoenix afternoon. The first thing I do is find Evan. Although he's probably less than thrilled to see me again, he remains polite and suggests that I check the seating chart for the game. I do, and am delighted to find that I've been given a spot on the upper press row. Finally I can relax, enjoying the fact that I'm no longer a nomad.

Once again I partake of free food at the press lunch, and during the time I spend in the media area I see only one player: Lakers forward Cedric Ceballos, dressed in street clothes with a bandage on the injured hand that will keep him from playing for the West in today's game.

As it draws closer to the 4:10 PM tip-off, I make my way back to the upper press box, not surprised to find that most of the seats are occupied for the game. Down on the court, the teams are warming up in their new All-Star uniforms, which utilize the Suns' colors of orange and purple, with a dash of pale green added for an extra touch of style.

Of course, the uniforms are only a small portion of the colorful decorations found in America West to commemorate the event, and part of the thrill of attending an All-Star Game is seeing how the host arena dresses up for the big show. The entire weekend has become the NBA's midseason party, and the game itself is only one part of the festivities.

That's a good thing, because the game turns out to be a blowout, as an East team with an awful lot of young players can't keep up with a more experienced West squad that builds a 72-56 lead at halftime.

I'm still enjoying myself, holding on to the hope that either Shaq or Penny will explode and win the MVP award, or that perhaps Barkley can take home the trophy for the second time. Although I'm disappointed that the game isn't remotely close, I guess I should be used to such a lopsided score—the 1992 event in Orlando ended in a 153-113 win for the West.

Still, the biggest damper to my enjoyment isn't the occasionally ragged play on the floor, but rather my nearly constant exposure to the media. To my right are an editor from one of the annual basketball preview magazines and a social columnist from a local newspaper, and I'm sitting too close to be able to ignore their conversation. For the entire fourth quarter, the two journalists sit and whine about basketball. They complain about the players, the fans, the lavish nature of All-Star Weekend, the crush of media people, and the fact that things used to be so much better back when Magic and Bird were still playing.

The social columnist offers this bit of insight: "You know, you could measure the combined depth of character of all the guys on the Eastern team with a foot-long ruler. Come to think of it, you could do the same thing with the Western team too, with the exception of David Robinson." I'm terribly offended by this—so somehow he's familiar with the character of all the NBA All-Stars?—but the guy from the basketball annual couldn't agree more. He then makes this observation: "Well, if you paid me such a huge amount of money when I was that young, I'd probably be a jerk too."

I'm convinced that it's his idea of being gracious, and all I can think is that I know plenty of literate, intelligent basketball fans who would love to have his job, myself included, if he hates the game so much. Unless such work inevitably transforms you into the kind of cynical elitists that these snobs have become, in which case I'll pass, and just remain a fan.

The West wins the game 139-112, the third-biggest blowout in All-Star history (the Orlando game was the second-biggest of all time—I sure can pick the ones to see). Shaq, Penny, and Barkley all play well, but the MVP goes to the guy who would be the next choice on my list: Mitch Richmond of the Kings, who leads all scorers with 23 points.

Back in the media room, I watch as Mitch seems dazzled by it all, suddenly thrust in the limelight after years of relative obscurity in Sacramento. I watch him answer questions on the podium, then he moves to do a short segment for ESPN in a corner of the interview room. Several TV reporters are jockeying to shoot video segments, and Mitch shakes a few hands as he moves from spot to spot, even autographing a game program for a foreign journalist who doesn't speak English but gestures his request.

Richmond just won the MVP award perhaps a half-hour ago, and he is the guy who waved at me in Orlando after I shouted to him. Besides, Jerry from Sacramento, the guy who sold me the ticket for the Kings–Bulls game, told me that Richmond is a nice guy.

So I swallow my pride, position myself near his exit route, and wait for Richmond to finish his interviews. As he's being led to the locker room, he pauses for a moment, and I see that I have one quick chance.

"Mitch!" I say, much like I had from the stands in Orlando, and Richmond turns and looks at me.

"Good game," I say, again just like in the O'rena, and offer my hand to him. Richmond smiles, shakes my hand with a softer grip than I might have imagined, and thanks me. Richmond continues on his way, and I feel both excited and embarrassed. I may have looked like a starstruck bumpkin, but I know that it's a moment I'll always remember.

Even though the game has been over for a little while, the weekend has one last memory to offer me.

Barkley takes to the podium for his postgame interview, and the unofficial host doesn't mince words.

"First of all, I want to address something," Sir Charles begins. "I hear ESPN's trying to f-word me, and you guys are trying to make a controversy. There's not going to be a controversy. I was joking around with one of my friends, and that's it. If you don't like it, f-word you and your families, too. Now let's talk about the game."

Of course, Sir Charles didn't say "f-word," but actually used the f-word. He's spent ten years swimming with the media sharks, and as usual he's not afraid to bite back.

ESPN will later show footage of the rather harsh opening, but they won't show what follows: Barkley calmly answering questions about the weekend, with no trace of animosity or bitterness.

As the press conference ends, Barkley makes his way out past me, stopping for a few moments to talk to a young boy and his parents. He's congenial and friendly, taking his time with the family and joking with the kid that he should be sure to buy *Shut Up and Jam*, Barkley's video game.

Sir Charles then moves to another group of people outside the locker room. Fueled by my success with Richmond, I try to find an opening to shake Barkley's hand, but he has learned through the years how to move quickly from place to place to avoid unwanted attention, and as a result I don't get the chance that I did earlier. He disappears through a door a few moments later, and I'm disappointed at the missed opportunity. Still, I'm glad to see firsthand that, despite the weekend's controversy, Barkley has remained level-headed and gracious toward the fans.

And if I ever do get to meet Sir Charles, I'd certainly prefer not to be wearing press credentials at the time.

As I walk back to my hotel through the warm night, I find myself reflecting on the previous 36 hours. The weekend has been the kind of experience that makes all the lonely miles worthwhile, not just one of the highlights of the trip, but one of the most exciting events of my life as well.

Empire of the Suns

PHOENIX SUNS

Founded: 1968
1993–94 Record: 56-26
Team Colors: Purple, Orange, Copper, Black

Monday, February 13–Friday, February 17

As I settled in on Monday morning, I read in a local paper that the Suns would be playing the Jazz on Sunday night. I'd planned to stay and see Phoenix host Portland on Wednesday and Golden State on Friday before leaving on Saturday, a schedule that would give me time to stop at the Grand Canyon before continuing on to Salt Lake City. But I'd already visited Arizona's most famous natural landmark during my first trip, and with the Suns and Jazz playing so well I decided to stay where I was for an extra couple of days so I could see the Jazz game.

But there would be no extra game for me in Phoenix, and the reason was hard to believe. A horse show and a bilingual conference were scheduled in the area over the weekend, and as a result every hotel room within 50 miles was booked after Thursday.

Not only would I be unable to stay over, I'd also have to switch from my nice hotel to a Motel 6 on Tuesday.

> **Previous Suns Games at America West Arena:**
>
> **1992–93 season:** San Antonio (Suns 125-110)/Dallas (Suns 126-105)

The main reason why I wanted to see an extra game in Phoenix was that I love the Suns, the team that I consider to be my second-favorite in the NBA, behind only the Magic.

There are several reasons for my appreciation of Phoenix, many of them similar to the things that led me to be a Warriors fan. Like Golden State, Phoenix was among the league's most exciting NBA teams in the first few seasons I had season-tickets. Not only did the two clubs play the kind of up-tempo basketball usually associated with the Western Conference, they also featured several players I liked, including Tim Hardaway and Chris Mullin of the Warriors, and Kevin Johnson and Dan Majerle of the Suns.

But in the summer of 1992, Phoenix made the move that, for me at least, would put them above all the other teams outside Orlando: They traded for Charles Barkley. As I mentioned earlier, I'm a big fan of Barkley, and his move from the Sixers, a team that didn't do much for me, to the Suns, who already had my respect, sealed the deal.

Sir Charles began his career in Phoenix during the '92–93 season, a year when the Suns made several other dramatic changes, including hiring Paul Westphal, one of their most acclaimed former players, to be their head coach; unveiling new uniforms that were among the best-looking in the league; celebrating their twenty-fifth season in the NBA; and moving into an arena that has since been acknowledged as the league's best, at least according to a survey of basketball insiders taken during the '93–94 season.

After my first visit in '92–93, the season that had to be the most exciting in team history, I came away with the same impression as the people who voted in the poll, and if anyone demanded that I choose a favorite arena, I would usually name Phoenix. Inside and out, in just about every detail, America West does it all.

Located in the southwest part of downtown Phoenix, the arena has an exterior design that is an attractive combination of curves and lines. The main building is basically rectangular, constructed of tan and gray bricks with brown accents, although each corner is flattened rather than sharp. On the south and east sides, which are virtually identical, the building has large entrances and many small windows, both on the main concourse level and on the luxury-suite levels located in the center of the building. Just below the gently ascending roof, the arena has an indented section that runs around the building, which gives a view into the back of the upper-level stands and hints at the interior design.

America West would be a great-looking arena even if it were similar on all four sides, but it's not. On the west side is an attached 900-space parking garage, constructed of the same materials as the building, that complements the arena without overwhelming it. The north side extends out from the main building as well, ending in a 10,000-square-foot restaurant and bar called the Copper Club, which has a huge entrance on the northwest corner of the building, the area considered to be the front of the arena.

Although the south and east sides of America West are pleasant enough, the view at the northwest corner is the best the facility offers. In between the parking garage on the right and the Copper Club on the left, fans walk through a lush plaza on their way to the main entrance. The plaza consists of brick sidewalks that match the arena's colors, as well as several fountains, sculptures, trees, and patches of grass. Before the games, the plaza is alive with activity, usually including live bands (a nice touch outside the arena) and several clowns (who are both annoying and creepy, in my opinion). The entrance itself is dark gray, a curving wall of stone that offers a nice contrast to the building's straight lines in other places. Fans looking for tickets can try the box office, which is located between the main entrance and the parking garage.

But if you don't have a ticket, the box office will rarely do any good. Asking about the game on Sunday against the Jazz, I found out that there were no tickets left for the rest of the season. Still, if I'd been able to stay, I could have bought a ticket without much trouble, as scalping is legal in Phoenix as long as it's not done on arena grounds. In fact, there is a small lot across from America West that is designated for the ticket business, and anyone who wants can usually find a ticket there for just about any location in the arena, as long as they can afford a healthy markup of the face value.

Fortunately, I wouldn't need to utilize the booming scalpers' market for either of the two games I planned to see, as the Suns' front office had agreed to sell me a single ticket for each of those nights. Still, my love for the Suns was in jeopardy after I began to organize my second trip.

Phoenix's media director had flat-out refused to help me, and the team became cooperative only after I contacted the Suns' vice-president who had assisted me during my first trip.

After years as a Suns fan, I was disappointed to have such difficulties with the team, but I guess every relationship has its ups and downs.

⚙ AMERICA WEST
ARENA
Opened: 1992
Capacity: 19,023
Phoenix, Arizona

Wednesday, February 15, 1995—7:00 PM

PHOENIX SUNS (38-10) VS. PORTLAND TRAIL BLAZERS (25-21)

Are the Suns still my favorite team outside of Orlando?

The question occurs to me as I park at a bank a block away from America West's main entrance. As the Magic develop into one of the league's best teams, I find myself much less interested in other teams anyway, but I suppose the Suns still take second place in my heart. While some of their team officials have tarnished my enjoyment of visiting their arena, others have been friendly, and I guess I can forgive and forget.

But it's not as if my feelings affect the club one way or another. Traveling the NBA is like a religious experience, as I devote time to a huge entity that rarely offers concrete recognition of my efforts.

Speaking of devotion—maybe the reason some members of the Suns' front office have an attitude problem is that the people of Phoenix absolutely love their team. As I make my way through the crowd toward the main entrance, the Suns' faithful surround me, filling the air with electric energy.

It's going to be an interesting game, for a couple of reasons. The Blazers come into town without Clyde Drexler, who got a Valentine's Day present yesterday when he was traded to the Rockets for Otis Thorpe. It will be only the Blazers' second game without their superstar, and Thorpe isn't available to play yet. The other memorable characteristic about tonight's matchup is that it is the first rematch I'll see on my trip, after watching the Suns play the Blazers in Portland four weeks ago.

As I make my way through the main entrance, to my left is the Suns' team shop, arguably the nicest in the league, and past that is an equally impressive food court, with several counters offering name-brand hamburgers, pizza, sandwiches, and Mexican food.

The concourse, as might be expected, is clean and modern, with a good variety of concession and souvenir stands. Like most arenas, it's located at the top of the lower bowl, with fans in the upper levels using stairs to reach their seats.

For the first of my two games, the Suns have sold me a ticket in a lower corner, only about forty feet from the court. As I settle in for the action, I'm surrounded by affluent season-ticket holders who spend much of their time discussing golfing, boating, and recent vacations. They seem like decent people, but they don't strike me as pure NBA fans, and I don't end up chatting to any of them about the game.

A few minutes after I settle in, the Suns go through their dramatic opening—just the kind of high-tech affair that one would expect in such a plush arena. Because of the All-Star break, it's the first home game for Phoenix in ten days, as the Suns had finished their first-half schedule with road wins in Dallas and Utah. After such a long stretch without a game, the arena seems especially energetic, as the fans enjoy the start of the second half of the season with their team holding the best record in the league.

Still, the Suns had to come from behind in both of their wins against the Mavericks and Jazz, and as the game begins they find themselves on the short end of the score again. The Blazers seem unflustered by the loss of their top player, and to my surprise lead at the end of the first quarter 32-26. Portland guard Rod Strickland is distributing the ball beautifully, center Chris Dudley is pulling down rebounds, and just about every Blazer is hitting his shots.

Phoenix gets a lift from guard Danny Ainge, who scores 9 points in the second quarter, but Portland continues to shoot the ball well and takes a 61-58 edge at halftime.

As one of the Suns will later describe it, both the crowd and the team seem rather nonchalant in the first half. Perhaps Phoenix has become overconfident in their ability to come back from a deficit, but without injured players Kevin Johnson, Wayman Tisdale, and Danny Manning, the undermanned Suns just might be letting one slip away.

During the halftime break, I take a few minutes to look around the now-familiar sight of America West Arena. The interior design is just as impressive as the outside, with seats running right up to the floor on three sides of the court. The lower level has thirty rows of seats, while the upper level has only fourteen. In between the levels are two rows of luxury suites running around the entire length of the building. The layout is similar to the arenas in Sacramento and Milwaukee, with a squared appearance, rather than the oval shape found in many arenas with separate lower and upper sections.

The center hanging scoreboard has message and player boards, while video monitors are hung on each side of the building in the center above the upper level. A variety of extra scoreboards and message boards are found around the building, mounted between the two levels of luxury suites. In an interesting touch, the 24-second clock is displayed on that upper row of scoreboards, which gives easy reference for fans who pay attention to that aspect of the game.

America West's reputation as a state-of-the-art arena is enhanced by the interior design, and by such features as the sound system, which broadcasts both the p.a. announcer and the incidental music impressively.

In short, it's easy to see why no game in the arena's short history has failed to sell out. The question tonight is whether the Suns can provide the full house with a victory.

In the third quarter, the Blazers come out playing as well as they have all night, and push the lead as high as 17 points. Midway through the quarter, the crowd is restless with frustration, and after the Blazers score to go ahead 85-70 with five minutes left in the third, a woman behind me clicks her tongue and loudly announces, "This game's over."

The Suns go on a small run, but still find themselves down by twelve at the end of the quarter, 92-80. The Blazers have shot a sizzling 58.2 percent through three periods, and both Strickland and Dudley are close to having career nights. Things look bad for the home team, but basketball fans know that anything can happen with a full quarter to play.

The displays in America West are certainly colorful, and there's one message unique to Phoenix that I really enjoy. After a questionable call by the refs, the message boards show an "Official's Eye Chart," with the letters arranged in a pyramid shape like an optometrist's chart. Looking closely, I can make out two messages during the game: In one display, the letters spell out, "Everyone but you knows that was clean," while the other one I can decipher reads, "This isn't football, dude." Maybe the officials don't appreciate such treatment, but I think the messages are pretty clever.

The game has all the makings of an embarrassing home loss for the Suns, a sloppy effort against a less-skilled team. But as the fourth quarter begins, the p.a. announcer spurs the crowd to life, and the Suns faithful roar their support for their team. The full house has pumped things up a notch, and it's up to the Suns to respond.

Slowly they do, climbing back into the game by taking better shots and playing stronger defense. The Portland lead is down to six nearly halfway through the quarter when Dudley, lying on the floor after a play, gets tangled with Ainge's leg. After a moment's pause, Ainge decides that Dudley has held on for a little too long, and swings a forearm at the big Portland center before crashing to the court himself.

The crowd is incensed by what they feel was a deliberate attempt to injure their player, and as Ainge limps off the arena is filled with a thundering chorus of boos. To make matters worse, after a brief huddle the officials announce that Ainge has been ejected for the play (which seems a little pointless, considering he had to be assisted off the floor), and that Dudley is awarded two free throws. The fans are outraged at the call, but Dudley, one of the worst free-throw shooters in league history, hits them both to put the Blazers up by eight with 6:15 left.

The Suns haven't gone on an offensive tear, but the Blazers are ice-cold, and are fortunate to hold a 102-96 lead with just under two minutes left. With KJ injured and Ainge gone, it's up to the other Phoenix guards to boost their level of play, and Elliott Perry does just that. Stripping the ball from Strickland, Perry races up the floor and feeds Barkley, who is fouled and makes both. On the next possession, Perry steps into a passing lane and makes another steal, racing up the floor to hit a layup and bring the Suns within two.

Strickland scores a basket, but so does Suns forward A.C. Green; Strickland misses with 14 seconds left, and Phoenix calls a timeout. With the Suns down by two, everyone in the building is looking to Sir Charles, but that doesn't mean he can be stopped: Barkley takes the inbounds pass near the top of the key, dribbles down the right side of the lane, then does a little up-and-under move to score on a layup. The Blazers have one more chance to avoid overtime, but after working the ball around the key they settle for an off-balance Strickland jumper that only draws iron. So after 29 games on the road, I finally get to see some overtime.

Once Phoenix forces the OT, however, Portland is clearly doomed. The Suns continue to execute and score, while the Blazers, who had 92 points in the first three quarters but only 12 in the fourth, can't buy a basket. Although the Suns lose Barkley with 2:17 left after he picks up his second technical foul, he leaves with 35 points and 14 rebounds, and with his team ahead by four. Ironically, it's the third game in a row the Suns will finish without their superstar, as Barkley was ejected in Dallas and injured in Utah.

In the end, the Suns outscore the Blazers 16-9 in the overtime period, and from the start of the fourth quarter through the end of the game Portland ends up making only 6 of 30 shots. Strickland finishes with an impressive triple-double of 26 points, 11 rebounds, and 18 assists, but he has to be disappointed: His Blazers really should have won the game.

From my perspective, it's been a satisfying evening. Even though the Magic and Suns are in a close race for the league's best record, I still can't help but be pleased for the Phoenix players and fans after their incredible comeback. The experience of visiting a packed America West Arena during a close, exciting game has made the week's frustrations seem worthwhile, especially since Barkley not only posted big numbers but got tossed as well—it was vintage Sir Charles. Final score: Suns 120, Trail Blazers 113 in overtime.

Nothing very exciting happens on Thursday, as I spend the day in my room doing a little writing. I haven't been able to find a room for Friday night, and even the Motel 6 is booked after Thursday. As a result, I have no choice but to pack everything into my car on Friday morning, check out just before noon, and then wait for the second Suns' home game on my schedule to tip-off. Fortunately, the start is going to be at 6 PM, an hour earlier than usual, because the game will be broadcast nationally on TNT.

I spend Friday afternoon hanging out at a local mall and seeing a movie, then head back into the city an hour before the game. Although crime seems to be no worse in Phoenix than in many other cities I've visited, I am still somewhat paranoid about leaving my car parked in the downtown area while fully loaded with all my gear, but I can't think of an alternative plan. All I can do is pack as much of the valuable stuff into the trunk as I can, and hope that the bags and suitcases in the back seat don't look too inviting to any nearby thieves. There is one other thing I do to prevent total disaster: I take a floppy disk with a copy of my half-finished manuscript to keep in my pocket during the game. That way, if someone does clean out my car, at least they won't get the only copies of my writing (although if they were smart, I guess they could finish the manuscript and sell it themselves).

It seems like a lot of trouble for a game that everyone predicts will be pretty boring. The Suns are facing the Warriors, who are 14-33 overall and a miserable 5-20 on the road. After so many come-from-behind victories, everyone figures that Phoenix will take advantage of Golden State's misfortunes to stomp the poor Warriors. Even though Danny Ainge is suspended for the game because of his swing at Chris Dudley two nights ago, the Suns have reason to be confident: Golden State hasn't won a game in Phoenix in almost eight years, a streak of 19 consecutive losses.

In the first quarter, the Suns appear to have finally gotten their act together, and by the end of the period they lead the Warriors 37-30. Golden State shows signs of life in the second, but Phoenix still holds a 3-point edge at halftime.

I spend a fair amount of time talking to the guy next to me. Vince is a high school freshman from Kearny, a town about 60 miles east of Phoenix, and after being surrounded by jaded season-ticket holders two nights ago, it is nice to talk to a fan who only sees a couple of games a year. His parents have a friend in the Suns' ticket office, which explains how they were able to get such good seats—we're in the dead center near the top of the lower level.

If nothing else, I like meeting people just so I can offer them some of my valuable insight, rather than having to keep my observations to myself. For example, the Suns' Gorilla comes out and attempts to duplicate a catapult trick he had introduced during the All-Star Game, where he dunked from near the 3-point line with the help of a supercharged springboard. While the Gorilla had no trouble with the trick on Sunday, come Friday night he fails on his first two attempts, and it is only during a later break that he is finally able to complete the stunt. I turn to Vince to tell him another one of my endless theories about the sport.

"That's a bad sign," I say in a haughty, know-it-all manner. "Any time a mascot or dance team screws up a trick or routine, the home team will almost certainly lose."

Probably inspired by the mascot's difficulties, the Warriors come out looking like an NBA powerhouse, and in the third they outscore the Suns by 12 to take a convincing 96-87 lead into the fourth quarter. Suddenly, despite all the signs of a well-needed blowout, Phoenix has to make another comeback.

And damned if they don't. Unlike the Blazers, the Warriors continue their solid play right up to the final buzzer, but the Suns still close the gap, setting the stage for another dramatic finish. Latrell Sprewell hits two free throws with 16 seconds left to give the Warriors a 121-118 lead, and the crowd holds their breath as the Suns look for their shot to tie. Charles Barkley, who is having another monster game, works free for an open 3-pointer, but his shot finds the rim, and as the seconds tick down the ball bounces off of Golden State's Carlos Rogers and out of bounds. With only 3.8 seconds left, the Suns work up a play during a timeout, then come out of the huddle to see if they have another miracle left.

Barkley inbounds a pass to rookie guard Wesley Person, who quickly dribbles to his left to avoid the onrushing Sprewell, then launches a long three from well behind the arc. The crowd lets out a collective gasp as— boom!—the ball hits nothing but net.

Not surprisingly, the arena erupts in glorious cheers, a madhouse of energetic fans, and the Suns pound Person's back as they head to the bench. There is still half a second left on the clock, but the Warriors are unable to get off a decent shot, and suddenly we have overtime for the second time in three nights.

But the Warriors have come too far to collapse the way the Blazers had, and Golden State comes out playing like they are happy to have extra time on the court. The Suns and their fans, understandably confident after Person's miracle of a moment before, quickly find themselves buried under a 9-2 run to start overtime. Try as they might, Phoenix can't pull any closer than three the rest of the way, as the Warriors hit all eight shots they take in the extra period. Barkley scores a season-high 38 points and pulls down 13 rebounds before fouling out in overtime, extending his streak of early exits to four games. Final score: Warriors 139, Suns 128 in overtime.

Average 1994–95 ticket cost: $38.00 (second highest in the NBA)

Beer: $3.50 (14 oz.)

Soda: $2.00 (16 oz.—Coca-Cola products)

Hot Dog: $2.25

Parking: $5.00

Mascot: The Gorilla

Cheerleaders: Phoenix Suns Dance Team

Remote-controlled blimp: none

Other teams that play full-time in America West Arena: Arizona Rattlers (Arena Football League), Arizona Sand Sharks (Continental Indoor Soccer League)

What I'd change about America West Arena: Not much, although I wouldn't mind if they got rid of the clowns. And it would be nice if the video monitors were on the center scoreboard, rather than high above the upper level.

What I love about America West Arena: The plaza, the team shop, the layout, the team—just about everything.

Statistics from Team Marketing Report, Inc.

Fly the Friendly Arena

Founded: 1974
1993–94 Record: 53-29
Team Colors: Purple, Green, Gold

Friday, February 17–Wednesday, February 22

Since I had no place to stay in Phoenix on Friday night, the evening's excitement didn't end after the game. Instead, I left America West and hurried to my car, relieved to see that everything was still intact. Instead of my usual short trip back to a hotel room in town, I had to drive far enough to find someplace with a vacancy.

I left Phoenix just before nine that night, and after nearly a hundred miles of driving through the dark desert countryside, I reached the town of Camp Verde, the first to offer any lodging since I left Phoenix city limits. Even then, the first hotel I visited was booked, and I began to think that I was trapped in some sort of bizarre alternate dimension where there were no rooms left in the entire state of Arizona.

My nightmare finally ended on the other side of town, where I found a nice hotel with an available room. Exhausted by my full day, I decided to take a break from my travels and stay in Camp Verde until Sunday.

On Saturday I worked on the book and spent a little time relaxing outside my room. The hotel looked out on a majestic valley, and the view was made all the more scenic by a small corral on the hotel grounds. A local cowboy named Bill Jones ran a business called Blazing Trails, offering visitors scenic trips on horseback through the surrounding area. Still discouraged that I couldn't see the Suns play the Jazz on Sunday, I decided to take advantage of the opportunity and ride a horse for the first time in my life.

Just after ten on Sunday morning, we set out from the hotel toward the canyon. I was the only rider in the group of seven who had no experience, so I was glad to find that my mount was a mild-tempered horse named Shadow who seemed to know where he was going.

By the end of the ride, my affection for Shadow had grown immeasurably, mainly because I was still alive. What I thought would be a pleasant little ride had turned into something much more adventurous, as Bill led us on a journey I'll never forget. We crossed rivers, navigated steep hills, and traveled through miles of beautiful Arizona landscape. It was a cool, sunny day, and the journey through the desert was stunning.

In the end, we rode for four and a half hours, causing me some concern that I might be terribly sore for a while. Still, Bill delivered on his promise of a memorable day, and I left Camp Verde having experienced more than just a glorified pony ride.

Immediately after my adventures on horseback, I continued on my way north, this time using a more traditional means of transportation, namely my Volkswagen. After an hour on the road I passed through Flagstaff, turning on a small highway that took me toward the northern part of the state. The road went through more of the spectacular Arizona countryside on the way to Page, the last town before the Utah border. By the time I entered Page, I'd driven nearly 200 miles, and I continued on for a few more minutes until I reached the Wahweap Lodge.

The area was the single most beautiful place I would stay on either trip. Located in Glen Canyon National Recreation Area, the hotel is part of a fairly large resort, but the land around it is majestically undeveloped. My room looked out on Lake Powell, a massive body of clear, blue water that stretches for nearly 200 miles into Utah. Surrounding the lake are multi-colored sandstone cliffs that complement the water's beauty.

I stayed at the Wahweap Lodge until Tuesday morning, and then checked out and continued on my way, crossing into Utah at a quarter of one, only a few miles into a long day's drive. The small highway headed northwest for roughly fifty miles, then turned due north toward Salt Lake City. Even after leaving an area as beautiful as Lake Powell, I was still impressed by the view during that day's drive, as I spent hours crossing through the towns, valleys, and mountains in the heart of the state.

It was close to 7 PM before I arrived in Salt Lake City, having traveled a total of 415 miles on that Tuesday. Although the Jazz game I planned to see was on the following evening, I could see crowds of people moving through the city streets near the Delta Center. An exterior message board in front of the arena showed the reason: The Grateful Dead were playing a concert that night.

So that was how my journey from Phoenix to Salt Lake City ended: in a motel two blocks north of the Delta Center, surrounded by rooms full of Deadheads. And what a long, strange trip it had been.

Previous Jazz Games at the Delta Center:

1992–93 season: Cavaliers (Jazz 113-96)

In my experience, the Jazz are the best team that seem to have no fans outside their city. Despite years of success, and two of the most skilled players in the NBA, I guess the Jazz are the kind of franchise that only someone from Utah could love. Even though Karl Malone, consistently the NBA's most productive power forward, and John Stockton, the league's best distributing point guard, both play for the Jazz, fans across the country still have a hard time embracing the boys in purple, green, and gold (although the combination of those three colors may have something to do with it).

Maybe it's because Stockton shuns the spotlight, playing in an unassuming fashion, that he doesn't get the same press as some other point guards. And perhaps Malone's aggressive style gives him a reputation as a dirty player. Or maybe people are put off because the Jazz have the NBA's strangest nickname—since when is Salt Lake City a jazzy town? (Although I'm sure most fans know the history behind it: The Jazz were founded in 1974 in New Orleans, and played there for five seasons before moving to Utah in 1979. Although that explains the origin of the name, why they decided to keep it after the move remains a mystery to me.)

I can only speculate on why the Jazz seem to attract few fans, but after seeing the tandem of Stockton and Malone work together in an amazing display of synergy on the Jazz, in All-Star Games, and on the Dream Team, I have to admit that I'm a rebel—I enjoy watching the Jazz play.

Heck, the '94–95 Jazz I saw were playing so well, I began to think of myself as a full-fledged fan. Even though Felton Spencer, their starting center, had suffered a season-ending injury a month before I arrived in Salt Lake City, the Jazz still were deeper than they had been in years. And with former All-Star Jeff Hornacek added to the mix at shooting guard, a scary Jazz team had become even more frightening. Or perhaps I just liked the Jazz because I'd visited the sparkling arena where they play.

Not only is Salt Lake City a beautiful metropolis, it also provides a feeling of safety and civility often missing in the larger urban areas around the country. And in the middle of this nice city, with its nearby mountains, lakes, and other displays of natural beauty, the Jazz play basketball in an arena that is nearly as beautiful.

Built in 1991, the Delta Center is unlike any other facility in the NBA. A nearly square building with notched corners, it offers the kinds of amenities found in other modern arenas, including ample concessions, upper and lower concourses, and a capacity of close to 20,000 fans. But like some of the older buildings, such as those in Portland and Oakland, the Delta Center has huge windows throughout the building, offering an unparalleled view of the back of the stands inside.

Located in the center of downtown Salt Lake City, the Delta Center stands in the middle of a city block, constructed at an angle that runs diagonally to the streets around it. There are no parking lots on the arena grounds; the rest of the block surrounding the building contains a courtyard, complete with small trees, bushes, and several large, metal statues. Despite the lack of parking on site, there are plenty of lots in the immediate area, so driving to the arena isn't a problem.

If America West is my favorite arena, then the Delta Center is my pick as the dark horse. If nothing else, I love the view as you walk to a Jazz game, the sight of the fans moving through the two concourses beneath the huge structure of the arena's stands. Sure, it looks the most like an office building of all the NBA venues, but the design works for me.

✪ THE DELTA
CENTER
Opened: 1991
Capacity: 19,911
Salt Lake City, Utah

Wednesday, February 22, 1995—7:00 PM

UTAH JAZZ (37-15) VS. L.A. CLIPPERS (9-43)

For the second time in as many visits, I head to the ticket windows at the Delta Center only to find that I'm not on their list. During my first visit, the Jazz eventually found me a spot on their upper press row, but on this night the oversight will work to my advantage in a big way. The Clippers have come to town with only a couple of members of the L.A. media to cover them, and as a result there are plenty of empty spaces in the lower press area at courtside. A few minutes before tip-off, I find myself in the second row of seats, so close I can practically hear the players sweating during warmups.

The location is a little surprising, but I'm pleased that the Clippers' unpopularity would allow me to sit right next to the action. Not only am I at dead-center court, I'm also directly behind the p.a. announcer, as well as a woman who is controlling the music playing over the arena's sound system.

As I marvel at the location—if I were any closer, they'd have to give me a uniform—I figure that the close-up view from the courtside seat is going to offer the only real entertainment of the evening, given that the Clippers are tonight's opponent. And if the Jazz needed any extra motivation, they have spent three days being scolded in the local press. Utah blew a 7-point lead with only 2:30 left in the game I had wanted to see in Phoenix on Sunday, as the Suns scored the last 10 points to win 110-107.

Still, as tonight's matchup begins, it's almost an exact replay of the game I saw these teams play in L.A. two weeks ago. The Clippers come out playing smart basketball, executing and shooting well while building an 8-point lead by the end of the first quarter.

As the Jazz go down by as many as 13 in the second, I have a great time watching the p.a. announcer at work. Although he has a smooth, professional delivery on the microphone, his behavior off-microphone is a different story. He curses loudly every time the Jazz turn the ball over or miss a shot, using a few choice words that would get him fired if they were broadcast over the p.a. system. Even though the Jazz cut the lead to 7 by halftime, he's still not happy, fuming as the break begins.

I'm so close to the floor that the building's design rarely enters my field of vision. Still, I take a few moments to look around during breaks in the action, because the Delta Center boasts an interesting layout.

The building has an upper and lower level with luxury boxes above the lower bowl, a design much like the one found in Phoenix (although the stands have a slightly curved look that is less rectangular than America West). Yet the seats at the Delta Center are remarkable for a couple of reasons.

First, the lower level surrounds the court like no other arena. On the three sides without the scorer's table, the seats run right up the sideline, and the walkways that the players use to reach the court are so small as to be nearly invisible. Second, the slope in both the lower and upper levels is very steep, which in many locations makes the stands seem to rise above the floor, rather than away from it.

Although the extreme slope may be a little disorienting to someone familiar with other arenas, the overall effect is amazing: The Delta Center is filled with seats in every corner of the lower level, with only a minimal amount of space cleared for the court. As a result, the Jazz play right in the midst of the fans, who are packed closely around them.

In most other ways, the Delta Center's design is much more predictable. The building has a couple of spacious concourses, complete with a full array of souvenir and concession stands, as well as two large team stores. Inside, a center scoreboard has video monitors on each of its four sides, although it hangs almost directly over my head and is impossible for me to see from courtside. The rest of the arena's scoreboards and message boards, mounted in the customary positions at the base of the upper bowl, are functional if unexceptional. Overall, the Delta Center offers the kind of clean, comfortable surroundings you'd expect in one of the NBA's modern arenas.

In another eerie parallel to the game in L.A., the Jazz turn things around in the second half, taking the lead with a 12-2 run to start the third quarter. Still, the Clippers aren't ready to fold just yet, and manage to keep the score close through the rest of the period. At the end of the third, the Utah lead, which has grown to as many as 8 points, is down to 91-88, and the announcer begins his colorful off-microphone complaints once again, to my amusement. Then again, I suppose I shouldn't be surprised at such behavior from a guy who refers to Jeff Hornacek as "Horny."

In the fourth quarter, the Clippers cut the lead to one with seven and a half minutes left, but the Jazz respond with a 9-0 run. It is during that stretch that Stockton provides the first of two highlights that, for me, elevate the game from merely average to memorable.

Stockton dribbles to the top of the 3-point arc on the left side of the floor. My view is over his shoulder, and the angle from my seat gives me a pretty good approximation of his view of the court. Suddenly, Stockton whips the ball through the lane, bouncing a pass between three Clippers. There's nobody even close to the ball, and I have time to register a quick moment of confusion—why is he throwing the ball away?—before Jazz forward Adam Keefe appears out of nowhere to catch the pass in full stride and lay the ball up and in. Not only did Stockton deliver the pass from the top of the key all the way to the low post on the opposite side, but as I watched from behind him I never even caught a glimpse of Keefe before the ball arrived in his hands. It was a dramatic demonstration of Stockton's uncanny ability to find the open man and get him the ball.

The Clippers stop the run with a basket to cut the lead to 8, and on the next play Malone commits an offensive foul, which not only gives the ball back to L.A. but also puts an end to his time on the floor, as it's his sixth personal of the game. The Clips score again to make it 108-102 with 2:33 left.

The second highlight of the game is a much more typical play than the pass a few minutes ago, but it's still exciting to see from close by. Stockton again dribbles to the top left side of the arc, then dumps a bounce pass to forward Antoine Carr on the left block. Stockton's defender sags off him to double-team Carr, who passes the ball back out to his point guard. Stockton again passes into the post before getting the ball back, but this time his defender has strayed a little too far, and Stockton launches up a three. Once again, my seat offers a perfect over-the-shoulder view, and I can appreciate the beauty of his form as I watch the ball arc through the air before dropping crisply through the net. I'm even close enough to hear the snap of the cords, the sweet sound that is music to any shooter's ears.

Stockton's three with 2:12 left pushes the lead to 9 and effectively ends any hope of a comeback, as once again the Clippers have hung tough throughout the game, only to have the clock run out on their efforts to steal a win. It's the last time I'll see the league's worst team on my trip, but they've played well enough, both at home and away, that I can't complain. Final score: Jazz 118, Clippers 109.

Average 1994–95 ticket cost: $30.23 (12th highest in the NBA)

Beer: $3.00 (16 oz.)

Soda: $1.50 (16 oz.—Coca-Cola products)

Hot Dog: $1.50

Parking: $5.00

Mascot: Bear (you guessed it—a bear wearing a Jazz uniform)

Cheerleaders: Jazz Dancers

Remote-controlled blimp: yes

Other teams that play full-time in the Delta Center: Utah Grizzlies (International Hockey League)

What I'd change about the Delta Center: It would be nice if the slope in both the lower and upper levels was a little less steep.

What I love about the Delta Center: The view of the back of the stands from outside the arena, the way the seats run right up to the court, the beautiful city, and the loyal fans.

Statistics from Team Marketing Report, Inc.

Nuggies and the Big Mac

Founded: 1967
1993–94 Record: 42-40
Team Colors: Gold, Red, Blue

Thursday, February 23–Sunday, February 26

I stayed an extra day in Salt Lake City, then headed out on Friday for Denver. On my first trip, I'd driven between the two cities through the Rocky Mountains of western Colorado, but this time I decided to use a quicker (if less scenic) route and travel through Wyoming.

I'd skipped the Cowboy State on my first trip, and as I spent a couple of days driving through it I could see I hadn't missed much. After crossing into Wyoming at 1:15 PM on Friday, I drove for hours through miles of seemingly endless prairie, with only the occasional valley or cliff to liven things up. Perhaps I'd been on the road too long, but I barely noticed the landscape during most of my time traveling east on I-80.

One thing I did take note of, however, was the weather. By the time I'd reached Portland, I knew that I was having an exceptional string of meteorological good luck. After the great warm spell in the Pacific Northwest, I figured that Utah and Colorado would be the last two stops where I would face true winter weather. But Salt Lake City was experiencing near-record high temperatures, and after three beautiful days in Utah I began to wonder what was going on. On Friday night, I stopped in Rawlins, Wyoming after a day's drive of 300 miles, and tuned in the Weather

Channel, only to learn that I was in the midst of a winter heat wave of epic proportions. Heck, many of the local areas were experiencing temperatures similar to those in Orlando.

It took me a good portion of Friday and Saturday to make my way across Wyoming. I reached Cheyenne late on Saturday afternoon and turned south onto I-25, crossing the state line into Colorado soon after 3:30 PM. A hundred miles later I reached Westminster, a suburb just north of Denver, and found a hotel for the night. Friday's drive had covered 300 miles, with 235 more on Saturday, but my stay in Denver wouldn't give me much time to rest. The Nuggets–Jazz game I was going to see had an early afternoon tip-off on Sunday, and my schedule required that I continue on right after the game ended, making my stop in Denver the shortest in the Western Conference.

The flat highway and the gorgeous weather had made the trip from Salt Lake City to Denver relatively easy, and with only four more cities to go, I had begun to feel I was in the home stretch of my trip. It was an ironic indication of the vast scale of my travels that I was in Denver, almost 2,000 miles from Orlando, when I began to feel like I was almost home.

Previous Nuggets Games at McNichols Arena:

1992-93 season: Cleveland (Nuggets 97-95)

In Cleveland, people call their team the Cavs, short for Cavaliers. In Portland, they're usually the Blazers, not the Trail Blazers. It's a tradition to shorten a lengthy name for easier use in conversation. But is the name Nuggets really too long?

Apparently so. The most startling thing I learned on my visits to Colorado was that fans in Denver often refer to their team as the Nuggies. To me, the shortened nickname sounds like a bunch of cute and fuzzy creatures on a Saturday morning cartoon show.

Still, the Nuggies of '93–94 had proven to be anything but cute and fuzzy, roaring through the start of the playoffs by upsetting top-ranked Seattle, then extending the Jazz to seven games before bowing out in the second round. It was heralded as Denver's return to the ranks of the NBA's quality teams, an exciting turnaround for a club that had posted the league's worst record only three seasons before. After improving through the draft (despite picking no higher than third), making several smart deals, and hiring former player Dan Issel as head coach, Denver had rebuilt quickly with only a brief stretch as a losing team. Although most fans regarded the Nuggies as one of the more exciting young teams in the league by the end of the '93–94 season, their subsequent taste of playoff success only made the future seem brighter.

But just like the Warriors, the Nuggets found '94–95 to be a season of broken promises. First power forward LaPhonso Ellis injured his knee before opening day, almost certainly ending his year. Then came the big shocker—with the Nuggets cruising along at 18-16 in mid-January, Issel surprised everyone by resigning from the team, saying he wasn't comfortable as a head coach. Combined with Ellis's absence, some other key injuries, and several players unhappy with their roles on the team, Issel's departure led to a five-game losing streak under interim coach Gene Littles (the Nuggets–Sonics game I saw in Tacoma was the last game of the slide, ten days after Issel's resignation).

For five weeks, Littles tried his best to keep the Nuggets on track, but on February 20, the Monday before I arrived in Denver, he found himself ousted after leading the Nuggets to a dismal 3-13 record. Replacing Littles on the bench was general manager Bernie Bickerstaff, who had five years of experience coaching the Sonics. Bickerstaff's first two games as coach were home blowouts, as Denver beat the Clippers on Tuesday and the Sixers on Thursday before traveling to Tacoma to face Bernie's former team on Friday night. Even though the Nuggets lost to the Sonics 90-86, Denver's players seemed revitalized by the second coaching change, and optimistic Nuggets fans knew that a playoff berth wasn't out of reach yet, although three coaches in one season couldn't be considered an omen of good fortune.

Even if things weren't going smoothly on the court or in the front office, the Nuggets were enjoying unprecedented success in attendance. The team was founded in the American Basketball Association as the Denver

Rockets in 1967, changed their name to the Nuggets in 1974, moved into McNichols Sports Arena in 1975, and joined the NBA with three other ex-ABA teams in 1976. Despite successful seasons both in the ABA and NBA, Denver had never won a championship in either league, and as the years passed there were several stretches where the team didn't draw many fans. But the Nuggets' exciting rebirth had led to strong attendance in '93–94, as the team averaged 16,433 fans per game, second-highest in their history, and set a club record for their NBA era with 27 sellouts.

(Of course, it didn't hurt that the team introduced new uniforms that season, complete with a redesigned logo and revamped colors. I never did understand why the '92–93 Nuggets claimed seven team colors without including gold. The team wisely trimmed the list to three, a much more attractive combination of gold, red, and blue.)

Yet as well as things had gone the year before, the '94–95 Nuggets were truly capitalizing on their success, as every single game before my arrival had sold out. In fact, the Nuggets–Jazz game would be the twenty-eighth home game of the season, breaking the record for full houses set the year before. Although they probably weren't happy with the way much of the season had gone, Nuggets fans still hadn't left a ticket sitting in the box office all year.

The fans might keep coming because McNichols Sports Arena is a decent place to see a game. Located adjacent to Mile High Stadium, the huge facility where the NFL's Broncos play, McNichols has also been given a cute nickname by Denver fans: the Big Mac. Surprisingly, McDonald's has neither filed a lawsuit nor used the nickname in a major promotion, at least to the best of my knowledge.

The Big Mac is oval-shaped, although the building's curves are broken up by hard corners that notch around the arena, making the twenty-year-old facility look somewhat futuristic. Built into the side of a small hill, McNichols has a white exterior, with a top section that overhangs the bottom and is supported by several large wedges that are arranged like buttresses around the building.

The complex is near the geographical center of the city, and even though the surrounding neighborhood is relatively suburban, fans can look to the east for a spectacular view of the downtown skyline. Although I'm not a huge football fan, I would imagine that the people of Denver enjoy the opportunity to steal a glimpse at the stadium when they come to see the Nuggies play, especially since Broncos games in Mile High Stadium have a reputation as being among the most exciting in the NFL.

✪ MCNICHOLS
SPORTS ARENA
Opened: 1975
Capacity: 17,171
Denver, Colorado

Sunday, February 26, 1995—1:30 PM

DENVER NUGGETS (23-30) VS. UTAH JAZZ (38-15)

The weather is still glorious, a preview of summer in late February, and as I park in a lot near Mile High Stadium I see that several fans on their way to the arena are dressed in shorts and T-shirts in the bright afternoon sun.

Just like during the Suns–Warriors game at America West, I have all my things packed in my car for today's game, so I hide as much as I can in the trunk and grab a copy of my computer files on a floppy disc before carefully locking up. I'm not too worried—there are several police officers and parking attendants nearby, and my car should be relatively safe in the daylight of a Sunday afternoon.

I join a stream of fans and walk across the parking lot below the Big Mac at the base of the small hill. The concourse level is located in the center of the arena, and to reach it I have to walk up a long flight of exterior stairs. As I do, I pass a plaque on the side of the building that reads: "McNichols Sports Arena—Elevation 5,280." Without an altimeter, I can't tell if the sign is accurate or not, but it's certainly romantic to think that the arena is exactly a mile above sea level. If nothing else, such an elevation would make the name Mile High Stadium amazingly accurate.

There's no ticket for me at the will-call window, so I check the media entrance and find that the Nuggets have left me a press pass for the game. I didn't expect to have media credentials for a second game in a row, but I'm not terribly surprised, as Denver has always treated me exceptionally well. During my first trip, the Nuggets' media director not only left me a pair of comp seats, he also made it a point to meet me during my visit. By the time I took to the road again, the job had passed to someone else, but the new media director turned out to be just as friendly as the first, an encouraging sign that Denver has a quality front office.

My day improves even more when I learn that I have a courtside seat for the game. This time, I'm next to the center section where the official scorers are located, no longer at midcourt but even closer to the players than I had been in the Delta Center.

Don't ask me to explain why, but the interior of the Big Mac reminds me of the Spectrum in Philadelphia. Even though the two buildings look completely different from the outside, were built nearly ten years apart, and are located across the country from each other, they share enough common characteristics to make the connection in my subconscious, even if it is difficult for me to pinpoint the exact reasons. There are a couple of similarities I can see. The concourses and entrance portals in both arenas are pretty similar, and McNichols does have an oval-shaped design like the Spectrum, with an upper bowl that overhangs the lower level, and luxury boxes at the top of each of the lower sections. Both the arenas make fans feel close to the action, in part because the legroom in most of the rows is very cramped. As long as nobody's trying to get past you, however, the view from the stands in McNichols or the Spectrum is usually pretty good.

Actually, it's easier to notice the differences between Denver and Philadelphia. For one thing, McNichols has only two levels, not three like the Spectrum. Also, the Big Mac has more added amenities than most other arenas in the league, including no less than three restaurants and a bar, as well as a full team shop. And perhaps the most striking feature of the Big Mac is that it has no center hanging scoreboard, one of only two such arenas in the NBA (not including Tacoma Dome).

Even though the Big Mac has no center scoreboard, the arena does have huge video screens built on each end of the lower bowl among the seats—high-quality monitors that are used to broadcast the game and replays.

Denver's opening is typically busy, and my favorite part comes at the end of the player announcements. The Nuggets' seven-foot center Dikembe Mutombo is introduced last, and the p.a. announcer uses his full name: "Dikembe Mutombo Mpolondo Mukamba Jean Jacque Wamutombo."

Without any warning, the outcome is virtually decided in the first quarter. On top of that, it's not even a typical blowout, but a game unlike any I can remember seeing.

It starts with Utah playing a nearly flawless quarter. Executing with a harmony that suits their melodious nickname, the Jazz are perfect from the floor and the line, and with 5:42 left in the first build a 22-8 lead, forcing the Nuggets to call their third timeout in less than seven minutes of play. After the huddle, Denver guard Mahmoud Abdul-Rauf provides a brief spark by hitting a 3-pointer (when he does, the sound system offers the refrain "Rauf! There it is!" to the tune of the NBA staple "Whoop! There it is!"), but the Jazz won't quit in their quest for perfection.

With 1:29 left, Jeff Hornacek hits a driving layup to put Utah ahead 34-15, the Nuggets take their fourth timeout, the crowd boos mercilessly, and things appear to be over practically before they've begun. With ten seconds left in the quarter, Jazz forward David Benoit bricks a 3-pointer, the first shot of any kind that Utah has missed all game. The period ends with Utah shooting 12-for-13 from the floor, an incredible 92.3 percent, and 8-for-8 from the line. It's the finest quarter of basketball I've ever seen.

The Jazz actually appear mortal as the second quarter begins, going scoreless for more than four minutes while the Nuggets put together a 16-0 run to pull within three. But Mutombo has left the game, his mouth a bloody mess after a nasty collision, and Utah heats up again to build the lead back to 14 by halftime. The Jazz shoot 69 percent in the first half, and it will take a miracle for the Nuggets to climb back into this one.

Like most teams, the Nuggets have a much better record at home than on the road, but in Denver's case the altitude is rumored to be one of the contributing factors. I don't know if there is any truth behind that perception (after all, nobody talks about the fact that Salt Lake City is at almost as high an elevation as Denver), but it did lead to the creation of one of the best NBA T-shirts I would see during my travels. A fan behind me is wearing it; above the Nuggets logo, the shirt reads "Mt. Mutombo—5,287 feet."

In the third quarter, the Nuggets briefly cut the lead to eight, but the Jazz push their advantage back into double-digits, and Denver will get no closer than 10 points for the rest of the game.

There is one odd characteristic to this afternoon's match-up: After the Jazz outscored the Nuggets 34-20 in the first quarter, the two teams played dead even in each of the final three periods, both scoring 24 in the second, 23 in the third, and 29 in the fourth. If any game ever went against my theory that the first quarter is meaningless, this certainly was it.

The Nuggets–Jazz game will be the last on my trip where I sit at press row. During my travels, I've seen games at courtside press tables in San Antonio, Minnesota, Boston, Utah, and Denver, and at lower-level press rows in New York, Portland, L.A.'s Memorial Sports Arena, and Phoenix during All-Star Weekend. Although the view from press row is usually pretty good, another benefit is the vast amount of information that teams provide for members of the media.

Before every NBA game, each arena's media room has detailed notes about that night's matchup available to the journalists, as well as media guides and other publications that provide information about the home team and the league in general.

After tip-off, a team of statisticians keeps track of all the action, updating an extensive computer program that crunches all the numbers. Monitors on press row provide instantly updated game stats, and the team distributes paper copies of the play-by-play and box score soon after each quarter concludes. Not only are the reporters spoiled by such an incredible amount of information, but in many arenas they are also provided with typed quotes from players and coaches after the game, and as a result some of the less-motivated journalists can file a complete story without having to speak to anyone.

Not to mention the free food. It's discouraging that the people who get the best treatment at the games are often the ones who seem to want to be anywhere else but at the arena.

The Nuggets–Jazz game is also probably the last I'll see at McNichols. In one more similarity to the Spectrum, the Big Mac is scheduled to be replaced in a couple of seasons. A new arena known as the Pepsi Center will be built at a location near McNichols, opening in time for the '97–98 season. (Denver must be a thirsty town—their new baseball stadium is Coors Field, and soon they'll have the Pepsi Center.) I have no major complaints about McNichols, but with a renewed interest in the Nuggets sweeping through Denver, I can understand why the team decided to make a move. After the controversy surrounding Gund Arena, however, I just hope that seeing a game at the Pepsi Center doesn't make fans hungry for the Big Mac. Final score: Jazz 110, Nuggets 96.

Average 1994–95 ticket cost: $21.14 (27th highest in the NBA)

Beer: $3.00 (14 oz.)

Soda: $1.50 (16 oz.—Pepsi products)

Hot Dog: $1.75

Parking: $4.50

Mascot: Rocky (mountain lion in a warmup suit with a lightning-bolt tail)

Cheerleaders: Nuggets Performance Dance Team

Remote-controlled blimp: yes—two

Other teams that play full-time in McNichols Sports Arena: The Quebec Nordiques of the NHL move to McNichols in the fall of '95 to become the Colorado Avalanche.

What I'd change about McNichols Sports Arena: Increase the leg room.

What I love about McNichols Sports Arena: The altitude plaque, the replay screens built behind the lower-bowl seats, the prices, and the way the Nuggets have treated me during my travels.

Statistics from Team Marketing Report, Inc.

6
Texas
February 27–March 7, 1995

NBA standings as of Monday, February 27, 1995:

EASTERN CONFERENCE
Atlantic Division

	W	L	Pct	GB	Home	Away
Orlando Magic	42	13	.764	—	27-1	15-12
New York Knicks	35	18	.660	6	20-7	15-11
Boston Celtics	22	31	.415	19	13-14	9-17
New Jersey Nets	22	34	.393	20.5	15-12	7-22
Miami Heat	20	33	.377	21	14-12	6-21
Philadelphia 76ers	15	40	.273	27	8-18	7-22
Washington Bullets	13	40	.245	28	7-19	6-21

Central Division

	W	L	Pct	GB	Home	Away
Cleveland Cavaliers	33	20	.623	—	17-10	16-10
Indiana Pacers	33	20	.623	—	20-5	13-15
Charlotte Hornets	34	21	.618	—	21-7	13-14
Atlanta Hawks	26	28	.481	7.5	14-14	12-14
Chicago Bulls	26	29	.473	8	15-11	11-18
Milwaukee Bucks	21	33	.389	12.5	12-14	9-19
Detroit Pistons	19	34	.358	14	15-12	4-22

WESTERN CONFERENCE
Midwest Division

	W	L	Pct	GB	Home	Away
Utah Jazz	39	16	.709	—	22-7	17-9
San Antonio Spurs	36	16	.692	1.5	19-6	16-10
Houston Rockets	34	19	.642	4	18-8	16-11
Denver Nuggets	23	31	.426	15.5	15-13	8-18
Dallas Mavericks	20	32	.385	17.5	11-17	9-15
Minnesota Timberwolves	14	40	.259	24.5	8-19	6-21

Pacific Division

	W	L	Pct	GB	Home	Away
Phoenix Suns	42	13	.764	—	24-5	18-8
Seattle SuperSonics	37	15	.712	3.5	22-5	15-10
L.A. Lakers	34	18	.654	6.5	18-6	16-10
Portland Trail Blazers	29	23	.558	11.5	18-9	11-14
Sacramento Kings	28	24	.538	12.5	20-7	8-17
Golden State Warriors	16	37	.302	25	10-15	6-21
L.A. Clippers	10	45	.182	32	7-19	3-26

Weathering the Storm

Founded: 1980
1993–94 Record: 13-69
Team Colors: Blue, Green

Sunday, February 26–Thursday, March 2

Less than a half-hour after the Nuggets–Jazz game ended on Sunday, I got back in my car and began the long trip to Dallas. Nearly 800 miles separates McNichols and Reunion Arena, and I wanted to reach "Big D" by Tuesday night so I could see the Mavericks host the Rockets.

I listened to the Nuggets' postgame radio show as I made my way east out of Denver on I-70, and after twenty minutes I left the city limits and started across the rural Colorado countryside. The sun began to set behind me, and I found myself growing weary of driving as darkness fell on the road ahead.

After only a hundred miles, I quit for the evening in Limon, a small town that stood at the crossroads of several highways, and settled into a motel for the night. That evening, I studied my maps and debated between the different routes I could take to Dallas, all the while trying not to think about the long miles that still lay ahead.

By Monday morning, I had decided to head down highway 287, a relatively small two-lane road that cut through the southeastern part of Colorado. It took me most of the morning and the early afternoon to travel through the rest of the state, finally reaching the Oklahoma border at 2:45 PM. A short 45 minutes later I entered Texas and continued south toward Amarillo, following the highway as it turned southeast.

It was well into the evening by the time I reached the town of Childress, where I found a motel after covering 450 miles on the road that day. As I unpacked my gear, the Texas night was cold and windy, and what had started for me as a pleasantly warm day in central Colorado had ended in a nasty evening.

Tuesday wasn't much better, as the skies of north Texas were overcast and chilly. Although the game I was rushing to see was scheduled for that night, I still had more than four hours left on the road before I reached Dallas, so I sucked it up and settled in for some more time on the rustic highway.

Late that afternoon, I turned onto I-35E north of Dallas and followed the major highway south into the city. The day's drive was 260 miles, and both the journey from Denver and the lengthy duration of my trip were weighing heavily on me. A drizzling downpour in the Dallas area didn't help my mood either, so I decided to blow a little extra money from my book advance and stay at the Hyatt Regency, a massive hotel across the street from the arena. The room would cost a little more, but I could use a few days in a nicer place than the hotels where I'd been staying.

I checked in only a couple of hours before tip-off, and tried to rest up as much as I could during the short break. Before I reached my room, however, I had an unexpected NBA encounter in the hotel lobby—the Rockets were checking out after staying at the Hyatt, and as I made my way to the elevators Clyde Drexler walked by.

> **Previous Mavericks Games at Reunion Arena:**
>
> **1992–93 season:** Denver (Nuggets 110-94)

The Mavericks were in their fifteenth season during my second trip, and in their relatively brief history they had experienced both ends of the NBA spectrum.

An expansion team in 1980–81, the Mavs won the Midwest Division in their seventh season, and the following year came within a game of making it to the 1988 NBA Finals. As the 1990s began, the Mavericks' front office made some moves to try to improve their team, and most NBA fans thought that Dallas would be a contender for the title over the next few seasons.

Instead, the Mavericks crumbled like a house of cards, a collapse caused by an improbable mix of serious injuries, poor draft picks, a prolonged holdout, and the suspension of a key player for substance abuse. I don't have the space to detail all the reasons here, but if you want to have nightmares about how quickly your favorite team could collapse, do a little reading about what happened to the Mavericks.

The '92–93 Mavericks flirted all season with breaking the record for fewest victories in league history, eventually winning a couple of late games to finish at 11-71, barely topping the '72–73 Sixers, who posted a 9-73 record. Still, the difference was, the Sixers won 30 games the year before their record-breaking season and 25 the year after. The Mavs managed to win only two more games in '93–94, despite signing Jim Jackson, their 1992 draft pick who had held out for almost the entire previous season, and adding Jamal Mashburn, one of the most explosive scorers in the 1993 draft. For the fourth straight year, the once-promising Mavericks had won less than thirty games, a cruel streak for a team that so recently seemed primed to go all the way.

But the '94–95 Mavericks had climbed out of the basement, building a young nucleus of talent that had led the team back to the ranks of the respectable. Although Jackson and Mashburn were developing well, the crucial addition might have been the third "J": Jason Kidd, the Mavs' selection with the second pick of the 1994 draft, had demonstrated the most talent of any point guard coming out of the college ranks in years. Dallas was 11-17 at home on the day I arrived, and if nothing else, the typical experience of seeing a Mavericks game at Reunion Arena had gone from being painful to promising.

Actually, I'd be a Mavericks fan no matter how well they were playing. In April 1992, only a week after I sent my initial group of letters requesting tickets for the first trip, I received a large envelope from Dallas's director of media services, my first response ever from an NBA team. Not only did he promise to leave me a comp ticket during my visit the following season, he also sent me copies of the two most recent issues of the Mavericks' fan magazine.

Leafing through the publications only a week after I started my preparations, I realized that my adventure truly had begun, and that I would always appreciate the Mavericks for their thoughtfulness. A cynic might suggest that the Mavs were only being gracious because they had begun their downward spiral, but I've certainly learned that the quality of a team's play often has little effect on the temperament of their front office. Besides, the offer of a free seat during the '92–93 season might not have been a big deal, but the Mavericks still took good care of me for two games in '94–95, when tickets were much more valuable.

The lone expansion team of the early 1980s, the Mavericks moved into a brand-new arena when they began play during the '80–81 season. Reunion Arena stands in the southwest part of downtown Dallas, a square building made of tan brick. The plain walls are dwarfed by a huge overhang, which juts out over the arena on all four sides and is supported by pillars at each of the rounded corners. While the walls have no windows, the overhang is made of glass and steel beams, allowing fans outside to see into the arena's roofing structure.

The two main entrances, which offer a slight glimpse into the concourse area, are built into the southeast and northwest corners. It's an odd design, as the windows at the top of the arena don't give fans much of a view into the building, and I have to admit that Reunion's exterior leaves me unimpressed. Still, the grounds around the arena are nicely decorated with greenery (although a major highway does pass by the arena a short distance to the west), and the building is close enough to the downtown area to offer a nice view of the Dallas skyline. With a decent amount of parking spaces and a location close to the heart of the city, I guess I can forgive a disappointing exterior design. Besides, you watch games inside the building, not from the parking lot.

Tuesday, February 28, 1995—7:30 P.M.

DALLAS MAVERICKS (20-32) VS. HOUSTON ROCKETS (35-19)

Darkness has fallen in the short time since I arrived in Dallas, and gusts of wind rip across the city as I make the quick walk from the Hyatt to the

✪ REUNION ARENA
Opened: 1980
Capacity: 17,502
Dallas, Texas

arena. Although I feel a little more rested, the night is still cold and damp, and the weather conditions are the type I'd expected in Utah or Colorado, not Texas.

Still, the miserable storm doesn't dampen my spirits too much, as the Mavericks–Rockets game promises to be a little more interesting than the average NBA regular-season matchup. For one thing, Dallas guard Scott Brooks, who was traded from the Rockets only five days ago, is set to make his home debut in a Mavericks uniform. For another, Dallas forward Roy Tarpley, back on the team after a two-year suspension for alleged substance abuse, is scheduled to return to action after missing 20 games over the last six weeks due to various injuries. And finally, Rockets guard Vernon Maxwell will play his first game following a 10-game suspension for going into the stands in Portland to take a swing at a fan.

To me, however, the most attractive thing about tonight's game is that it will be a Texas showdown between two local rivals. And even though the Mavs will be missing one of their "J"s (guard Jim Jackson suffered an ankle injury four nights ago in New Jersey and will probably sit out the rest of the season), Houston is without three of their regular forwards: Robert Horry and Carl Herrera are injured, and Otis Thorpe was traded to the Blazers two weeks ago for Clyde Drexler.

On paper, at least, it looks like a good matchup, and I'm glad that I busted my butt to get to Dallas in time to see it.

Although the outside is a disappointment, once I'm inside the main entrance I begin to enjoy Reunion Arena. Decorated in the Mavericks' colors of blue and green, the concourse includes plenty of concession stands, information booths, and a nice team shop. The walkway itself is rather narrow, and during sold-out games there are frequent traffic jams outside the stands, but in every other way Reunion offers decent facilities on the concourse area.

The Mavs have left me a single seat in the lower bowl, more on the end than I would prefer but at a level that gives me an acceptable view of the action. In another indication of the Mavericks' rebirth, the stands are full by the opening announcements, and I'm pleased to get the chance to be part of a packed house at Reunion Arena.

The Mavericks are one of only two teams that chose not to perform the national anthem before each game, offering "God Bless America" instead. (The Heat perform "America the Beautiful.") The rest of the opening involves the customary hoopla during the player introductions, including spotlights, video clips, and thundering music, in this case a selection from the "Phantom of the Opera" score.

The Mavs struggle in the first quarter, much to the delight of the numerous Rockets fans in attendance. With just under two minutes left in the period, Houston leads 31-21, and I begin to worry that the Mavs might not be able to make as strong a showing as I'd hoped.

But Dallas ends the period with a 5-0 run, then plays evenly with the Rockets in the second, cutting the lead to 4 points at halftime. The biggest scare comes just before the break, when Kidd aggravates his sprained right ankle and has to be helped off the court, but at least the Mavericks are still in the game.

After sitting among the members of the media in Utah and Denver, I was hoping to spend a little time chatting with an average fan, but the people around me are involved in their own conversations, so I spend my time concentrating on the game and checking out the arena.

The stands are laid out in a basic oval arrangement, with the upper bowl overhanging the lower. The walls behind the stands are white, marked with large numbers to designate the different sections. Sizable groups of folding chairs run right up to the court on three sides, with a wide aisle between the floor sections and the permanent seats in the lower bowl.

During my first visit, most of Reunion's seats were the Mavericks' shade of green, interspersed with several blue rows running around both the lower and upper bowls. Since that time, however, the seats have been reupholstered in a darker shade of green to match one of the team colors of Reunion's newest tenant, the NHL's Dallas Stars. As much as I can understand the desire to honor the new team in town, I'm disappointed at the change, because Reunion had been one of the few NBA arenas that had been entirely decorated in the team's colors.

Hanging over the court is a four-sided scoreboard, complete with video screens and player boards. In addition to the usual message boards and scoreboards mounted to the base of the upper bowl, two opposite corners above the upper bowl each have a "hustle board" that shows total rebounds, blocks and steals, which the Mavericks have appropriately designated the "Big 'D' Board."

Most noticeably missing are any luxury boxes, a fact that has become increasingly significant in recent seasons. Even though Reunion is a great place to see a game, with good sightlines and no obstructed views, the absence of the revenue-generating suites has become a source of concern for Mavericks' ownership, and negotiations have begun for the team to move to a new arena. With no practical way to add luxury boxes to the existing building, Reunion's days as the home of the Mavericks are numbered.

In all likelihood, the new arena will be built outside of the city, as the team's management is considering several suburban locations as potential sites. As much as I appreciate their desire to move to a more modern building, it's unfortunate that such a nice arena has to be replaced, especially if the change involves moving to an isolated area far from downtown.

The game tightens up in the third quarter, as Kidd returns to the court and the Mavs manage to tie the score. Tarpley is playing well, Maxwell is being relatively quiet, but the most interesting element in the game is Brooks: The diminutive guard is making the most of his Dallas debut by diving for loose balls, distributing effectively, and hitting his jumpers. The third quarter ends with the score tied at 80, and the crowd is charged with excitement, caught up in the action of a terrific game.

Although the Mavs have a small dance team, no mascot, and no remote-controlled blimp, the team still offers their own brand of extras. Taking advantage of an impressive video system, Reunion features an amazing variety of video clips, to the point where a Mavericks game sometimes has the feel of a night at the movies. After forward Popeye Jones scores, for example, the screens show a clip of the cartoon Popeye playing basketball. In addition, during every game there is "Players on Film," a taped segment where two Mavericks spend a few minutes discussing one of their favorite movies—on this night, their choice is *Animal House*. It's not a bad way to liven up the game, as the extensive video clips provide unobtrusive entertainment that can easily be ignored if it's not to your liking.

On this night, however, the extras are unnecessary. The game itself is all the entertainment any fan could want.

The Mavericks play Kidd and Brooks together for much of the fourth quarter, and Dallas is able to build a five-point lead with nine minutes left. Still, the Rockets battle back, and for the rest of the quarter the lead changes back and forth, with neither team able to pull away.

The lead has changed hands eleven times by the final minute of play, and as the clock ticks down the Mavs trail by two. With 30 seconds left, Mashburn spins free and puts up a driving shot from 10 feet. Up to this point, he's made some clutch baskets, but the shot bounces off the rim toward the weak side. Popeye Jones is in good position for the rebound, and as Rockets forward Chucky Brown grabs his left arm, Jones reaches up with his right and taps the ball in before tumbling to the floor. The play happens at the basket in front of me, and I get a great view as the crowd erupts and the refs whistle Brown for the obvious foul. With 23.9

seconds left, Jones calmly buries the free throw, and the Rockets call a timeout, suddenly down by one.

After the huddle, Houston brings the ball the length of the court, and work around the perimeter to find a decent shot to win the game. As the clock winds down, Jones manages to knock away a pass intended for Hakeem Olajuwon in the low post, and the ball rolls into the backcourt.

As the crowd noise grows to a deafening level, Drexler tracks down the ball and passes to guard Sam Cassell with six seconds left. Cassell swings the ball to Olajuwon, who has worked free of his defender and is alone at the foul line. The crowd gasps, Olajuwon takes the open 14-footer with two seconds left, and the ball arcs through the air and rebounds off the back iron. The buzzer sounds, and the crowd erupts in a glorious out-pouring of cheers that one reporter will later claim is the loudest noise level heard at Reunion Arena in the past two seasons. Of all the positive steps that the Mavericks have taken this year, perhaps Olajuwon's unlikely miss at the buzzer is the best indication that Dallas has truly weathered the storm, with only brighter days on the horizon. Final score: Mavericks 102, Rockets 101.

It continues to rain on Wednesday, a wet, nasty afternoon that I watch from my seventeenth-floor window at the Hyatt Regency. After twelve weeks with only an occasionally pleasant view, the panorama of down-town Dallas is a nice change, but the weather certainly isn't helping.

The matchup on Thursday does little to improve my dreary outlook, especially since the Mavericks will face the Cavaliers, who are still playing some of the most meticulous, deliberately paced basketball seen in years.

At least I am going to the game with somebody. The third and final person I will meet from the pro basketball group on the Internet is Patricia, following in the footsteps of Jim in Washington and Ted in Seattle. Among the people who frequent the group, Patricia is legendary for her incredibly detailed and informative messages about the NBA, many of which focus on the Mavericks. Although she works with com-puters in Austin, Patricia grew up in Dallas, and since she frequently vis-its her parents in the area, she took me up on my offer to see the game.

Patricia likes to go early to watch the players warm up, and so we enter the arena about an hour before tip-off. The Mavs have left us a pair of tickets on one end of the lower bowl, and they are closer to the floor and have a better angle to the action than my seat on Tuesday. As Patricia and I spend the time before the game talking about basketball, she keeps a close eye on Jamal Mashburn, who is moving gingerly up and down the court to see if he will be able to play.

Mashburn's injury is literally a pain in the butt. He has been battling a case of the flu, and after talking a penicillin shot in his right buttock, he has found it difficult to flex the muscle. By game time, it is clear that he can't run, and Dallas is missing its two top scorers.

Still, the Cavs aren't exactly healthy either, as both Mark Price and Tyrone Hill are sidelined. With both teams shorthanded, the Mavs seem to be getting the best of things through the early going, and at halftime Dallas leads 49-41. I am thankful to have someone to talk to, because the game isn't nearly as interesting as Tuesday's. It is apparent from the attendance: Reunion is only about two-thirds full.

I had thought that I might be intensely involved in the game, because Dallas was the last of the six cities where I had not seen the home team win during the first trip, but after the Mavs' victory over the Rockets that was no longer an issue. Still, soon after halftime Patricia returns from the concourse level with a first-half box score, and we realize that there is at least one noteworthy development: The Cavs had committed only one turnover in the entire first half. (The fact that the Mavericks provide copies of the box score to any fans who want them only increases my appreciation for the team.) So if nothing else, I am curious to see if the Cavs can break the NBA record for fewest turnovers in a game.

The Mavericks' lead is down to four at the end of the third quarter, and the Cavs still have only one turnover charged against them. Unfortunately for Mavs fans, Cleveland goes on a 14-3 run to take the lead with 4:25 left, and unfortunately for me, they commit three turnovers during that stretch.

Jason Kidd takes control in the final minutes, tying the score at 76 with a pair of free throws, then posting a 3-point play to give the Mavericks a lead they won't lose. In the last three and a half minutes, Kidd has five points, two assists, and a rebound, and Dallas manages to survive with only one of their three young stars healthy.

Cleveland ends the game with four turnovers, one more than the league record, so Patricia and I are denied the chance to witness NBA history. If the Cavs had shot better than 35.6 percent, their impressive protection of the ball might receive more recognition, but Cleveland's grind-it-out style of play has most fans paying little attention. Final score: Mavericks 90, Cavaliers 84.

Average 1994–95 ticket cost: $25.16 (21st highest in the NBA)

Beer: $3.00 (14 oz.)

Soda: $1.50 (14 oz.—Coca-Cola products)

Hot Dog: $1.75

Parking: $5.00

Mascot: none

Cheerleaders: Dallas Mavericks Dancers

Remote-controlled blimp: none

Other teams that play full-time in Reunion Arena: Dallas Stars (National Hockey League), Dallas Sidekicks (Continental Indoor Soccer League)

What I'd change about Reunion Arena: I'm not a big fan of the exterior design, and the concourse could be a little wider.

What I love about Reunion Arena: The interior design, the mix of video and graphics, and the team's gracious front office, the first to reply.

Statistics from Team Marketing Report, Inc.

Remember the Alamodome

Founded: 1967
1993–94 Record: 55-27
Team Colors: Metallic Silver, Black
Secondary Colors: Teal, Fuchsia, Orange

Friday, March 3–Sunday, March 5

The rain was still falling on Friday morning, and it was with tremendous relief that I packed my car and got out of town. With all the gray skies, I was beginning to think that Dallas had somehow been magically transported to the Pacific Northwest.

It would take me nearly five hours to reach San Antonio, located about 280 miles southwest of Dallas on I-35. There was no tricky navigation required, but the drive would still be a long one, made somewhat urgent because the Magic were going to play the Spurs at the Alamodome that night.

Although the day remained overcast throughout my journey, the precipitation stopped an hour after I left Dallas, and I reached San Antonio safely just after 5 PM. I checked into a budget hotel on the north side of town, but once I unpacked my gear I had less than an hour to rest before heading out to the arena. After the various uncertain moments I'd faced on my trip—no ticket for the Kings–Bulls game, no assigned seat at All-Star Weekend, and no hotel room in Phoenix—I had one final challenge left: I didn't have a ticket for the game that night. I knew that I wouldn't be able to relax until I solved that problem, so I grabbed a handful of cash and headed out the door almost an hour and a half before the 7:30 PM tip-off.

San Antonio, a proud Texas city most famous for the historic Alamo mission, is the center of a thriving metropolitan area, but still ranks far

Previous Spurs Games at the HemisFair Arena:

1992-93 season: Denver (Spurs 121-110)

Previous Spurs Games at the Alamodome:

1993-94 season: Minnesota (Spurs 101-89)/Denver
(Nuggets 83-78)

behind Dallas and Houston in overall population. Yet if their new NBA building is any indication, the people of Texas's third-largest city must be aching to do whatever is necessary to try to catch up, at least in terms of sports facilities. San Antonio didn't just build an arena, they raised a behemoth.

The Spurs were founded in 1967 as the Dallas Chaparrals of the ABA, playing there for six seasons before moving to San Antonio and adopting a new team name in 1973. The ABA lasted three more seasons, and when the league folded in 1976 the Spurs joined the NBA along with fellow refugees New Jersey, Indiana, and Denver.

From their arrival in 1973 through the end of the '92–93 season, the Spurs made their home in the HemisFair Arena, a 16,000-seat building that had opened in the downtown area in 1968. HemisFair was a small arena with an unusual design that offered a wide variety of views of the court from different seat locations. But there was one problem: Too many of those views were obstructed, as the arena had been renovated several times to increase capacity, with the unfortunate result that some people found themselves sitting behind support columns. Even though HemisFair was a loud building with an intimate feel, with so many unacceptable seats the team decided it was time for a change.

It was no surprise that the Spurs wanted to move to an arena with a capacity of more than 20,000 fans. What was a little unusual, however, was that their new building would be able to hold more than three times that many.

Even though San Antonio has no other major teams, the civic leaders decided to build a giant facility that would be heralded as the "third generation of domed stadiums." While many NBA teams share their buildings with hockey teams, the Spurs would play in a venue that could not only host hockey but football games as well. Strange as the idea may have sounded, whoever came up with it got his or her wish, and in the fall of 1993 the Spurs moved into the brand-new Alamodome.

Located less than a mile from both the real Alamo and the HemisFair Arena, the Alamodome stands next to one of the downtown highways, a massive structure that seems like it would dwarf even the United Center. The tan and white stadium is rectangular, decorated with brown stripes around large bay windows that extend out from all four sides. In each corner is a sizable curved section that only extends about halfway up the structure, giving the building a notched look.

But the most striking element of the Alamodome's design is the pillars that rise more than 300 feet above the four corners, each connected to huge yellow cables that run down to support the roof. The towers, which were built to eliminate the need for interior columns, resemble a quartet of ship's masts, and whenever I visit the Alamodome I always get an image of the building raising sail and floating away.

The $186 million facility has configurations for almost any kind of event, ranging from a 5,000-seat layout for conventions all the way up to a full capacity of 65,000 for football games. The Spurs' '92–93 media guide gave a glimpse of the city's aspirations, subtly mentioning that the building's capacity could "expand to 72,000 seats for events like a Super Bowl game." Not to hint or anything.

Perhaps the strangest thing of all about the move was that the HemisFair Arena was a domed building, while the Alamodome is not. Despite its misleading name, the new facility has a flat roof that gently slopes toward the center, which could hardly be mistaken for a dome.

The Spurs' move came at a good time. Ever since center David Robinson's arrival in 1989, the team has been exciting to watch and competitive on the court. The people of San Antonio love their club, which isn't surprising when you consider that the Spurs are the only big-league game in town. As might be expected, the NBA cities with no other teams have some of the most devoted crowds in the league.

✪ THE ALAMODOME
Opened: 1993
Capacity: 20,662/34,402
San Antonio, Texas

Friday, March 3, 1995—7:30 PM

SAN ANTONIO SPURS (37-16) VS. ORLANDO MAGIC (44-13)

The light is fading in the overcast sky as I park at a bank lot in downtown San Antonio. Even with its huge capacity, the Alamodome has no on-site parking spaces available to the general public, but fans can leave their cars at several nearby garages or use public transportation to get to the game.

The stadium is located across the highway from the downtown area, but a wide walkway runs under the road to provide easy access on foot. The scalpers have taken up positions along the sidewalk, and I spend a few minutes gauging the market for tickets.

I have one big advantage: The Alamodome usually holds nearly 21,000 fans, but for important games the Spurs open the upper-level stands to increase the capacity to nearly 35,000 people. Although Orlando's only appearance at the Alamodome is probably the city's biggest regular-season game all year, with so many tickets available I figure that I can afford to be a little picky in finding a seat.

The first three scalpers I approach don't have any good seats and ask for huge markups on the ones they do. The fourth, however, has a $45 ticket in the lower level, and after a few minutes of dealing I agree to pay $75 for it. Although the seat is near the top of one of the corner sections, I figure it's a fair deal, and that the markup is acceptable considering how few good seats seem to be available from the scalpers.

Given the demand for tickets to tonight's game, it was no surprise that the Spurs had turned down my request for a seat, but during my travels they have provided me with media credentials for two games and pairs of comps for two others. In fact, after dealing with San Antonio's front office on three separate occasions, I've learned that the Spurs' director of media services is among the most courteous and professional in the league.

Although the Spurs were still playing in the HemisFair Arena during my first trip in January 1993, I had traveled to San Antonio in April 1994 to see two games in the NBA's only new arena that season. As a result of that earlier visit, I find the sight of the Alamodome quite familiar as I make my way under the highway.

The walkway leads to a courtyard on the north side of the stadium, and there I weave through an impressive crowd of people to reach the main entrance. Once inside, the concourse is spacious if unspectacular, with numerous concession and souvenir stands built against the gray concrete walls. It's only a short walk to my section, where I get the chance to see my seat for the evening.

Since the Spurs are the Alamodome's primary tenant, the stadium has a special configuration for hosting NBA games, utilizing an elaborate system to mask the building's unused space. The court is located on the north side of the Alamodome, adjacent to the permanent seats on three sides, but occupying less than half of the stadium floor. On the fourth side, near where the 50-yard line would be found on the football field, the Spurs hang a huge blue curtain, which closes off the empty southern half of the building. Extending the width of the stadium and rising more than 90 feet, the curtain not only creates a temporary wall, but is also used to hang a group of banners, both the ones that commemorate the Spurs' NBA division titles and a special pair of portraits honoring George Gervin and James Silas, the only two players in team history to have their numbers retired. The 50-foot-high banners depict Gervin and Silas in action with the team, and the gargantuan cloth images hover over the court as a constant reminder of years past.

Since the main cameras are located on that side of the court, the curtain doesn't appear on television very frequently, but the blue wall is hard to ignore at a Spurs game, unless you're sitting in the bleachers that are set up in front of it.

In the normal configuration of 20,662 seats, the Alamodome's upper level is closed, and fans must sit in the lower stands that stretch far back from the floor on every side but the south. Unlike most cheap seats in the NBA, the Alamodome's lowest price is for locations not very far above the court, but instead a sizable distance behind the baselines.

Above the main stands is a club level, which includes luxury suites and more than 3,500 seats. Although people sitting in that area get such added amenities as extra legroom, waitress service, and a private concourse, the seats are somewhat far from the court, and as a result the club-level tickets aren't much more expensive than the regular seats. There is one other benefit to sitting in the club level: Although the Alamodome has two restaurants, access to them is limited to those people who rent luxury boxes or buy club seats.

On the other end of the scale, the Spurs have the capacity to offer a tremendous number of cheap seats when a particular game generates enough interest. There are huge upper sections located above the club level, and in the basketball configuration the top level is opened at discount prices. With the notched corners separating them, there are three distinct locations: a middle section at $8 per seat, and two end sections at $5 a ticket. With approximately 15,000 seats in the upper level, Spurs games can be cheap entertainment for an awful lot of fans, but the ticket prices give an indication of the quality of the view—the stands were built for football, after all.

On the nights with lower capacity, the upper level is masked by a series of thirty-six blue banners, which hang from the catwalks down to the top of the club level, hiding the huge empty space of the vacant upper stands. The 90-by-15-foot banners have slight gaps between them, which give fans a glimpse of the upper level, but they effectively keep the stadium from dwarfing the basketball crowd that occupies only a third of its permanent seats. With all the banners in place, the Alamodome does a fair imitation of an NBA arena, only giving slight clues that it's really a vast multipurpose facility.

Still, once I reach my seat I decide that I'm not a big fan of the Alamodome. The location is right where I thought it would be, about three-quarters of the way up the lower level but between the baskets, and as soon as I sit down I'm disappointed—the court is just too far away. The slope contributes to the problem: With so many seats on one level, the incline from the court is too shallow. I will luck out tonight, however, as the seat in front of me will remain empty during the game, and for that reason I won't have my view partially blocked by a head in front of me.

My only real solace is that I'm part of the NBA's biggest crowd—the upper level was closed during my two previous visits, but tonight every seat is filled, and the sight and sound of more than 35,000 fans at a basketball game is undeniably exciting. But with the middle section of the upper level above and behind me, it's hard for me to appreciate the enormity of the crowd.

By tip-off I'm already friendly with everyone around me, an indication of how warm I've found the people of San Antonio to be. To my right are Royce and Beverly, a married couple I guess to be in their fifties. I also get to know Pam and Meaghan on my left, a mother and her preteen daughter from Hallettsville, about a hundred miles east of San Antonio. Even a group of young men in front of us get into the act, and from all three sides I find myself answering questions about my trip and talking about the game. Probably the most surprising thing is that everyone stays just as friendly, even after they find out I'm from Orlando.

Gracious fans aside, I'm terribly nervous at tip-off. Even though the Magic are a game ahead of Phoenix for the best record in the NBA, with a virtual lock on the top playoff spot in the Eastern Conference, the prospect of seeing the team play in person again is just too nerve-racking—remember the 32-point loss in Chicago?

After a relatively tame opening routine, the game begins far differently than the nightmare at the United Center on January 10th. The Magic begin scoring early, stylish in their new blue uniforms that they alternate with their regular black road jerseys, and at the end of an exciting first quarter the Spurs lead 30-29. With the prospect of a start-to-finish blowout eliminated, I can relax a little, but in the second quarter the Spurs begin to open up their lead, running the break and taking advantage of Orlando misses. By halftime, my hometown boys are down by 10, but they are playing well enough to give me hope for a comeback.

Not only is the game a matchup between two of the league's best teams, it also comes at an interesting time: The Magic have been on a tear this week, beating the Knicks at home on Tuesday before flying to Houston and topping the Rockets last night, giving Shaquille O'Neal two quick victories over rival centers Patrick Ewing and Hakeem Olajuwon. But in this final game of three in a row against superstar centers, Shaq is facing David Robinson and a San Antonio team that has won six games in a row. The Magic have never beaten the Spurs during Shaquille's time with the team, and as far as I can tell the two star centers really don't like each other. Even as harmony reigns in the stands between the Spurs fans and me, the war on the court seems to be a little bit personal between the two big men.

The Magic fail to make any sort of dramatic run in the third quarter, and the Spurs widen their lead to 97-83 by the end of the period. The score wouldn't bother me so much, except that a major factor in San Antonio's success is Dennis Rodman, who is having his usual monster game on the boards. I respect Rodman as a player, and I know that most of those nice Spurs fans like him, but in the last few years his behavior has begun to get on my nerves. Tonight he's got his hair dyed a light tan shade that he describes as "camel," accented by a Band-Aid across his nose. Rodman may pull down a ton of rebounds, but I still have to wonder if his recent antics might be hurting the Spurs.

As the lead widens, I take note of some design details. Despite the curtain and the unique seating layout of the Alamodome, the displays are pretty traditional, including a four-sided center hanging scoreboard that provides both video screens and detailed player boards that list assists and rebounds in addition to points and fouls. The sound system and graphics are solid, and my impression is that the Spurs have done a competent job of incorporating the displays found in a typical NBA arena.

After talking freely with Royce, Beverly, Pam, and Meaghan throughout the game, our conversations become less and less frequent in the fourth quarter, and with good reason. With 8:06 left, the Spurs' lead is 105-90, and everybody thinks the rest of the game will be garbage time.

Everybody except Shaq. Led by O'Neal's 12 points, the Magic go on a tear, and despite several desperate timeouts the Spurs can't do anything to stop the boys in blue. Minute by minute, the lead shrinks and the fans get more and more quiet, until Horace Grant finishes a 21-4 Magic run by tipping in a Shaq miss to give the Magic a 111-109 lead with 29.8 seconds left. San Antonio calls another timeout, and suddenly the Spurs fans around me are silent as I sit stoically and enjoy the remarkable turnaround. I'm concerned that my new friends might be a little less hospitable if their team loses, but I'm pretty sure I could live with that if it meant a Magic victory.

Out of the huddle, the Spurs work the ball to Robinson, who is fouled after only a couple of seconds tick off the clock. The Admiral makes the first but misses the second (who says only Shaq misses free throws?), but I'm heartbroken as the Spurs manage to tip the rebound and regain control.

Robinson gets the ball again, but the Magic collapse on him, and he's forced to pass out. As the shot clock and game clock both wind down to under ten seconds, San Antonio can't find even a remotely good shot, and suddenly the ball is in Doc Rivers' hands beyond the 3-point line. He's got no choice, so Rivers sends up a terrible shot, and as it arcs toward the basket I realize that the Magic will have a one-point victory as soon as it rebounds off the rim.

Sure enough, the shot misses, but there is no rim involved—the ball drops down without touching the iron, and who is there to collect the airball? None other than Rodman, who snatches the shot and lays it up and in. The crowd roars its approval, and I feel sick as I look up at the clock: 3.7 seconds left.

After another timeout, Anfernee Hardaway's 19-footer at the buzzer is off, and the game ends in a San Antonio victory. The game has lived up to the hype, and suddenly everyone around me is as friendly as before, but I'm still steamed—if Rivers' shot hits the rim, either the Magic get the rebound or the clock runs out before any of the Spurs can put the ball back up. Instead, the horrible shot became a perfect pass, and the Magic's impressive comeback and solid defensive stand are wasted.

Apparently, I'm not the only one a little angry. To the delight of the fans who remain in the building, Rodman comes onto the court to do the postgame radio interview, and Royce tells me I'm lucky, as the Worm rarely takes part in the ritual. Funny—I don't feel very lucky.

Rodman is mad as well, but for a different reason. "We should've won this game by 25 points," he says. "It just pisses me off."

I click my tongue as the crowd cheers, in love with their bad boy, but the Worm isn't done yet. Asked for his outlook on the season, Dennis doesn't mince words: "We kick ass," he says, "and with the help of the fans, we're gonna keep kicking ass."

Good for you, Dennis—do you kiss your mother with that mouth? Final score: Spurs 112, Magic 111.

By the weekend, it has become obvious what is happening: I am paying my dues in Texas for all that great weather out west. Having reached that conclusion, I'm not surprised that Saturday is just as overcast as every day has been since I crossed into Texas on Monday. I take solace that to-morrow will bring another Texas matchup, as the Rockets come to San Antonio for a noon game that will be broadcast on NBC.

Sunday proves that there can be nice weather in Texas. The sky has finally cleared to a glorious blue, and the temperature rises to a level much more to my liking. I plan to leave San Antonio right after the game, so I pack all my gear in my car and check out of the hotel, driving to a lot at a shopping mall in the northern part of the city, where I catch a bus to the Alamodome. Joining me is Julie, a Spurs fan I'd met during my first visit to San Antonio.

Just like on Friday, the upper level of the stadium is opened for the game, and the attendance is once again announced at 35,818, an especially impressive figure for a day game. Still, the Rockets are slumping, and I expect that the Spurs will have little trouble winning their eighth game in a row.

Houston fans make up a large part of the crowd at the Alamodome, but they will have little to cheer about on this afternoon. The Spurs go ahead by 11 with 6:49 to play in the first half, and for the rest of the game the Rockets can't get the lead below double-digits. Although I've seen worse games during my trip, the fact that I'm indoors during such a beautiful afternoon makes the Spurs–Rockets matchup all the more tedious. For me, the only highlight comes after the final buzzer, as the stadium begins to empty. A man dressed in Spurs apparel is walking up the bleachers with his son, who is decked out in Rockets gear. As the father passes, I can see that he is wearing a T-shirt with a custom message printed on it: "I did not raise my son to be a Houston fan—Forgive him." Final score: Spurs 124, Rockets 103.

Average 1994–95 ticket cost: $29.93 (13th highest in the NBA)

Beer: $3.00 (16 oz.)

Soda: $1.75 (16 oz.—Coca-Cola products)

Hot Dog: $1.75

Parking: $5.00

Mascot: The Coyote (dressed in Spurs uniform)

Cheerleaders: Spurs Silver Dancers

Remote-controlled blimp: none

Other teams that play full-time in the Alamodome: San Antonio Texans (Canadian Football League)

What I'd change about the Alamodome: Most of the seats are way too far from the floor, and while the stadium has a functional basketball layout, it's hard to forget that the building is more suited for the NFL than the NBA.

What I love about the Alamodome: The unique exterior design, the friendly people, and the excitement of 35,000 fans when the upper level is open.

Statistics from Team Marketing Report, Inc.

Splashdown

HOUSTON ROCKETS

Founded: 1967
1993–94 Record: 58-24
Team Colors: Red, Gold

Sunday, March 5–Tuesday, March 7

Not surprisingly, my car had survived the early afternoon without incident, and so I said good-bye to Julie before taking off for Houston. Crossing the 200 miles between the two cities on I-10, I reached the final NBA city on my trip three hours later as the sun set for the evening. The Rockets wouldn't play the Suns until Tuesday night, so I settled into a hotel room to wait for one last game before heading home.

> **Previous Rockets Games at The Summit:**
>
> **1992–93 season:** New York (Rockets 104-102)

Unlike the Jazz, the Rockets were lucky: After beginning play as the San Diego Rockets in 1967, the team moved to Houston in 1971 with the perfect nickname already in place. Four years later, the club settled into The Summit, a new arena located within a group of buildings in Greenway Plaza. Although the city's largest skyscrapers are found several miles away in the downtown area, the plaza boasts a group of impressive buildings as well, and The Summit is overshadowed by the larger structures.

The arena is a square, reddish-brown building dominated by large windows on all four sides. Built on top of a small hill, The Summit looks deceptively small because its lower level is located under the hill, and only the concourse level and upper bowl are visible from the outside. Less than a hundred feet to the south of the arena is one of the city's major highways, with only a small stretch of grass between them. A large group of flagpoles stand near the southwest corner, but the arena has few other decorative touches, and with its square design and spacious windows Houston's NBA venue bears a strong resemblance to Portland's Memorial Coliseum.

During my travels, The Summit would be the first and last arena I visited, and as a result the length of time between the games I saw in Houston was the longest of any city. In the nearly 26-month period between my visits, the Rockets had seen quite a variety of changes, both in the team and the arena where they play.

When I first visited The Summit in '92–93, Hakeem Olajuwon was leading a Rockets team that had recently added coach Rudy Tomjanovich and rookie forward Robert Horry, and the club's solid play hinted that the Rockets might have a few promising seasons left during the rest of The Dream's career. Yet the Rockets' fan base was weak, with relatively few die-hard supporters, and although attendance at The Summit was near 90 percent of capacity, sellouts were uncommon. The problem may not have been disappointment specifically directed at the Rockets, but rather a citywide malaise about sports in general. Houston teams had failed to produce a championship in any major sport, and after notorious near-misses by football's Oilers and baseball's Astros, Texas's largest metropolis had become known in the world of professional athletics as "Choke City."

But things change, and the '93–94 season brought an end to many traits associated with the Rockets. Just before the season began, after every NBA fan had consigned the championship trophy to the Bulls for the fourth straight year, Michael Jordan retired to pursue a career in baseball, throwing the hunt for the title wide open. The Rockets took advantage of His Airness' absence to claim their first championship, beating the Knicks in a seven-game Finals series. So what if neither team scored a hundred points in a game, the only time since the introduction of the shot clock that nobody's reached the century mark in the Finals? And who cares that the fifth game of the series was overshadowed by a rather dramatic low-speed chase involving a Ford Bronco that distracted many viewers from the game? The Houston Rockets had become the fourteenth existing team

✪ THE SUMMIT
Opened: 1975
Capacity: 16,611
Houston, Texas

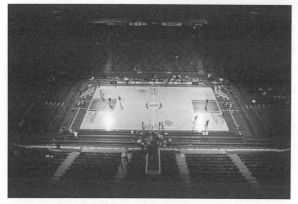

to win an NBA title, and in the process they created a new nickname for their home: "Clutch City."

Yet the Rockets barely had time to register the term as a team trademark before things changed again. Rockets owner Leslie L. Alexander, who had purchased the team after the '92–93 season, decided to take advantage of Houston's inaugural championship by raising ticket prices a whopping 33 percent, vaulting the average cost of a Rockets ticket from just below the league average to third most expensive in the NBA. Just as Houston fans finally found a reason to feel good, many couldn't afford to see games at The Summit anymore.

To make matters worse, the '94–95 Rockets hadn't exactly been confident defenders of their title, slipping to sixth place in the Western Conference while having to endure a series of major injuries, the 10-game suspension of Vernon Maxwell for hitting a fan, and the trade of perennial power forward Otis Thorpe to Portland for Clyde Drexler. Losers of four straight after the blowout in San Antonio, Rockets fans could only wonder if their reign as Clutch City had already passed.

Tuesday, March 7, 1995—7:00 PM

HOUSTON ROCKETS (35-23) VS. PHOENIX SUNS (45-14)

The final game on my trip will have an early tip-off, and as a result it is still light out as I make the ten-minute drive from my hotel to The Summit. Stealing a glimpse of the arena as I pass it on the highway, I take the next exit and double back, crossing a bridge to find a place to park. Attendants are waving cars into an underground garage near the arena, and I follow their directions through a series of snaking rampways.

Alexander's changes went much further than just raising ticket prices. One of his first acts after buying the team was to clean out the Rockets' front office, replacing many of the staff members in the summer of 1993. As a result, I've dealt with two entirely separate media departments. The first time I traveled, the Rockets were helpful but asked me to pay, selling me a ticket about halfway up the lower bowl off of one of the corners. For my current trip, the team's new media services manager has promised me a free ticket, which I soon discover is only one row below the top of the lower bowl, almost on the dead end behind the baseline. It's a question I've pondered many times during my travels—would I rather pay for a good seat, or get a fair seat for free? Actually, all of my dealings with the Rockets have been positive, and occasionally the team has been downright friendly, so it's not a question of which of the two Houston media staffs treated me better. Still, I have to admit that I would have liked a little better seat for my final game.

More changes: The Summit has undergone several renovations since I visited two years ago, and the place looks much better. After entering the concourse level, I see that the team has replaced the section numbers above the entrance portals, updating from a futuristic style that screamed 1970s to a more attractive design. A 30,000-square-foot expansion has created a splashy new food court on the arena's north side, which includes thirteen different stands and a ring of twenty-two video monitors to provide fans with a view of the action while they eat.

The rest of the concourse is much as I remember, with wide walkways and numerous concession stands located both against the walls and in the corners of the building in small glass structures that resemble greenhouses. While everything else checks out, the one area where The Summit comes up short is in souvenirs, as the team has no team shop and only a few merchandise stands throughout the building, each of which offers a woefully small selection of merchandise.

The view from the concourse is pleasant, with the large buildings of Greenway Plaza giving the panorama through the windows a nice urban feel. I take a few moments to watch the sun set on the west side of the arena, and as the daylight fades I wonder if the Rockets are in their twilight as well.

During my first game at The Summit, the Rockets introduced their starters while playing Herbie Hancock's "Rockit," but not anymore. Tonight, Houston starts things off with an impressive sound mix as the team takes to the floor, a combination of music, NASA broadcasts and play-by-play clips from last year's championship season. Next, the lights drop for the opening announcements, and red rockets shoot up from the goals as part of an elaborate fireworks display. I'm flabbergasted—the Rockets used to be so much more tame. I guess the team wanted to give the fans a little something extra to justify the price increase.

As the game begins, the Rockets match the intensity of their opening hoopla, and at the end of a spirited first quarter Houston leads Phoenix 35-32. But the Suns storm back in the second, and by the halftime break the visitors are on top 63-57.

Just like many of the Houston fans at the arena, I'm rather nervous during the break, and not just because the Rockets have lost four games in a row. My concern is that I might be a personal jinx for the team. Remembering the unlikely loss to the Clippers in L.A. just before the All-Star break, then Olajuwon's miss at the buzzer in Dallas a week ago, not to mention the embarrassing drubbing in the Alamodome on Sunday, I'm beginning to think that, depending on what happens tonight, the Rockets might not want to give me any more tickets.

Still, after two games in San Antonio's oversized combination NBA/NFL facility, I'm pleased to be back in a more conventional arena. The Summit is a classic example of the lower bowl/upper bowl tiered design, with the oval-shaped stands having an equal number of rows throughout the upper level. The unobtrusive luxury boxes are located above the regular seats, and with the arena's relatively small capacity The Summit has an intimate feel. If nothing else, The Summit reminds me of home, as the O'rena shares almost exactly the same interior design.

Still, obvious differences remind me that I'm not back in Florida yet. For one thing, The Summit has the same multicolored seat design found at The Omni in Atlanta, a seemingly random mixture of red, yellow, orange, and purple seats in the stands. Fortunately, I've arrived late enough that most of the rows are occupied, sparing me the ugly sight of that color scheme.

The Summit also has no hanging scoreboard, the only regular arena outside of Denver not to offer this feature. Still, the Rockets manage to make do nearly as well as the Nuggets by hanging video screens and player boards at each end above the seats, as well as by placing message boards and scoreboards at the base of the upper bowl on both sides. While the rear-projection video screens offer an acceptable picture and the various scoreboards are easy to see, one thing bothers me: The Summit is one of the arenas where there is no display that shows time-outs remaining. Considering that it's a single-digit number, it is amazing that this information would be missing in any arena.

There are times in the third quarter when both teams appear ready to break the game open, but the score remains close, and at the end of the period the Rockets have pulled within one.

It's been a quiet game for me, as neither of my neighbors seems interested in engaging in a conversation, so I spend some time taking note of the way the Rockets present the game. During my first trip, I came away with the impression that the team was contest-crazed: It seemed that every break saw fans competing on the court in a variety of activities for some prize. Happily, the Rockets have toned things down, and instead of the nonstop contests the team offers other distractions, including more performances by the dance team.

Actually, the Rocket Power Dancers provide the highlight of my evening. After frequent outfit changes, their final choice is a combination of white T-shirts and black shorts. I can see that the shirts have some sort of design on them, so I pick up my binoculars for a closer look.

Printed in red and gold block letters, a message is sandwiched above and below a Rockets logo, with black shapes behind the design. "All Animals Have Rights" the shirts read, and the shapes are silhouettes of birds, elephants, giraffes, and other creatures. Only later will I learn the reason for the politically correct message: Owner Alexander and his wife are big-time animal rights activists who apparently think that an NBA game is a good place to make a statement. I would imagine that by raising his ticket prices to be the third-highest in the league, Alexander might be concerned that only rich people would be in the stands during Rockets games, not the kind of crowd you would expect to strongly support animal rights.

The fourth quarter begins with the Suns ahead 82-81, and I try to convince myself that the game will be a masterpiece, an exciting contest to finish my travels.

For a little while I get my wish: The first four minutes of the quarter are even, and with 8:12 left in the game a Charles Barkley slam puts the Suns up 90-88. On the next play, Olajuwon gets tangled with Suns guard Kevin Johnson, back from the injury that kept him out of action when I was in Phoenix, and the refs give the Houston center a technical foul for what they see as excessive force. I'm not a big Rockets fan, but I can understand why the crowd begins jeering: It's a questionable call.

Johnson hits a jumper, and on their next three possessions the Suns run isolation plays for KJ, who breaks down the Houston defense to score twice and create two Dan Majerle free throws the other time. Meanwhile, the Rockets can't put the ball in the hole, and Olajuwon picks up a couple of quick fouls as the Suns build their lead to 97-88.

Barkley adds a 3-pointer with 4:54 left to put the Suns up 102-92, and less than a minute later Phoenix center Danny Schayes draws his second offensive foul on Olajuwon in the quarter, giving The Dream a total of six personals and an early departure from the game. The crowd is incensed with the officials, and the boos are mixed with a ugly chant that seems appropriate for the farmlands of Texas—something about steer manure. After a tie game with a little more than eight minutes left, the last four will be meaningless, as the Rockets pull no closer than ten the rest of the way. My trip has come to a close with one of the more disappointing quarters I will see all season.

Of all the changes I notice about The Summit, probably the most dramatic is in my own feelings toward the arena. During my first trip, I thought that Houston's building seemed plain and outdated, but after visiting all the other NBA venues, I had begun to appreciate the more intimate arenas that still offered some extras. All it took was two trips and a little renovation by the Rockets to change my opinion of their arena. Final score: Suns 113, Rockets 102.

Average 1994–95 ticket cost: $36.55 (third highest in the NBA)

Beer: $3.75 (20 oz.)

Soda: $2.75 (16 oz.—Coca-Cola products)

Hot Dog: $1.50

Parking: free (included in ticket price)

Mascot: Turbo (absent on the night I visited; he's described as a guy looking like a spaceman in a red-and-yellow outfit)

Cheerleaders: Rocket Power Dancers

Remote-controlled blimp: yes (shaped like a cartoon airplane)

Other teams that play full-time in the Summit: Houston Aeros (International Hockey League), Houston Hotshots (Continental Indoor Soccer League)

What I'd change about the Summit: Add a team store, refurnish the seats in one color, and lower the ticket prices.

What I love about the Summit: The free parking, the new food court, and the decent sightlines.

Statistics from Team Marketing Report, Inc.

NBA standings as of Wednesday, March 8, 1995:

EASTERN CONFERENCE
Atlantic Division

	W	L	Pct	GB	Home	Away
Orlando Magic	45	14	.763	—	29-1	16-13
New York Knicks	38	19	.667	6	22-7	16-12
Boston Celtics	24	34	.414	20.5	14-16	10-18
Miami Heat	23	35	.397	21.5	16-12	7-23
New Jersey Nets	23	36	.390	22	16-13	7-23
Philadelphia 76ers	17	41	.293	27.5	8-19	9-22
Washington Bullets	15	42	.263	29	8-20	7-22

Central Division

	W	L	Pct	GB	Home	Away
Charlotte Hornets	37	22	.627	—	21-7	16-15
Indiana Pacers	35	23	.603	1.5	20-6	15-17
Cleveland Cavaliers	34	24	.586	2.5	18-11	16-13
Chicago Bulls	30	30	.500	7.5	18-11	12-19
Atlanta Hawks	28	30	.483	8.5	16-14	12-16
Detroit Pistons	22	36	.379	14.5	17-12	5-24
Milwaukee Bucks	22	38	.367	15.5	13-16	9-22

WESTERN CONFERENCE
Midwest Division

	W	L	Pct	GB	Home	Away
Utah Jazz	43	16	.729	—	23-7	20-9
San Antonio Spurs	39	17	.696	2.5	23-7	16-10
Houston Rockets	35	24	.593	8	19-10	16-14
Denver Nuggets	27	31	.466	15.5	17-13	10-18
Dallas Mavericks	22	34	.393	19.5	13-19	9-15
Minnesota Timberwolves	16	43	.271	27	9-19	7-24

Pacific Division

	W	L	Pct	GB	Home	Away
Phoenix Suns	46	14	.767	—	25-5	21-9
Seattle SuperSonics	38	18	.679	6	22-7	16-11
L.A. Lakers	36	21	.632	8.5	20-8	16-13
Portland Trail Blazers	31	26	.544	13.5	19-10	12-16
Sacramento Kings	29	28	.509	15.5	21-9	8-19
Golden State Warriors	17	40	.298	27.5	10-18	7-22
L.A. Clippers	12	48	.200	34	9-21	3-27

First Home, Then to the Air

Wednesday, March 8–Friday, March 10

So that was it. The Rockets–Suns game was the last one on my schedule, and come Wednesday morning all that I had left to do was turn my car east and begin the trip back to Orlando. The only problem was, the drive back home was almost a thousand miles long, and during my trip only the journey between Minneapolis and Portland was a longer drive between two cities.

I had spent three days driving to Houston from Orlando on my first trip, but for my return I decided to suck it up and make it home in two. If nothing else, I was tired of hauling my gear in and out of hotel rooms, and was ready to drive like a maniac if I could avoid even one extra night on the road.

Traveling east on I-10 all day, I cut through the rest of Texas and crossed into Louisiana just after 2 PM, then traversed the Mississippi River around 5 PM. I reached the Mississippi state line just after 7 PM, followed by Alabama a little more than an hour later. The big moment arrived at 9:22 PM, when I returned to Florida after my three-month absence, but I was too tired to get excited, especially since I was in the state's panhandle and still had a formidable distance to go. It was almost 10:30 PM when I quit in DeFuniak Springs. At 620 miles, it had been the longest driving day of my second trip, and just for the hell of it I booked a room at the same Best Western where I had stayed on January 13, 1993—my first night of traveling.

During the many hours on the road on Wednesday, I had plenty of time to think about what I'd accomplished. The trip had gone well, with surprisingly agreeable weather and few dull spots. While I was disappointed with the overall quality of play in the Eastern Conference, the teams in the West were exciting to watch, and I had seen many more good games than bad. I came surprisingly close to completing my goal of eventually seeing at least one home victory by every team: The home wins by the Bulls, Blazers, Warriors, and Mavericks took them off the list, and only the losses at the Spectrum and The Palace kept me two teams shy of the mark. (Although once the Canadian teams joined the league, I guess I'll have to add them to the list.)

The trip had also been made easier by my previous traveling experience. My familiarity with the NBA cities and arenas had helped to make the second trip less stressful, and I had become accustomed to the long hours on the road and occasional bouts of loneliness. My only regret was that the end of the Rockets–Suns game had been so disappointing—it made me a little sad to think that my travels would end with an ugly fourth quarter marred by Houston's collapse and the vindictive wrath of the Rockets fans toward the officials.

On Thursday I packed my things for the final time, watching *SportsCenter* on ESPN as I did. It had become somewhat of a ritual for me on the road, but that morning's broadcast was anything but routine.

Michael Jordan was quitting baseball and returning to the Chicago Bulls. There had been no official announcement yet, but reliable sources had indicated that Mike would be back on the court within a couple of weeks. As I listened to the report, all I could think of was the incredible irony of it all: On the same day that I returned home from a three-month trip around the country to watch basketball, word leaks out that Jordan wants to play after all.

It just didn't seem fair.

Even though I was back in Florida, it would still take me most of Thursday to get home. At 12:45 PM, I crossed the line into the Eastern time zone, costing me another hour. At 4:30 PM, I reached the intersection of I-10 and I-75, the crossroads I had passed on the morning of December 9th as I made my way to Atlanta. It was there, at the symbolic close of my circle around the country, that I turned south on I-75 toward

Orlando. It took me an hour and a half to reach the Florida Turnpike, and 45 minutes later I entered the northwest part of Orlando. After the day's drive of 390 miles, the first thing I did was stop at my favorite sportscard store to buy some of the new basketball cards that had been released during my trip. Almost an hour later, I completed my travels by heading back to my apartment, arriving home just before 8 PM.

It was a strange feeling—everything seemed so familiar, but the months on the road had changed my perspective enough to give my return a surreal edge. After so much time living out of my car, it would take me several days to adjust back to life in Orlando, but I was happy to make the switch.

One adjustment concerned the basketball I would be seeing. No longer would I be at games that offered limited emotional involvement—I was a Magic fan again, and I couldn't wait to catch my team playing in their home whites.

Astoundingly, the Magic were still in a close race with Phoenix for the best record in the league, and had an unbelievable 30-1 mark at home. On Friday they played the Blazers, and it was then that I made my return to the O'rena.

It was a surprisingly physical matchup, but the Magic still prevailed, outrebounding Portland on the way to a 97-85 victory. In another unexpected coincidence relating to my trip, the Magic–Blazers game turned out to have some significance: With the win, Orlando clinched their second playoff berth in team history. Although most of the Orlando faithful took the game in stride, for me it was a special night, and I was glad to be back in my element, no longer a temporary fan.

Monday, March 13–Saturday, March 25

By early the following week things were nearly back to normal, as I had settled back into my Orlando lifestyle while working toward finishing the book. The Jordan rumors were still flying, but there had been no official confirmation that he would return to the Bulls. Meanwhile, my post-trip NBA action had been pretty satisfying, especially when I saw the Magic stomp the Spurs at the O'rena on the Sunday after I returned to Orlando, a little payback for the one-point loss in the Alamodome nine days earlier.

I was working at my apartment one afternoon when Rachel called me from Atlanta. I'd spoken to her a few times since we saw the Hawks play the Knicks at The Omni in December, and I figured she was calling to find out if I had gotten home safely. We talked for a few minutes, and then she told me that she had bought a pair of tickets for the Hawks–Bulls game at The Omni on March 25th, in the hope that Jordan would return.

"Good for you," I said. "It sounds like he'll be back by then."

"Uh-huh," Rachel said. "So, do you want to go?"

Jordan kept the world in suspense for the rest of the week, then announced on Saturday, March 18th, that he had decided to return to play for the Bulls in their game the following day against the Pacers at Market Square Arena. Chicago had a 34-31 record at that point, giving Jordan 17 games to see how well he could do with the team before the playoffs began. Amidst a media frenzy not seen in basketball in a long time, Michael donned a jersey sporting his new number 45 and jogged onto an NBA court for the first time in 21 months.

The game in Indiana proved to be an inauspicious return, as Jordan struggled during an overtime loss. The next stop was Boston on Wednesday night, where Michael looked better: Although hampered by foul trouble, His Airness still scored 27 points in only 26 minutes on the floor.

Friday saw the event that many thought would never happen—Michael Jordan playing for the Bulls in the United Center. It was hard to judge whether Michael's return at Indiana or his United Center debut generated more hype, but we Magic fans knew which meant more to us: The Friday game was against Orlando.

In a proud moment for our boys, the Magic held Jordan to 21 points on 7-for-23 shooting and beat the Bulls 106-99. Chicago had lost two of three since Mike's return, and NBA fans had to wonder if Jordan would ever regain the form that was captured on his statue outside the Bulls' new arena.

The next day was Saturday, March 25th, and late that morning I caught a flight out of Orlando Airport. It was Rachel's idea, and it made perfect sense: Instead of missing Jordan's return, why not revisit Atlanta to see him play? She had tickets for the game, and after my publisher agreed to extend my book deadline the circumstances were just too good for me not to spring for a plane ticket.

After landing in Atlanta, I took the subway downtown to the store where Rachel worked in Underground Atlanta, an upscale shopping district not far from The Omni. We had lunch together soon after my arrival, and I spent the rest of the afternoon in the mall, waiting for her to get off of work.

Saturday, March 25, 1995—7:30 PM

ATLANTA HAWKS (33-34) VS. CHICAGO BULLS (35-33)

It is a night for the unexpected—Jordan is back playing basketball, and I'm traveling again two weeks after my trip was supposed to end.

Rachel and I arrive at the arena early, and the courtyard surrounding The Omni is packed with more fans than I would have imagined possible in Atlanta. For the first time all year, a game at The Omni has created serious demand for tickets.

Most of the crowd is here to see Jordan, of course, a situation made worse by the lack of die-hard Hawks fans, and one of the Atlanta players has suggested that the Hawks should wear their road uniforms tonight.

Still, there is one nice thing for the Hawks fans in attendance: They'll have the rare privilege of seeing The Omni filled with people, many decked out in red. Unfortunately, the vast majority will be wearing the red and black of the Bulls, rather than the red and gold of the Hawks.

We reach our seats in the second row of the upper bowl about twenty minutes before tip-off. The location is behind one of the baskets, but since we're near the bottom of the section the view really isn't that bad. After my previous experiences in Atlanta, I never thought I would see a full house at The Omni, but as I look around the packed arena I realize that everything about tonight is a little strange.

All the distractions of Jordan's return aside, the game is pretty even in the first quarter, with His Airness playing only an average role in the action. People are hanging on his every move, of course, but I'm pleased to see that a large part of the crowd is actively cheering for the Hawks. Jordan once said that the fans who come to see Chicago play in other cities always want him to score 50 while the Bulls lose by two, and it's a good sign for Atlanta that many of the people in the crowd seem to feel that way tonight; at least it means that they haven't abandoned the Hawks altogether.

In the second the Bulls grab a big lead, capped by a Jordan dunk that is the first real flashback of the evening, but the Hawks respond by going on a 17-0 run to pull ahead by seven. At halftime Atlanta is up by nine, and it looks as if perhaps Michael should still be playing baseball. This is his fourth game back, and Jordan has yet to demonstrate that he still has the intangible greatness that made him the most universally revered player in NBA history.

That all changes in the second half.

In the third quarter comes the show that every basketball fan has been waiting for, as Jordan explodes for 18 points on 8-of-11 shooting, mixing jumpers with dunks to put the Bulls back on top at the end of the quarter by two, 80-78. It is vintage Jordan, and it comes at a time when the Bulls need it most, as neither team has taken control of the game.

As the fourth period begins, all I ask is for a decent quarter, the kind I didn't get in Houston. Jordan begins to look mortal again, and even though the Hawks go through a five-minute stretch where they score only one point, the game still remains close throughout.

Times have changed: With 1:25 to play, Jordan goes for a jumper, and I'm shocked to see Hawks guard Steve Smith simply outjump His Airness to swat the ball away. Smith feeds Mookie Blaylock for a layup, and suddenly everybody in the stands has to wonder if Michael's lost it, if his play during the third quarter was a happy fluke.

The Hawks hit a jumper with 47.3 seconds left to go ahead 98-97, and on the next possession Blaylock steals a Chicago pass. As the clock winds down, Atlanta has trouble finding a good look at the basket, and Jordan rebounds a missed shot and calls a timeout with 5.9 seconds left.

Down by one, the Bulls make their plans in the huddle, and the crowd buzzes with excitement. As I wait for the game to resume, I make one more wish: If the Bulls are going to win, at least let Jordan be the deciding factor. The Hawks have played too well on their home court, in front of thousands of people rooting for the visiting team, to lose on a shot by anyone else.

With so little time left, I'm surprised to see that the Bulls will be inbounding the ball in their backcourt, rather than moving up to the frontcourt and running a play from there. Still, that's their decision, and Jordan comes back to my end of the court to take the pass.

He dribbles toward the far basket, with Smith backpedaling in front of him and no play developing as far as I can see. Jordan picks up speed, and I have a clear view as he makes his move: Stutter-stepping near midcourt, Michael fakes left, fakes right, then elevates on the right side near the top of the key. There's been no screens or passes, and Smith steps up as Jordan takes the 18-footer. Jordan hasn't created much of an opening, but to my surprise he manages to arc the ball cleanly over Smith's outstretched hand. As the shot travels toward the hoop, I hear the buzzer sound and have time to register a quick thought: It wasn't much of a play to get a decent last shot.

But my surprise turns to amazement: This hurried shot, a contested jumper without the benefit of even a simple pick to create a little space, drops through the hoop, and as the sound of the crowd in The Omni becomes deafening Jordan turns toward my end, bends down to pump his fist and slap the court twice, and then dashes off the floor with his teammates.

The crowd keeps cheering long after he's gone, as the image of one more bit of Jordan wizardry remains with us. After a week of media hype and fan hysteria, Michael has surprised and delighted the basketball world by showing that he really isn't through yet.

And for me, he's provided a memory unlike any other during my travels: There's no question that his last-second shot is the highlight of all the games I've seen outside Orlando. Final score: Bulls 99, Hawks 98.

Sunday, March 26

The next day, I catch an early flight out of Atlanta and arrive back in Orlando by mid-morning. I'm in a terrific mood, mostly because I know that the game I saw last night will long be remembered as the true return of Michael Jordan. I relax for a few minutes at my apartment, letting it sink in that Jordan's buzzer-beater has marked the end of my travels—I am finally home from the NBA road.

Then I get up and head to the O'rena, because the Magic are playing the Warriors at noon.

Final NBA standings, 1994–95 season:

EASTERN CONFERENCE
Atlantic Division

	W	L	Pct	GB	Home	Away
Orlando Magic	57	25	.695	—	39-2	18-23
New York Knicks	55	27	.671	2	29-12	26-15
Boston Celtics	35	47	.427	22	20-21	15-26
Miami Heat	32	50	.390	25	22-19	10-31
New Jersey Nets	30	52	.366	27	20-21	10-31
Philadelphia 76ers	24	58	.293	33	14-27	10-31
Washington Bullets	21	61	.256	36	13-28	8-33

Central Division

	W	L	Pct	GB	Home	Away
Indiana Pacers	52	30	.634	—	33-8	19-22
Charlotte Hornets	50	32	.610	2	29-12	21-20
Chicago Bulls	47	35	.573	5	28-13	19-22
Cleveland Cavaliers	43	39	.524	9	26-15	17-24
Atlanta Hawks	42	40	.512	10	24-17	18-23
Milwaukee Bucks	34	48	.415	18	22-19	12-29
Detroit Pistons	28	54	.341	24	22-19	6-35

WESTERN CONFERENCE
Midwest Division

	W	L	Pct	GB	Home	Away
San Antonio Spurs	62	20	.756	—	33-8	29-12
Utah Jazz	60	22	.732	2	33-8	27-14
Houston Rockets	47	35	.573	15	25-16	22-19
Denver Nuggets	41	41	.500	21	23-18	18-23
Dallas Mavericks	36	46	.439	26	19-22	17-24
Minnesota Timberwolves	21	61	.256	41	13-28	8-33

Pacific Division

	W	L	Pct	GB	Home	Away
Phoenix Suns	59	23	.720	—	32-9	27-14
Seattle SuperSonics	57	25	.695	2	32-9	25-16
L.A. Lakers	48	34	.585	11	29-12	19-22
Portland Trail Blazers	44	38	.537	15	26-15	18-23
Sacramento Kings	39	43	.476	20	27-14	12-29
Golden State Warriors	26	56	.317	33	15-26	11-30
L.A. Clippers	17	65	.207	42	13-28	4-37

Observations

Now that I've completed two trips around the NBA, I thought I'd offer a few quick observations and perspectives.

Dance Teams: The NBA has become a haven for dance teams, the modern equivalent of the traditional cheerleading squads. Although several NBA clubs showcase their dancers only during certain games, most present them all the time, and apparently dance teams must be more popular than ever—during the '94–95 season, only the Celtics and Pistons failed to field a squad. I'm no arts critic, but most NBA dance teams demonstrate much less talent than I would have expected. Perhaps I'm spoiled by Orlando's dancers, a talented squad who obviously work hard at their routines. They are close behind the Laker Girls in terms of overall quality, and a few other dance teams around the league perform well, but there are quite a few franchises that should consider either improving their dance teams or dropping them altogether.

Mascots: Unlike dance teams, I have a soft spot in my heart for mascots. A good costumed character can keep a dull game entertaining, as I learned during the early years of the Magic, when Stuff the Magic Dragon would provide a seemingly endless series of diversions during the times when Orlando was getting blown out of the building. Of the twenty-seven teams in the league during the '94–95 season, nineteen had mascots. While many do little during the games except walk around the stands and clown around with fans, a few are pretty impressive, including Phoenix's famous Gorilla, San Antonio's Coyote, Minnesota's CRUNCH, and Charlotte's Hugo.

But my pick for most entertaining mascot is Rocky, the Denver Nuggets' mountain lion. His stunts may not be as flashy as some of the others in the league, but Rocky displayed an amazing variety of routines during the two games I saw at the Big Mac. Not only that, but he exhibits a boundless enthusiasm that fits perfectly with a young team like the Nuggets. Denver fans are lucky to have him.

Blimps: Another popular item, the remote-controlled blimps fly around many NBA buildings during breaks in the action, usually at half-time and between quarters. By my count, thirteen teams utilize the air-ships, among them Seattle and Denver, who each fly two at the same time. Most are relatively simple, but a few are quite impressive and elaborate, including the ones in Atlanta, Charlotte, and Chicago that are shaped like the teams' mascots. Houston's blimp looks like a cartoonish airplane, while Sacramento's is shaped like a traditional hot air balloon, complete with a small hanging basket.

Soda: As a loyal Diet Pepsi drinker, I was curious to see which brand of soda was found at each arena. It turns out that only three serve Pepsi products: Denver, Philadelphia, and, luckily for me, Orlando. Every other building offers the Coca-Cola product line. Still, the cola war isn't over yet—the underdog will get a big boost in publicity when the Nuggets move to the Pepsi Center in a couple of years.

Programs: Nearly all NBA teams have a standard program, which is a combination of the monthly *Hoop* magazine published by the league and pages of information about the individual team. The covers of the programs usually feature the visiting team's star player, but on some nights will show a member of the home team or a general picture related to basketball. Most teams have some sort of insert in the program to provide updated information about that night's game.

A few cities make an extra effort regarding programs, including Chicago and Minnesota, who provide fans with two publications, a magazine produced by the team as well as the latest issue of *Hoop*. But the best programs are in San Antonio, where the *Hoop* pages are combined with a much larger publication that includes material about the game and the Spurs in general. Packed with information, the San Antonio program is nearly as extensive as some teams' media guides, and as a bonus even includes a poster in every issue.

Instant Replay: Everybody has message boards, even Boston Garden. But if you want to see a replay of the action, there are a few places where you'll be out of luck. During the '94–95 season, twenty-two arenas offered video monitors. Some work better than others (remember Miami's misshapen screens?), but nearly all provide an acceptable image of the action. The teams that don't have instant replay are the Hawks, Celtics, Sonics, Warriors, and Clippers, but that number will shrink in '95–96 after Boston and Seattle move into their new arenas.

ARENA RANKINGS

All jobs have certain responsibilities, and if my job from November 1994 to March 1995 was visiting and writing about NBA arenas, I guess I should make a few judgments about what I saw. So here it is, a completely arbitrary ranking of the twenty-seven NBA arenas occupied during the '94–95 season. These rankings are based on a combination of each arena's physical design, location, fans, general atmosphere, and intangible characteristics that I experienced during my visits. Rather than try to determine exact positions, I've grouped them in six categories, with the teams divided alphabetically within each group:

The best four:

New York Knicks: An exciting building in an equally exciting city. In addition to decent sightlines and exceptional graphics, Madison Square Garden is boosted by rowdy fans, prominent celebrities, and employees who are generally more friendly than you might expect.

Orlando Magic: Sure, I'm biased toward my favorite team's arena, but I think anyone familiar with all the NBA buildings would agree that the O'rena is exceptional. With an accessible downtown location, a beautiful exterior design, and an intimate feel, Orlando Arena is the nicest small arena in the league, and boasts a great balance between NBA action and extracurricular entertainment.

Phoenix Suns: The model for all others. Virtually everything about America West Arena is top-notch, including the location in the heart of Phoenix, the striking exterior design, and the effective layout of the seats.

It doesn't hurt that Suns fans worship their team and loudly demonstrate their affection during home games.

Utah Jazz: Another downtown building, the Delta Center offers a dazzling view from outside the arena, as well as all the comforts of a modern NBA facility. In addition, the mass of seats in the lower level, including the dozens of rows packed directly around the floor, almost make the fans appear to be part of the game.

The exceptional five:

Boston Celtics: What Boston Garden lacks in modern conveniences (which is just about all of them), it makes up for in sheer tradition. Seeing a game under the dozens of commemorative banners is close to a religious experience for true NBA fans, and more than adequately compensates for the wooden seats and occasionally obstructed views.

Charlotte Hornets: Although you might have someone's head in your view, the energetic crowd at the Charlotte Coliseum will more than make up for it. With reasonable prices, large concourses, plentiful concessions, and some of the loudest fans in the league, Hornets games are among the most exciting in the NBA

Chicago Bulls: Bigger than I normally like, the United Center still offers a solid balance between luxury suites and the more traditional seats. Its relatively isolated location might have dropped it to a lower category, but the interactive displays on the concourses, the Michael Jordan statue, and the fact that His Airness has returned to play for the Bulls help compensate for any shortcomings.

Detroit Pistons: Another huge arena with a design much like the United Center's, The Palace of Auburn Hills is also more isolated than I would like, but the Pistons still rate highly in several other ways. Not only is The Palace a clean, spacious building, but the Pistons nicely balance the game with music, graphics, and just the right combination of frills. Detroit gets bonus points for offering an atmosphere where basketball comes first, without the distractions of dancers and excessive fan contests—I hope they keep that balance intact in future seasons.

Sacramento Kings: The little details make ARCO Arena one of my favorites, like the wooden floors, the restaurant and lounge on the upper concourse, and the strong sightlines. As much as the team has improved

recently, part of the charm of seeing a game in Sacramento is the devotion of the fans, who continue to pack their building through good times
and bad.

The great five:

Dallas Mavericks: Reunion Arena could use a facelift, and fans who look
for extra amenities will be disappointed. But the arena has all the things
I need at a game: good sightlines, solid video monitors, an attractive
interior design, and a great location near downtown Dallas. It's unfortunate that the Mavs plan to move.

Houston Rockets: Just like Reunion Arena, The Summit doesn't offer as
many frills as some other NBA buildings, but its recent renovations have
improved the experience of seeing a Rockets game. The arena not only has
a good location, it also provides a relatively intimate atmosphere for those
who can afford tickets.

Milwaukee Bucks: The Bradley Center's entrances are among the most
beautiful in the league, and the concourse level is sparkling as well. Nicely
incorporated into the downtown area, the arena's location is a plus. Still,
the layout is unexceptional, and during the Bucks' recent lean years many
games at the Bradley Center have been played in front of small crowds of
sluggish fans.

Minnesota Timberwolves: Another struggling team, the Timberwolves also
play in a nice arena. With a striking exterior design that incorporates the
elevated walkways of downtown Minneapolis, Target Center suffers from
its large capacity, which not only makes the upper seats a formidable distance from the court but also emphasizes the recent decline in attendance.

Portland Trail Blazers: While the building is old and somewhat basic,
three things vault Portland's Memorial Coliseum above most other
league buildings: the tiny capacity, which keeps every seat relatively
near the floor; terrific video monitors and scoreboards, including the
most detailed display of game stats in any arena; and the fans, whom I
consider to be the best in the NBA.

The good five:

Cleveland Cavaliers: Of the twelve arenas that have opened since 1988,
The Gund appears to be taking the most flack. While its exterior design

makes it among the most stylish buildings in the NBA, Gund Arena's seating design has come under fire, and the luxurious extras have failed to keep many Cavaliers fans from complaining about their new facility.

Denver Nuggets: There's good and bad about McNichols Sports Arena: While the venue offers a decent capacity and mostly good sightlines, legroom is often compromised. Still, as the team has improved the Big Mac has become much more exciting to visit, and the view of the downtown area from the arena is a nice bonus.

Golden State Warriors: Playing in a great metropolitan area, the Warriors enjoy a solid fan base and one of the league's smallest arenas. Still, the Oakland Coliseum Arena does show its age in some spots, and fans have to make do without video screens. There was a time when the extras didn't matter, but with the Warriors' recent struggles it's unfortunate that the building doesn't offer a few more amenities.

Miami Heat: With a poor choice of location, Miami Arena has been in trouble in recent years, and the oddly-shaped video screens added after the team's first season are but one example of several mistakes in planning by the team. Still, the exterior design is strikingly beautiful, and the relatively small capacity keeps fans near the court.

San Antonio Spurs: An NBA facility unique in virtually every way, the Alamodome is certainly memorable, especially when filled to a capacity near 36,000. But the stadium requires fans to sacrifice because of its enormous size, and many of the seats are a long distance from the court.

The adequate five:

Atlanta Hawks: Square to the extreme, The Omni offers many good seats, but loses points for a variety of reasons, including a somewhat scary location, a dingy exterior design, lukewarm fans who rarely fill the arena, and the absence of video monitors for replays.

Indiana Pacers: The only dome among the regular NBA arenas, Market Square Arena also boasts a unique elevated design. Still, the uniform slope of the interior stands is an unfortunate design choice, and the overall view from the stands is only mediocre in many locations.

L.A. Lakers: The Lakers' tradition of excellence and the frequent visits by celebrities don't compensate for an unattractive mixture of colors and a narrow concourse. Add in a windowless, plastic-looking exterior and a crowd that really does arrive late and leave early, and the Forum becomes one of the biggest disappointments of my travels.

New Jersey Nets: While the physical layout of the Meadowlands Arena is nice enough, the suburban location detracts from the building's appeal. With uninspired fans and frequently ill-tempered employees, a Nets game rarely generates much excitement, a situation made worse by traditionally poor attendance.

Philadelphia 76ers: Like the Meadowlands Arena, the Spectrum isn't a bad building, but the listless atmosphere created by the lack of real NBA fans greatly reduces the building's appeal. Like McNichols, the Spectrum has good qualities and bad, but the struggling Sixers need a better crowd to make their arena a memorable place to visit.

The worst three:

L.A. Clippers: As if playing in an old building in a bad neighborhood wasn't difficult enough, the Clippers' recent woes have only made things worse at the Sports Arena. The interior design offers a good view from just about every seat, but that doesn't matter when the stands are nearly always less than half full. The lack of any extras, especially replay screens, doesn't help the situation.

Seattle SuperSonics: Tacoma Dome is an acceptable temporary arena, but I wouldn't want to have to spend a season commuting to it. Not only does the building have uncomfortable seats and virtually no amenities, its suburban location creates traffic nightmares during Sonics games.

Washington Bullets: Dark and isolated, with a hideous exterior design, there is only one positive thought that comes to mind about USAir Arena: It will be replaced before long. Easily my least favorite NBA arena.

In the end, my basketball adventures proved to be every bit as rewarding as I'd hoped, especially when my first trip led to the opportunity to travel a second time and write this book about my experiences. And if I ever want to contemplate everything I've done, I can look at my complete set of NBA hats, each a souvenir from the team's arena. Nothing's changed since I was in the ninth grade: I still think that such a collection is just about the neatest thing a sports fan can have, especially when I recall the history behind it. And lucky me, I don't have just one such collection, but two.

After my return, it was still hard for me to believe what I'd done. From January to April 1993, I saw 32 games outside Orlando, driving 12,722 miles while spending just under $3,400 for lodging and gas. From late November 1994 to March 1995, I attended 39 games in other cities, a 12,367-mile tour of the NBA that cost slightly more than $5,400. It was a time when my love of basketball went from being just a part of my life to the main focus of it, and although my job as a wandering fan must come to a close, I'll always treasure the days and nights I spent traveling the NBA road.